# ROMANIAN-ENGLISH
# ENGLISH-ROMANIAN
## Dictionary & Phrasebook

# Dictionary & Phrasebooks

Albanian
Arabic (Eastern) *Romanized*
Australian
Azerbaijani
Basque
Bosnian
Breton
British
Cajun French
Chechen
Croatian
Czech
Danish
Esperanto
Estonian
Finnish
French
Georgian
German
Greek
Hebrew *Romanized & Script*
Hungarian
Igbo
Ilocano
Irish

Italian
Japanese *Romanized*
Lao *Romanized*
Lingala
Malagasy
Maltese
Mongolian
Nepali
Norwegian
Pilipino (Tagalog)
Polish
Québécois
Romansch
Russian *Revised*
Shona
Slovak
Somali
Spanish (Latin American)
Swahili
Swedish
Tajik
Thai *Romanized*
Turkish
Ukrainian
Uzbek

# ROMANIAN-ENGLISH
# ENGLISH-ROMANIAN
## Dictionary & Phrasebook

MIHAI MIROIU

HIPPOCRENE BOOKS INC.
*New York*

For information, address:
HIPPOCRENE BOOKS, INC.
171 Madison Avenue
New York, NY 10016
www.hippocrenebooks.com

*Library of Congress Cataloguing-in-Publication Data*

Miroiu, Mihai.
    Romanian-English, English-Romanian dictionary
  & phrasebook / Mihai Miroiu.
        p. cm.
    Includes bibliographical references.
    ISBN-10: 0-7818-0921-5
    ISBN-13: 978-0-7818-0921-4
      1. Romanian language--Dictionaries--English.
2. English language--Dictionaries--Romanian.
3. Romanian language--Conversation and phrasebooks--
English. I. Title: Romanian-English, English-Romanian
dictionary and phrasebook.
II. Title.

PC779.M58 2002
459'.321--dc21

                                        2002032906

# ACKNOWLEDGEMENTS

My work on this project has benefited from the expertise of many people whose dedication has inspired me over the years. They are too numerous to mention by name, but I owe them all an immense debt of gratitude.

I am indebted to professor William Kennedy of Cornell University for his constant encouragement and support, and to the faculty in the Department of Comparative Literature at Cornell for the stimulating intellectual environment that has made my stay as Fulbright scholar a rich and rewarding experience.

I would like to thank George Blagowidow of Hippocrene Books who included the Romanian Dictionary and Phrasebook in the series. Anne McBride, editor at Hippocrene Books, offered invaluable assistance in planning and editing the dictionary. She has my deepest thanks and gratitude.

Special thanks also go to the staff of Olin Library at Cornell in which some of my research was carried out.

Thanks are due to my sons, Mihai and Alexandru, who conscientiously perused my manuscript in draft and made useful suggestions. All along, they demonstrated how creative and surprising the young men of today could be.

It goes without saying that any errors or flaws that might be found in this book are, of course, entirely my own.

I dedicate this book to my mother and sister and to the memory of our dear father and brother.

# CONTENTS

# INTRODUCTION

Romanian is spoken by 23 million people living in Romania and by another 3 million living in the Republic of Moldova. No accurate census of the Romanian diaspora is available, but it is estimated that the number of Romanians living outside Romania, including the Romanians in America, is more than three million.

In the Latin linguistic family, composed of nine languages, Romanian has the fifth numerical place, after Italian, French, Spanish and Portuguese.

All other Romance languages are the offspring of the Latin of the Western Roman Empire, and are called West Romance languages. Romanian is the only survivor of the Latin languages spoken in the Eastern Roman Empire.

According to Herodotus and other ancient chroniclers, many centuries before our age, a people of Thracian origin called Dacians or Getae inhabited the land occupied today by the Romanians. Later Horace, Strabo, Dion Cassius, Eutropius and others, including Ovid, who spent his last years in exile on the shore of the Black Sea at Tomi (Constanța of today), where he is buried, give us more information about this "peaceful, content, yet courageous and independent people." Their country, Dacia, which once, in the reign of the famous king Burebista, controlled all Thrace, Macedonia and Illyria, was very rich in gold and mineral wealth, as well as in fertile fields and livestock. The Greeks, the Macedonians, the Persians, and later the Romans, often tried to subdue this people and conquer their land, but they were repelled with vigor.

The Roman emperor Trajan (A.D. 102) undertook a punitive expedition against this daring people; and after five years, in the year A.D. 107, the Dacian king Decebal and his army were defeated. As security against any future uprising, the country was intensively colonized by the Romans.

Dacia remained under Roman protection for 169 years, and its prosperity was so great that the country acquired the name of "Dacia Felix." In the year A.D. 275, however, the Emperor Aurelian, forced by the repeated incursions of the barbarians who at that time began to invade the Roman Empire from all sides, withdrew his legions and officials, abandoning the colonists.

The fifth century was crucial for the Roman Empire and for Europe. It was then that the Empire, with Rome itself, was finally overrun by the barbarians and permanently cut up into various separate regions that are at the root of today's Romance-speaking nations.

The process of Romanization in the Eastern Roman Empire was a similar one to that in the Western. Everywhere Roman administration and Latin culture caused the indigenous languages to be superseded by Latin. The breaking up of the unity of the Roman civilization—a consequence of the splitting of the Roman Empire—made it possible for different provinces to develop the Latin language along their own lines.

Being cut off from the Western Latin area through the settlement of the Slavs in South-Eastern Europe in the seventh century, and through the settlement of the Magyars in Central Europe in the ninth century, the Romanian language has had an evolution independent of the other Romance languages. Because this evolution did not continue to be influenced by medieval Latin, like the evolution of the Western Romance languages, Romanian is in some ways more conservative than the Western Romance languages, i.e. it is nearer to Latin.

It is difficult to determine with scientific certainty what happened to the Dacian population after the departure of the Roman legions and during the succeeding seven centuries of invasions. There is little doubt, however, that the Romanian-speaking people who reappeared in the ravaged former province after the period of invasions was over are the descendants of the earlier Latinized Daco-Romanian population. It is very likely that the Daco-Romanians took refuge in their stronghold in the Carpathians during the invasions and then returned to the foothills and plains of Moldavia, Wallachia, and Transylvania when the barbarians left.

On the eve of the tenth century, these Daco-Romans appear again in the limelight of world history. The Byzantine and Russian chroniclers began to mention them under the name of Blacki, Vlachi, Volochi or Wallachians. By that time they had succeeded in forming little "voevodates" or principalities governed by a prince (voevod), which later were united into larger states. In 1290, the principality of Wallachia (Muntenia) was formed, and in 1350, the principality of Moldavia. They prospered as a result of their strategic location on the trade route from the Black Sea to northern Europe. Soon afterward, the two principalities had to face a new threat from the south, the advancing Ottoman Turks. After the defeat of the Christian armies at Kossovo in Serbia in 1389, the rulers of Moldavia and Wallachia as well as of Transylvania tried, for more than a century, to hold the Turks at the Danube. They included such notable Wallachians as Mircea the Old and Vlad (Dracul) Ţepeş, "The Impaler;" Janos Hunyadi, the governor of Transylvania, who was of Romanian origin; and the Moldavian prince Stephen (Stefan) the Great, who earned from Pope Sextus IV the title of the "Athlete of Christ."

Despite a long series of hard-fought battles, by the early sixteenth century, both Moldavia and Wallachia had become Turkish vassal states.

Sporadic resistance to the Turks continued. Michael (Mihai) the Brave, who became the ruler of Wallachia in 1593, was especially successful. He defeated not only the Turkish forces in 1595, but also the Hungarian prince of Transylvania in 1599, uniting all three lands under his rule for the first time. His reign was brief (he was murdered in 1601) but long enough for him to become a symbol of Romanian unity.

Beginning with the fourteenth century, when the Romanians created their first greater political organizations, they used in the Church and in their political affairs the Middle Slavonic language, a form of the Old Church Slavonic of the ninth to the eleventh centuries, with local variations. It is through this language, which played in the life of the Orthodox peoples of Eastern Europe a similar role to that of Latin in the West, that the Romanians were in touch with Byzantine culture. A rich Slavonic literature of religious writings, annals, and pseudo-religious books was created in this language in the Romanian countries.

The first Romanian texts were written in the sixteenth century in northern Transylvania. They are reproductions of older manuscripts of the fifteenth century and are translations of parts of the Bible made under the influence of Hussitism and of the Reformation. The first Romanian book, the Gospels, was printed in 1560–61 by the Deacon Coresi. Of an earlier catechism, printed in 1544 in Sibiu under the influence of the Reformation, no copy has yet been found.

The seventeenth century was the golden epoch of Old Romanian culture, ecclesiastical as well as secular. The Bible is translated from Greek and printed in a monumental edition (1688). The chroniclers documented the Roman descent of the Romanians and awakened national consciousness.

In 1859, the Romanians succeeded in uniting the principality of Muntenia with Moldavia, and in 1877, through their courage and sacrifice, they earned their complete independence after four centuries of Ottoman domination. The nineteenth century brought both increased contact with the West and assimilation of Western ideas and the manifestation of Romanian originality. The old autochthonous culture, enriched by Byzantine elements, began to grow into a new unity. In the twentieth century, after the First World War, the Romanian people were united in one state that brought together all the territories historically inhabited by the Romanians.

Romanian culture reflects the country's geographic location at the intersection of Eastern and Western influences. Aspects of Roman culture from the second and third centuries were merged in subsequent centuries with those of medieval Byzantium and those of Islam brought by the Turks in the fifteenth century. In modern times, this mixture was overlaid by successive waves of West European culture. Beneath all these layers of foreign influence lies a remarkably rich native folk culture with deep historical roots. Folk art is rich and varied. There are significant regional differences in the styles, colors, and materials employed. Motifs typically stress abstract and geometric designs rather than figurative ones. Elaborate wood-carving, exhibited in house decorations, farmyard gates, furniture, household utensils and farm tools, is especially characteristic of the wooded areas of the Carpathians and Transylvania. Intricate embroideries adorn the traditional holiday costumes of men and women. Other examples of textile art are rugs, tablecloths, and wall hangings woven of linen, wool, hemp, or flax. Pottery, both black and red, is made for decorative as well as household uses, and many rural cottages still have beautiful ceramic stoves. Special peasant arts include the dyeing of Easter eggs in colorful patterns and the painting of religious icons on glass.

Throughout centuries of foreign domination, the Romanians built castles and monasteries that testify to their resilience and artistic genius. From the fourteenth century, distinctive religious and secular architectural styles developed in Moldavia, Wallachia, and Transylvania. The former two exhibit a strong Byzantine influence, with exterior frescoes and massive protective walls. Transylvanian architecture reflects the influence of West European styles, from the Romanesque to the Baroque. During the seventeenth century, the "Brancovan" style appeared, fostered by Prince Constantin Brîncoveanu. Its open, pillared porches and intricate floral carvings can be seen in the Mogoșoaia Palace in Bucharest.

While in Romania, no visitor would want to miss the wall-painted monasteries. They date from the fourteenth and fifteenth centuries, when frescoes were painted on the walls of churches and other religious buildings, depicting scriptural events, saints, and noble benefactors. Notable examples are the group of monasteries of northern Moldavia (Voroneț, Humor, Moldovița, Sucevița, and others), whose exterior walls are covered with murals that were painted in the fifteenth and sixteenth centuries.

They reflect local folk elements as well as a late Byzantine style and are still remarkably vivid.

The Romanians are also great lovers of music and dance. Folk music and folk dance exhibit great richness and variety and are basic components of folk festivals and celebrations, especially those connected with Christmas and New Year's Day, weddings and funerals, and seasonal rites.

# THE ROMANIAN
# WAY OF LIFE

Romanians are frank and open, gregarious and receptive, with a mild temperament. Optimism, humor, healthy laughter and zestful irony are among their characteristic features, as well as friendliness and hospitality.

Romanians are extremely sensitive to beauty and incline toward lyricism. They have never rejected what is new and modern, but they care less for the eccentric. The urban lifestyle of Romanians is very similar to that of other peoples of Europe. While older generations still preserve customs that have disappeared in Western countries, younger people have adopted general cultural trends worldwide.

The Romanian family has traditionally been a strong social unit. The family has had a strong influence on an individual's life; extended families, grandparents, and other family members would typically live near one another and see each other frequently.

Romanians can be described as individualists. One facet of this individualism is their tendency to call almost anything into question. This leads to original and creative thought, but it can also be a source of conflict. Conversations among friends may sound brusque and aggressive to foreigners, as if participants were trying to assert their viewpoints for the pure pleasure of it. As a population, Romanians enjoy discussion immensely, spending hours—usually around a table—debating everything from politics to sports and entertainment.

In politics, this critical spirit shows up as a spirit of confrontation rather than compromise. The average Romanian citizen mistrusts the intentions of politicians—indeed, of any institution or bureaucracy except the Church.

The handshake is customary on greeting and at leave-taking; when being introduced, both sexes give their last names. There is almost always some sort of physical contact when Romanian speakers greet each other. Casual acquaintances or coworkers shake hands briefly when they meet, even if they see each other every day. Friends and relatives exchange two or more kisses on the cheek. Men generally shake hands rather than exchange kisses. The gallant hand-kiss is still flourishing in Romania, but if it is not actually practiced—it is still symbolically referred to by men in their greeting or leave-taking of women: the phrase "*sărut mîna*" (I kiss the hand) is very common and is used when talking to women of all ages and to the elderly in general.

Education represents a fundamental value for Romanians, and families are willing to spend much on the education of their children. Most Romanians have graduated from high schools and many of them are university graduates.

Romanians are proud of their heritage and of their contributions to the world. Most of them are aware of their compatriots who have won world fame, such as composer George Enescu, sculptor Constantin Brâncuşi, playwright Eugene Ionesco, gymnast Nadia Comăneci, or tennis player Ilie Năstase.

For leisure, people choose to go out to restaurants and bars. Since one of the favorite forms of entertainment is dining and dancing, most restaurants have a dance floor, with music in the evening. During the summer season there are garden restaurants in the middle of parks or by the lakes.

Romanian consumers spend more on food than American consumers do, and as a group, they seem willing to pay more for high quality products, although the amount has been steadily decreasing over the past ten years.

Romanian cuisine is greatly appreciated by those who have had the opportunity to sample it in its homeland. From the culinary point of view, Romania is the crossroads where every "school" has met and left its mark. During the last century, French cuisine was the one generally adopted, but was yet unable to replace the national one. Additionally, it is not surprising that some of the most typical dishes from neighboring countries have also made their appearance in Romania. However, they only serve to garnish the varied and savory Romanian cuisine that is so tantalizing. Different regions have their own favorites, such as the Moldavian cuisine with its old traditions using sour cream; the Transylvanian, which specializes in sweetened sauces and spices; and the Oltenian, which favors soups, meat and fish, as well as highly spiced dishes.

Breakfast is usually served between 8–9 A.M., lunch between 1–4 P.M. and dinner around 9 P.M. However, restaurants are always ready to serve a good meal, whatever the time.

A meal generally begins with a *gustare* or "appetizer." This normally consists of one or more types of cheese, salami, fresh vegetables or olives. Romania has a great variety of very good cheeses ranging from sweet to salty, mild to strong. After the main course, the favorite dessert is *clătite* (crepes served with jam, flambé) and black coffee. At breakfast, coffee is served with milk.

Lunch (*prînzul*) is the main meal of the day. It usually consists of soup, the main dish and dessert. Nowadays, however, because of busy work or school schedules, Romanians take less time for lunch and prefer to have a larger evening meal (*cina*). Snacking is becoming very popular at the desk in the office or at home.

Dinner is in many cases a three-course meal, but more and more Romanians tend to limit themselves to one main dish and skip the traditional appetizers.

Some typical Romanian dishes include *ciorbă de perișoare* (soup with meat balls), *ciorbă pescărească* (soup with many varieties of fish), *ciorbă de potroace* (sour soup with giblets), *ciorbă țărănească* (meat and vegetable soup peasant-style), *ciorbă moldovenească* (a hearty sour meat soup), *borș de miel* (sour soup containing pieces of lamb), *sarmale* (ground meat, rolled in cabbage or vine leaves) with *mămăligă* (cornmeal mush), *sărmăluțe în foi de viță* (ground meat rolled in grape leaves, sprinkled with borsch, served with cream or yogurt), *tocană* (pork, beef or mutton stew, with onions, also usually served with *mămăligă*), *ghiveci* (a vegetable stew cooked in oil) also called *"călugăresc"* when served without meat, *saramură de crap* (grilled carp with pepper, also served with *mămăligă*), *ardei umpluţi* (sweet peppers stuffed with ground meat and rice), *pîrjoale moldoveneşti* (Moldavian hamburgers), *mititei*, which are made with highly seasoned ground meat and grilled, making tasty snacks that can be ordered in cafes and restaurants. *Mămăligă*, a cornmeal mush, is the Romanian all-purpose staple food. Hot, cold, fried, it is delicious in melted butter, sour cream or yogurt, garnished with salted herring and cottage cheese, or eaten with eggs for breakfast, and added to meat dishes.

For dessert, one can have *clătite* (crepes served with jam, flambé), *papanaşi* (ring doughnuts served with sour cream), *baklava* (cake with nuts and honey), *cataif* (cake with whipped cream), *colţunaşi cu smîntînă* (boiled triangular dumplings filled with cottage cheese and served with cream and sugar), *plăcinte poale-n-brîu* (turnovers).

Wine and beer are equally popular in Romania. The variety of wines is truly remarkable, ranging from international types such as Riesling, Cabernet and Muscat, to local wines from Romanian vineyards, which have gained not only numerous gold medals in international wine competitions but also lasting fame on the world market. Mixed with soda, they are delicious cold drinks—as "soft" as you wish them to be. Romanians drink *"spriţ"*—wine with soda—more often than pure wine.

"Before dinner" drinks include, beside *ţuică* (plum brandy), a wide selection of vermouths, cognacs, liqueurs, and more, thus catering to all tastes. An extensive assortment of soft drinks is also available, particularly refreshing fruit juices—*"nectar"*—made from plums, apricots, peaches, strawberries and many others. A tasty Romanian specialty is *"lapte bătut"* (turned over milk, slightly sour). Drink it for breakfast, with a croissant, or simply as a snack at any time of the day. If by chance you visit Romania in the fall, do not forget *"must"* (the *u* is pronounced like *oo* in *moose*)—fermented grape juice.

Romanians drink their coffee after a meal, when they consider it a must. Coffee in Romania automatically means

Turkish coffee—strong, black and sweet. If you want any other sort of coffee, you must be specific: espresso (Italian style coffee), Nescafe (instant, with or without milk), *cafea cu lapte* (coffee with milk).

In both English and Romanian, the context makes it clear whether a speaker is talking about A.M. or P.M. In Romanian, *dimineaţa* is used to specify A.M. To indicate P.M. *după amiază* is used for "in the afternoon", and *seara* is used for "in the evening" or "at night" (before midnight). Generally, these expressions are used only to tell the time on the hour.

To avoid all confusion, the 24-hour clock is used in official announcements—such as on TV, on the radio, and in train or plane schedules.

The official time is two hours ahead of Greenwich Mean Time (that is, seven hours ahead of EST in the U.S.) When it is noon in London, it is 2 P.M. in Bucharest.

In Romanian, the days of the week and the months of the year are not capitalized. The week starts on Monday on the Romanian calendar. When referring to dates, the day is usually followed by the month: 21 *martie* (March 21) abbreviated as 21/3. Dates in Romanian are expressed with cardinal numbers, with the exception of the first of the month: 1 *(întîi) ianuarie* (January 1).

In Romania and other countries with Orthodox (or Catholic) traditions, each day of the year is associated with a particular saint. Many personal first names are names of saints.

Power supply in Romania is 220 V. Before leaving, verify that your razor or other electrical appliances are suitable to that higher voltage.

Mailboxes, painted navy blue, can be found on streets, in hotels, at resorts, in stations, and other places. You can buy postage stamps at hotels, tobacco stores, newspaper stands, and post offices, among other retailers.

Public telephone booths are indicated by a small sign-board representing a receiver. In Romanian, telephone numbers are written and told in two-digit numbers.

In Romania, like everywhere in Europe, the temperature is measured on the Celsius, rather than the Fahrenheit scale, and the decimal system is uniformly used with weights and measures.

Romanian currency is the *leu,* which is divided into 100 *bani.*

Service is usually quite efficient, and where it lacks the professional touch, you'll find lots of goodwill. To communicate better with the locals, you should try and learn a few basic terms in Romanian, because not all waiters and porters speak a foreign language.

Handicraft traditions have survived in several areas. There are still many craftsmen who continue the tradition of pottery, woodcarving, embroidery, costumes, carpets, textile decoration, sewing and carpet weaving. The most comprehensive and concentrated collection of Romanian folk art is found in the Village Museum in Bucharest. This open-air museum of Romanian village life consists of furnished rural structures of the seventeenth to the twentieth century, from the different Romanian lands.

Folk costumes perhaps best represent the Romanians' soul and temperament. The peasant costumes excel in their variety and gold and silver threads were brilliantly embroidered on silk, before being ornamented with spangles and colored glass beads. The women's peasant blouses, made of the purest embroidered gauze, are fashionable all over the world.

You are sure to find all kinds of original articles that will later remind you of your visit to Romania. Arts and crafts shops sell fine carved and poker-work wooden articles; straw baskets, handbags, and all sorts of other straw articles made by hand; dolls dressed in all the regional costumes of Romania; hand-woven carpets in a multitude of colors and designs.

Folk pottery is well represented by that made at Horezu (colored) and by the black ceramics of North Moldavia and of Transylvania. The vases, jugs, plates and jars that decorate the walls of many peasant houses are renowned throughout the world.

The Romanian musical tradition is especially rich in folk music and folk dance. Both are basic components of folk festivals, especially those connected with major

Christian holidays, Christmas and New Year's Day, weddings, funerals, and seasonal rites. Instruments used by the folk musicians (*lăutari*) are the violin, the *cobza* (lute), the *ţambal* (cembalom), bagpipe, flutes (including panpipes), and accordion. Dances tend to be fast and intricate, including the familiar *horă* (round dance) and the ritual dances of which the *căluşari* (the Oltenian fertility dance with the dancers imitating horse-riders) has become emblematic of Romanian folk dance. Folk songs include ballads such as *Mioriţa*, the epic ballad of Transylvania and northern Moldavia, sentimental laments (the *doina*), and Christmas carols (*colinde*).

Some restaurants, beside the typical Romanian fare and décor, also have a folklore program. This is worthwhile seeking, since the bright, colorful costumes, the gay dances and the lyrical love songs will add an extra flavor to your Romanian meal. The great variety of Romanian folk dances and songs will not allow you to see everything, but you can get a good idea of the most famous dances, like the *calusari*, the most typical costumes, and a few examples of Romanian folk music. Often there is just a singer, who in addition to hit songs of today sings also a selection of Romanian folk tunes.

If you want to discover new places and meet new people, remember Romania. Romanians will welcome you into their homes, feed you well, and expect nothing in return other than friendship. When they say *"Bine aţi venit!"* (Welcome!), Romanians really mean it.

# BASIC GRAMMAR

## The Article

The definite article **the** is **(u)le** for masculine singular and **(u)a** for feminine singular.

The article **–l** is added at the end of all masculine nouns that end in **–u**:

bou-**l**, *the* ox
codru-**l**, *the forest*
tigru-**l**, *the tiger*

When the noun ends in a consonant, the vowel **u** is interpolated before the article, as in the following examples:

cal-**u**-l, *the horse*
pom-**u**-l, *the tree*
scaun-**u**-l, *the chair*

The article **–le** is added on the end of masculine or neuter nouns that end in **–e**, as:

frate-**le**, *the brother*
iepure-**le**, *the rabbit*
nume-**le**, *the name*

The article **–a** is added at the end of all feminine nouns that end in **–ă**. The letter **ă** drops before the article:

casă-**a**-casa, *the house*
masă-**a**-masa, *the table*
pisică-**a**-pisica, *the cat*

In feminine nouns ending in **–ea** or **–ia**, the vowel **u** is interpolated before the article:

stea-**u**-a, *the star*
cafea-**u**-a, *the coffee*
nuia-**u**-a, *the twig*

In feminine nouns ending in –e the article goes after the –e:

carte-**a**, *the book*
floare-**a**, *the flower*
vulpe-**a**, *the fox*

Exceptions are the nouns ending in –**ie**, as: prostie, *stupidity*; gelozie, *jealousy*; farmacie, *pharmacy*, etc., which drop the –**e** before the article, as: prosti-**a**, gelozi-**a**, farmaci-**a**, etc.

The indefinite articles for masculine nouns are **un** for singular and **nişte** for plural:

**un** bărbat, *a man*; **nişte** bărbaţi, *men.*
**un** fiu, *a son*; **nişte** fii, *sons*
**un** miner, *a miner*; **nişte** mineri, *miners*
**un** munte, *a mountain*; **nişte** munţi, *mountains*

The indefinite articles for feminine nouns are **o** for singular and **nişte** for plural:

**o** fată, *a girl*; **nişte** fete, *girls*
**o** cafea, *a coffee*; **nişte** cafele, *coffees.*

In form, the neuter appears as masculine singular and feminine plural:

autobuz**ul**, *the bus*; autobuz**ele**, *the buses*
hotel**ul**, *the hotel*; hotelur**ile**, *the hotels*
**un** autobus, *a bus*; **nişte** autobuze, *buses*
**un** hotel, *a hotel*; **nişte** hoteluri, *hotels*

## Gender

Romanian nouns are divided into three genders: masculine, feminine, and neuter. The form of the indefinite article that accompanies a noun and the ending of the noun indicate the gender to which it belongs. Masculine nouns take a consonant plus –**u**, -**e**, or –**i** endings and the plural is marked by a final –**i**:

bărbat, *man*; bărbați, *men*.
fiu, *son*; fii, *sons*
munte, *mountain*; munți, *mountains*
pui, *chicken*; pui, *chickens*.

Feminine nouns end in –**ă**, -**e**, -**ea**, -**a**. Plurals are marked by –**le**, -**e**, or –**i** endings:

saltea, *mattress*; saltele, *mattresses*
fată, *girl*; fete, *girls*
femeie, *woman*; femei, *women*.

## Number

There are four plural endings in Romanian:

1. -**i** for masculine nouns: lup-lupi, *wolf-wolves*; pantof-pantofi, *shoe-shoes*; codru-codri, *forest-forests*; leu-lei, *lion-lions*.
   -**i** for feminine nouns: floare-flori, *flower-flowers*; vulpe-vulpi, fox-*foxes*; regulă-reguli, *rule-rules*.

2. -**le** for feminine nouns: zi-zile, *day-days*; pijama-pijamale, *pajamas*; basma-basmale, *scarf-scarves*.

3. -**uri** for feminine nouns: vreme-vremuri, *time-times*; sare-săruri, *salt-salts*; treabă, treburi, *job-jobs*.
   -**uri** for neuter nouns: tren-trenuri, *train-trains*; val-valuri, *wave-waves*; raft-rafturi, *shelf-shelves*; ceas-ceasuri, *watch-watches*.

4. -**e** for neuter nouns: caiet-caiete, *notebook-notebooks*; roman-romane, *novel-novels*; scaun-scaune, *chair-chairs*; oraș-orașe, *town-towns*.

## Declension

Romanian is an inflected language, which means that all nouns have special endings depending on their role in the sentence. The Nominative and Accusative have identical endings, and so do the Genitive and Dative.

To form the masculine singular Genitive-Dative add **–ui** to the singular definite form:

Camera fiul**ui** meu este alături.
  *My son's room is next door.*
Dă-i acest caiet fiul**ui** tău.
  *Give this notebook to your son.*

To form the feminine singular Genitive-Dative add **-ei/-ii** to the plural indefinite form:

casa-case-cas**ei**
femeie-femei-feme**ii**
El stătea pe acoperișul cas**ei**.
  *He stood on the roof of the house.*
Transmite-i, te rog, mulțumiri feme**ii** care mă ajută.
  *Please give my thanks to the woman who helps me.*

To form the masculine and feminine plural Genitive-Dative add **–lor** to the plural indefinite form:

fiu-fii-fii**lor**
femeie-femei-feme**ilor**
casa-case-case**lor**.

Dictionaries provide the Nominative-Accusative form:

Fiul meu este student.
  (Subject) *My son is a student.*
Am cumpărat o carte interesantă.
  (Object) *I bought an interesting book.*
Ieri am fost la restaurant.
  (Object) *Yesterday I went to a restaurant.*

# Pronouns

| | |
|---|---|
| eu | *I* |
| tu | *you* |
| dumneata | *you* |
| dumneavoastră | *you* |
| el | *he* |
| ea | *she* |
| noi | *we* |
| voi | *you* |
| dumneavoastră | *you* |
| ei | *they* |
| ele | *they* |

In Romanian there are three different pronouns for the second person. The "tu" form is used when addressing family members, close friends, and children. The "dumneata" form is appropriate when addressing acquaintances and coworkers. "Dumneavoastră" is the official and polite form used when addressing adults.

## POSSESSIVE PRONOUNS/ADJECTIVES

These pronouns agree in gender and number with the "possessed object" and in number with the "possessor."

| English | Masc. Sing. | Masc. Plural |
|---|---|---|
| my | meu | mei |
| your | tău (dumitale, dumneavoastră) | tăi (dumitale, dumneavoastră) |
| his | său | săi |
| our | nostru | noştri |
| your | vostru (dumitale, dumneavoastră) | voştri (dumitale, dumneavoastră) |
| their | lor | lor |

Examples: cîinele **meu** *my dog*; cîinii **mei** *my dogs*; cîinii **noştri** *our dogs*

| English | Fem. Sing. | Fem. Plural |
|---------|-----------|-------------|
| my | mea | mele |
| your | ta (dumitale, dumneavoastră) | tale (dumitale, dumneavoastră) |
| her | sa | sale |
| our | noastră | noastre |
| your | voastră (dumitale, dumneavoastră) | voastre (dumitale, dumneavoastră) |
| their | sa | lor |

Examples: casa **mea** *my house*; casele **mele** *my houses*; casele **noastre** *our houses*.

## INTERROGATIVE RELATIVE PRONOUNS

| | |
|---|---|
| care | *which, that* |
| cine | *who* |
| ce | *what* |
| cît | *how much/many* |

**Care, cine** and **cît** follow the noun declension rules:

**Cine** a sunat?
   *Who called?*
Nu stiu **ce** vrei să spui.
   *I don't know what you mean.*
**Care** maşină este mai scumpă?
   *Which car is more expensive?*
**Cît** timp durează?
   *How long will it take?*
**A cui** este cartea?
   *Whose book is this?*
Am un prieten **al cărui** tată este actor.
   *I have a friend whose father is an actor.*

## DEMONSTRATIVE PRONOUNS

When accompanying a noun, it functions as an adjective, and agreement between the noun and the adjective is required.

| English | Masc. Sing. | Fem. Sing. |
|---|---|---|
| this | acest | aceasta |
| that | acel | acea |
| of/to this | acestui | acestei |
| of/to that | acelui | acelei |

| English | Masc. Plural | Fem. Plural |
|---|---|---|
| these | aceşti | aceste |
| those | acei | acele |
| of/to these | acestor | acestor |
| of/to those | acelor | acelor |

All these forms become definite by adding –a at the end: acest–acesta *this one*; aceşti–aceştia *these ones*; acel–acela *that one*.

Exceptions: aceasta–aceasta *this one*; acea–aceea *that one*.

## INDEFINITE PRONOUNS

The most common indefinite pronouns are:

| | |
|---|---|
| **alt, alta, alţi, alte** | *other* |
| **cineva** | *someone* |
| **ceva** | *something* |
| **fiecare** | *each, every* |
| **orice** | *anything* |
| **oricine** | *anyone* |

# Adjectives

In Romanian, adjectives agree with nouns in gender, number and case. Generally, the adjective follows the noun it qualifies. The feminine gender is formed by adding –ă to the masculine.

| English | Masc. Sing. | Fem. Sing. | Masc. Plural | Fem. Plural |
|---------|-------------|------------|--------------|-------------|
| young | tînăr | tînără | tineri | tinere |
| beautiful | frumos | frumoasă | frumoşi | frumoase |

When accompanying a noun the adjective agrees with the noun in gender and number:

băiat **frumos** *handsome boy*; băieţi **frumoşi** *handsome boys*
fată **frumoasă** *beautiful girl*; fete **frumoase** *beautiful girls*.

Some adjectives are invariable:

dulce–dulci, *sweet*
fierbinte–fierbinţi, *hot*
iute–iuţi, *hot, spicy*
limpede–limpezi, *clear*
mare (*masc. and fem. sing.*), mari (*masc and fem. pl.*) *big*
rece–reci, *cold*
verde–verzi, *green*

## COMPARISON OF ADJECTIVES

Positive: **puternic** *strong*

Comparative: **mai puternic decît/ca** *stronger than.*; **mai puţin puternic decît/ca** *less strong than*; **la fel de puternic ca** *as strong as.*

Superlative: **cel mai puternic** *the strongest*; **foarte/extraordinar de puternic** *very strong.*

# Adverbs

Adverbs are generally not inflected. Some follow the same degree of comparison rules as the adjectives:

| | |
|---|---|
| acasă | *at home* |
| acum | *now* |
| aseară | *last night* |
| atunci | *then* |
| cînd | *when* |
| cum | *how* |
| din nou | *again* |
| duminica | *on Sunday* |
| niciodată | *never* |
| pe de rost | *by heart* |
| pe neașteptate | *unexpectedly* |
| românește | *in Romanian* |
| unde | *where* |

Many adverbs and adjectives are similar in form:

| | |
|---|---|
| cald | *warmly* |
| frumos | *beautifully* |
| plăcut | *pleasantly* |
| rar | *slowly* |
| rece | *coldly* |
| repede | *quickly* |
| tare | *strongly, loudly* |

The degrees of comparison follow the same pattern as the one described for adjectives.

# Verbs

In Romanian, there are four regular conjugations

1. verbs ending in –a in the infinitive: **a cînta** *to sing*, **a lucra** *to work*, **a lega** *to tie*.

2. verbs ending in –ea: **a vedea** *to see*, **a plăcea** *to like*, **a cădea** *to fall*.

3. verbs ending in –e: **a face** *to do, to make*, **a plînge** *to cry*, **a decide** *to decide*.

4. verbs ending in –i/î: **a citi** *to read*, **a dormi** *to sleep*, **a coborî** *to go down*.

## AUXILIARY VERBS

The three Romanian auxiliary verbs, **a fi** *to be*, **a avea** *to have*, and **a voi** *to want* are used in combination with main verbs as parts of a compound tense. They can also be used as main verbs.

**a fi** *to be*
Indicative present: **eu sînt, tu eşti, el/ea este, noi sîntem, voi sînteţi, ei/ele sînt.**
Indicative imperfect: **eu eram, tu erai, el/ea era, noi eram, voi eraţi, ei/ele erau.**
Indicative compound past: **eu am fost, tu ai fost, el/ea a fost, noi am fost, voi aţi fost, ei/ele au fost.**
Indicative future: **eu voi fi, tu vei fi, el/ea va fi, noi vom fi, voi veţi fi, ei/ele vor fi.**
The subjunctive: **eu să fiu, tu să fii, el/ea să fie, noi să fim, voi să fiţi, ei/ele să fie.**
Conditional: **eu aş fi, tu ai fi, el/ea ar fi, noi am fi, voi aţi fi, ei/ele ar fi.**
Past participle: **fost**
Gerund: **fiind**

**a avea** *to have*
Indicative present: **eu am, tu ai, el/ea are, noi avem, voi aveţi, ei/ele au.**
Indicative imperfect: **eu aveam, tu aveai, el/ea avea, noi aveam, voi aveaţi, ei/ele aveau.**
Indicative compound perfect: **eu am avut, tu ai avut, el/ea a avut, noi am avut, voi aţi avut, ei/ele au avut.**
Indicative future: **eu voi avea, tu vei avea, el/ea va avea, noi vom avea, voi veţi avea, ei/ele vor avea.** There is also an informal future commonly used in ordinary

conversation: **eu o să am, tu o să ai, el/ea o să aibă, noi o să avem, voi o să aveți, ei/ele o să aibă.**

Subjunctive: **eu să am, tu să ai, el/ea să aibă, noi să avem, voi să aveți, ei/ele să aibă.**

Conditional: **eu aş avea, tu ai avea, el/ea ar avea, noi am avea, voi ați avea, ei/ele ar avea.**

Past participle: **avut.**

Gerund: **avînd.**

The verb **a voi** appears as an auxiliary verb in the future indicative (see above).

To form the negative, the adverb "nu" (not) is placed in front of the verb. Examples: eu am-eu **nu** am, eu am avut-eu **nu** am avut, eu voi avea-eu **nu** voi avea, etc.

Indicative present

First conjugation—**a cînta:** eu cînt-, tu cînți-**i**, el/ea cîntă-**ă**, noi cîntăm-**m**, voi cîntați-**ți**, ei/ele cîntă-**ă**.

**a lucra:** eu lucrez-**ez**, tu lucrezi-**ezi**, el/ea lucrează-**ează**, noi lucrăm-**m**, voi lucrați-**ți**, ei/ele lucrează-**ează**.

Second conjugation—**a vedea:** eu văd-, tu vezi-**i**, el/ea vede-**e**, noi vedem-**m**, voi vedeți-**ți**, ei/ele văd-.

Third conjugation—**a face:** eu fac-, tu faci-**i**, el/ea face-**e**, noi facem-**m**, voi faceți-**ți**, ei/ele fac-.

Fourth conjugation—**a dormi:** eu dorm-, tu dormi-**i**, el/ea doarme-**e**, noi dormim-**m**, voi dormiți-**ți**, ei/ele dorm-.

**a citi:** eu citesc-**esc**, tu citești-**ești**, el/ea citește-**ește**, noi citim-**m**, voi citiți-**ți**, ei/ele citesc-**esc**.

**a coborî:** eu cobor-, tu cobori-**i**, el/ea coboară-**ă**, noi coborîm-**m**, voi coborîți-**ți**, ei/ele coboară-**ă**.

To be able to conjugate a Romanian verb one should memorize a few basic forms, e.g. **a lucra:**

Indicative present, first person: **lucrez**

Subjunctive third person: **să lucreze**

Past participle: **lucrat**

Short infinitive: **lucra**

Once these forms have been memorized, all verbs follow a regular pattern:

Indicative present: **lucrez, lucrezi, lucrează, lucrăm, lucrați, lucrează**

Example: **Lucrez** ca programator. *I work as a programmer.*

Indicative imperfect (**stem of the verb + –am, -ai, -a, -am, -ați, -au**): **lucram, lucrai, lucra, lucram, lucrați, lucrau.**

Example: Cînd **lucram** la editură citeam foarte mult. *When I was working for a publisher I read a lot.*

Indicative compound past (**am, ai, a, am, ați, au + the past participle** of the main verb: **am lucrat, ai lucrat, a lucrat, am lucrat, ați lucrat, au lucrat.**

Example: In Romania **ați lucrat** și sîmbăta? *In Romania did you work on Saturdays too?*

Indicative future (**o + subjunctive** or **voi, vei, va, vom, veți, vor + short infinitive**): **o să lucrez, o să lucrezi, o să lucreze, o să lucrăm, o să lucrați, o să lucreze; voi lucra, vei lucra, va lucra, vom lucra, veți lucra, vor lucra.**

Example: Cînd **veți merge** în România, **o să vizitați** litoralul Marii Negre. *When you (will) go to Romania, you will visit the Black Sea coast.*

Subjunctive (identical with Indicative present, except for the third person singular and plural): **să lucrez, să lucrezi, să lucreze, să lucrăm, să lucrați, să lucreze.**

Example: Vreți **să mergeți** la petrecere deseară? *Do you want to go to the party tonight?*

Conditional (**aș, ai , ar, am, ați, ar + short infinitive**): **aș lucra, ai lucra, ar lucra, am lucra, ați lucra, ar lucra.**

Example: **Aș lucra** din greu pentru a termina proiectul. *I'd work hard to finish the project.*

Gerund (**stem of the main verb + -înd**): **lucrînd.**

Example: V-am văzut **lucrînd** seara tîrziu. *I saw you working late at night.*

## REFLEXIVE VERBS

The reflexive verb shows that the subject acts upon itself, or that the action is performed in its own behalf. When the subject acts upon itself, the verb is preceded by the accusative form of the personal pronoun: **mă, te, se, ne, vă, se**. When the action is performed on behalf of the subject, the dative forms of the personal pronoun precede the verb: **îmi, îți, își, ne, vă, își**:

**a se duce** (to go, to carry oneself to): Vara **mă duc** la piscină in fiecare zi. *In the summer I go to the pool every day.*

**a-și duce** (to carry): **Îmi duc** hainele la curățat în fiecare săptămînă. *I take my clothes to the cleaners every week.*

**a se spăla** (to wash oneself): Imediat ce mă scol, **mă spăl** și apoi pregătesc cafeaua. *As soon as I get up, I wash myself and then make coffee.*

**a-și spăla** (to wash one's...): **Îmi spăl** mașina în fața casei. *I wash my car in front of the house.*

## IRREGULAR VERBS

The verbs that deviate from the four regular conjugations are commonly called irregular. They follow the conjugation of the regular verbs, but undergo certain changes in the root. There are about a dozen irregular verbs including **a da** *to give*; **a lua** *to take*; **a mînca** *to eat*; **a bea** *to drink*; **a putea** *can*; and **a sta** *to stay*.

# Interrogation and Negation

In Romanian, the form of the verb in the interrogative is exactly the same as the affirmative. Interrogation is expressed by a rising inflection of the voice, and in writing by the use of the interrogative mark:

| | |
|---|---|
| **Au sosit?** | *Have they arrived?* |
| **Înțelegi?** | *Do you understand?* |

In Romanian the negative is expressed by the particle **nu**, which is placed in front of the verb:

**Nu** lucrez. *I don't work.*
**Nu** văd. *I do not see.*

The vowel **u** of the particle disappears before the vowel **a** of the auxiliary in compound tenses:

**N-am auzit**. *I did not hear.*
**N-aş spune asta**. *I wouldn't say so.*

In the tenses of the subjunctive, the negative particle is interpolated between the conjunction **să** and the verb:

**Să nu aud**. *That I may not hear*
**Să nu vorbească**. *That he may not speak.*

In the infinitive, the negative particle also goes between the preposition **a** and the verb:

**a nu face**, *not to do*
**a nu vedea**, *not to see*
**a nu fugi**, *not to run*

## Prepositions

Most prepositions, whether they are simple or compound, require the Accusative case:

| | |
|---|---|
| **cu** | *with* |
| **despre** | *about*, etc. |
| **în** | *in* |
| **înspre** | *toward* |
| **la** | *at* |
| **lîngă** | *beside* |
| **pe** | *on* |
| **pentru** | *for* |
| **peste** | *over* |
| **sub** | *under* |

Some prepositions, however, most of them in definite-like form, require the Genitive-Dative case:

| | |
|---|---|
| **asupra** | *about* |
| **contra, împotriva** | *against* |
| **datorită** | *because of* |
| **deasupra** | *over* |
| **din cauza** | *due to* |
| **grație, mulțumită** | *thanks to* |
| **în fața** | *in front of* |
| **în jurul** | *around* |

Fac aceasta **pentru fratele meu**.

    *I'm doing this for my brother* (Accusative).

El a făcut o călătorie **în jurul lumii**.

    *He made a trip around the world* (Genitive-Dative).

# GUIDE TO PRONUNCIATION

## Vowels

**a** like the vowel sound in bar, but the **r** should not be pronounced; e.g. **alfabet** (alphabet).

**ă** like the English vowel sound in hurt, but the **r** should not be pronounced; e.g. **masă** (table).

**â** has no exact equivalent in English; it resembles the **o** in lesson. It occurs only in a few words; e.g. **român** (Romanian).

**e** like the **e** in ten; e.g. **elev** (student).

**i**   1) like **ee** in bee; e.g. **bine** (well).

    2) if unstressed at the end of a word, it may be scarcely audible, softening the preceding consonant; e.g. **bani** (money).

**î** pronounced exactly like the **â** above; e.g. **între** (between), **hotărî** (decide).

**o** like the vowel sound in sport, without pronouncing the r; e.g. **copil** (child).

**u** like **oo** in moon; e.g. **munte** (mountain).

## Diphthongs

**ai** like **igh** in high; e.g. **mai** (May).

**au** like **ow** in cow; e.g. **stau** (stand).

**ău** like **o** in go; e.g. **rău** (bad).

**ea** has no exact equivalent in English; sounds almost like **ya** in **ya**cht; e.g. dimineaţa (morning), oprea (stopped).

**ei** like **ay** in d**ay**; e.g. lei (lions).

**eu** has no exact equivalent in English; start pronouncing the **e** of bed then draw your lips together to make a brief **oo** sound; e.g. leu (lion).

**ia** like **ya** in **ya**rd; e.g. iarba (grass).

**ie** like **ye** in **ye**llow; e.g. ieftin (cheap).

**io** like **yo** in **yo**nder; e.g. creion (pencil).

**iu** like **ew** in f**ew**; e.g. iubire (love).

**oa** like **wha** in **wha**t; e.g. poate (perhaps).

**oi** like **oy** in b**oy**; e.g. doi (two).

**ua** like **wa** in **wa**tch; e.g. aluat (dough).

**uă** similar to **ue** in infl**ue**nce; e.g. nouă (nine).

## Consonants

**c**   1) like **c** in **c**ake; e.g. cartof (potato).

    2) followed by **e** or **i,** like **ch** in **ch**eese; e.g. ceas (watch), cineva (somebody).

**ch** like **k** in **k**ettle; e.g. chibrit (match), chel (bald).

**g**   1) like **g** in **g**irl; e.g. gard (fence).

    2) when followed by **e** or **i,** like **g** in **g**ender; e.g. ginere (bridegroom), ger (frost).

**gh** like **g** in **g**arden; e.g. ghete (boots), ghindă (acorn).

**h** like **h** in **h**and; e.g. **h**artă (map).

**j** like **s** in plea**s**ure; e.g. **j**ucărie (toy).

**r** rolled consonant similar to the Scottish **r**; e.g. **r**oată (wheel).

**s** like **s** in **s**un; e.g. **s**tudent (student).

**ş** like **sh** in **sh**ort; e.g. **ş**iret (sly).

**ţ** like **ts** in bi**ts**; e.g. **ţ**ară (country).

**x** like **x** in e**x**treme before consonants, e.g. e**x**plica (to explain), and like **x** in e**x**act before vowels, e.g. e**x**emplu (example).

**b, d, f, l, m, n, p, t, v, z** are pronounced as in English.

# ABBREVIATIONS

| | |
|---|---|
| *adj.* | adjective |
| *adv.* | adverb |
| *art.* | article |
| *conj.* | conjunction |
| *det.* | determiner |
| *excl.* | exclamation |
| *f.* | feminine noun |
| *interj.* | interjection |
| *m.* | masculine noun |
| *n.* | noun |
| *neut.* | neuter noun |
| *num.* | numeral |
| *pl.* | plural |
| *pron.* | pronoun |
| *prep.* | preposition |
| *v.* | verb |
| *v.aux.* | auxiliary verb |
| *v.i.* | intransitive verb |
| *v.imp.* | impersonal verb |
| *v.mod.* | modal auxiliary verb |
| *v.r.* | reflexive verb |
| *v.t.* | transitive verb |

# ROMANIAN-ENGLISH DICTIONARY

## A

**abandona** *v.t.* to abandon
**abatere** *f.* diversion
**abătut** *adj.* downcast
**abdomen** *neut.* abdomen
**abia** *adv.* barely; hardly
**abil** *adj.* clever
**abilitate** *f.* skill
**abonament** *neut.* subscription
**aborda** *v.t.* to approach
**abrupt** *adj.* steep
**absent** *adj.* absent
**absență** *f.* absence
**absolut** *adj.* absolute
**absolvent** *m.* graduate
**absurd** *adj.* absurd
**abundent** *adj.* abundant
**abuz** *neut.* abuse
**ac** *neut.* needle
**academie** *f.* academy
**acasă** *adv.* at home
**accelera** *v.i.* to speed (up)
**accelerat** *neut.* fast train
**accelerator** *neut.* accelerator
**accent** *neut.* accent
**accepta** *v.t.* to admit
**accesibil** *adj.* accessible
**accident** *neut.* accident
**acea** *adj.* that
**aceasta** *pron.* this
**aceea** *pron.* that
**aceeași** *pron.* the same
**acei(a)** *pron.* those (ones)
**aceiași** *pron.* the same
**acel(a)** *pron.* that (one)
**același** *pron.* the same
**acele(a)** *pron.* those (ones)
**aceleași** *pron.* the same
**acest(a)** *pron.* this (one)
**aceste(a)** *pron.* these (ones)
**acești(a)** *pron.* these (ones)
**achita** *v.t.* to pay (off)

**achiziție** *f.* acquisition
**acolo** *adv.* there
**acomoda** *v.r.* to accommodate; to adapt oneself
**acomodare** *f.* accommodation
**acompania** *v.t.* to accompany
**acont** *neut.* advance
**acoperi** *v.t.* to cover
**acoperiș** *neut.* roof
**acord** *neut.* agreement
**acord, a fi de** to agree
**acorda** *v.t.*, *v.i.* to grant
**acru** *adj.* sour
**act** *neut.* act; deed
**activ** *adj.* active
**activitate** *f.* activity
**actor** *m.* actor
**actriță** *f.* actress
**actual** *adj.* present-day
**acționa** *v.i.* to act
**acționar** *m.* shareholder
**acțiune** *f.* action
**acuarelă** *f.* watercolor
**acum** *adv.* now
**acut** *adj.* sharp
**acuza** *v.t.* to charge
**adapta** *v.r.* to adjust
**adaptor** *neut.* adaptor
**adăpost** *neut.* shelter
**adăposti** *v.i.* to shelter
**adăuga** *v.t.* to add
**adecvat** *adj.* suitable
**adesea** *adv.* often
**adevăr** *neut.* truth
**adevărat** *adj.* true
**adeverință** *f.* certificate
**adeziv** *neut.*, *adj.* adhesive
**adică** *adv.* that is
**adineauri** *adv.* just now
**adio** *neut.* good-bye
**administra** (*medicine*) *v.t.* to medicate
**administrator** *m.* manager

admira *v.t.* to admire
admirabil *adj.* admirable
admiţînd că admitting that
adormi *v.i.* to sleep
adormit *adv.* asleep
adresă *f.* address
adresă de reexpediere
    forwarding address
aduce *v.t.* to bring
adult *m.* grown-up; adult
aduna *v.t.* to assemble
aer *neut.* air
aerobică *f.* aerobics
aeroplan *neut.* airplane
aeroport *neut.* airport
afacere *f.* business; deal
afaceri *f.pl.* business
afaceri, în interes de on
    business
afaceri, călătorie de business
    trip
afaceri, om de businessman
afară *adv.* out
afectare *f.* affectation
afirmaţie *f.* statement
afiş *neut.* poster
agenţie *f.* agency
agenţie de voiaj travel agency
agita *v.r.* to stir
agitaţie *f.* stir
aglomerat *adj.* crowded
agresiune *f.* aggression
agricol *adj.* agricultural
agricultură *f.* agriculture
agronom *m.* agronomist
aici *adv.* here
aiurea *adv.* astray
ajun *neut.* eve
ajunul, în on the eve
ajunge *v.i.* to reach
ajuta *v.t.* to help
ajutor *neut.* help
alcool *neut.* alcohol
alături de *adv.* beside
alb *adj.* white
albastru *adj.* blue
albină *f.* bee
alege *v.t.* to choose
alegere *f.* choice

alerga *v.i.* to run
alergic *adj.* allergic
alergie *f.* allergy
alfabet *neut.* alphabet
alo *interj.* hello
alt(a) *pron.* another
alta, o another
altceva *pron.* something else
altfel *adv.* otherwise
altul, un another
altul, unul pe each other
aluat *neut.* dough
aluneca *v.i.* to slip
amar *adj.* bitter
amator *m.* amateur
ambasadă *f.* embassy
ambasador *m.* ambassador
amenda *v.t.* to fine
amendă *f.* fine
ameninţa *v.t.* to threaten
ameninţare *f.* threat
America *f.* America
american *m.* American
amestec *neut.* mixture
amesteca *v.t.* to mix
ameţeală *f.* dizziness
ameţit *adj.* dizzy
amiază *f.* noon
amiază, după afternoon
amigdale *f.pl.* tonsils
aminti *v.r.* to remember; *v.i.* to
    remind
amurg *neut.* twilight
amuzant *adj.* funny
an *m.* year
anestetic *neut.* anesthetic
anestezist *m.* anesthesiologist
Anglia *f.* England
animal *neut.* animal
animal de casă *neut.* pet
antibiotic *neut.* antibiotic
antic *adj.* ancient, antique
anticipat *adj.* in advance
anticoncepţional *neut.*
    contraceptive
anula *v.t.* to cancel
anulare *f.* cancellation
anunţ *neut.* announcement
anunţa *v.t.* to announce

aparat *neut.* apparatus
aparat de ras razor
apartament *neut.* apartment
aparține *v.i.* to belong
apă *f.* water
apă distilată distilled water
apă minerală mineral water
apăra *v.t.* to defend
apărare *f.* defense
apărea *v.i.* to appear
apăsa *v.t.* to press; to squeeze
apel *neut.* appeal; call
apendice *neut.* appendix
apendicită *f.* appendicitis
aperitiv *neut.* appetizer
aplauze *f.pl.* applause
aprilie *m.* April
aproape *adv.* nearly; almost
aproba *v.t.* to approve
apropia *v.r.* to get near
apropiat *adj.* close; near
aproviziona *v.i.* to provide
apuca *v.t.* to seize
aramă *f.* copper
aranja *v.t.* to arrange; to settle
arăta *v.t.* to show
arde *v.i.* to burn
ardei *m.* pepper (*vegetable*)
aresta *v.t.* to arrest
arestat, a fi to be under arrest
argint *neut.* silver
argintiu *adj.* silver
arhitect *m.* architect
arhitectură *f.* architecture
aripă *f.* wing
armă *f.* gun
arogant *adj.* arrogant, haughty
arsură *f.* burn
artă *f.* art
arteră *f.* artery
articulație *f.* joint; articulation
artificial *adj.* artificial
artist *m.* artist
artizanat *neut.* handicrafts
artrită *f.* arthritis
arunca *v.t.* to throw away
ascensor *neut.* elevator
asculta *v.t.* to listen
ascultător *m.* listener

ascuțit *adj.* sharp
asediu *neut.* siege
asemănare *f.* resemblance
asemănător *adv.* like
asemenea, de *adv.* also
asigurare *f.* insurance
asigurare, poliță de
    insurance certificate
asocia *v.r.* to associate
asociat *m.* associate
aspirator *neut.* vacuum
    cleaner
aspirină *f.* aspirin
aspru *adj.* harsh; *adv.* rough
astăzi *adv.* today
astmă *f.* asthma
astupa *v.t.* to plug
așa *adv.* so
așezare *f.* locality
aștepta *v.t.* to wait; *v.r.* to
    expect
aștepta cu nerăbdare to look
    forward to
așteptare *f.* wait
așternut *neut.* bedding
atac *neut.* attack
ataca *v.t.* to attack
atașa *v.t.* to attach
atent *adj.* attentive
atenta *v.i.* to attempt
atentat *neut.* attempt
ateriza *v.i.* to land
ateroscleroză *f.*
    arteriosclerosis
atinge *v.t.* to touch
atitudine *f.* attitude
atlet *m.* athlete
atletism *neut.* athletics
atmosferă *f.* atmosphere
atracție *f.* attraction
atrage *v.t.* to attract
atrăgător *adj.* attractive
atunci *adv.* then
atunci, de since
ață *f.* thread
august *m.* August
aur *neut.* gold
Australia *f.* Australia
australian *n.*, *adj.* Australian

autentic *adj.* genuine
autobuz *neut.* bus
autobuz, linie de bus route
autobuz, staţie de bus stop
autogară *f.* bus station
autohton *adj.* native
automat *adj.* automatic
automobil *neut.* car
auto, piese car parts
autor *m.* author
autoritate *f.* authority
autorizaţie *f.* permit; license
autoservire *f.* self-service
auzi *v.t.* to hear
avantaj *neut.* advantage
avea *v.aux., v.t.* to have
avea voie may, to have
    permission
avere *f.* wealth
aversă *f.* shower (*rain*)
avertiza *v.t.* to warn
avion *neut.* aircraft
avion, par airmail
avocat *m.* lawyer

# B

bacşiş *neut.* tip
bagaj *neut.* baggage; luggage
bagaj de mînă hand luggage
bagaj excedentar excess
    luggage
baie *f.* bath
baie, a face to take a bath
baie, cadă de bathtub
baie, cameră de bathroom
baie, halat de bath robe
balcon *neut.* balcony
balon *neut.* balloon
banană *f.* banana
bancă *f.* bank
bancher *m.* banker
bancnotă *f.* banknote, bill
bancomat *neut.* ATM
bandaj *neut.* bandage
bandă *f.* magnetică tape
    (*recording*)
bani *m.pl.* money

bani gheaţă cash
bar *neut.* bar
barbă *f.* beard
barcă *f.* boat
barcă cu motor motorboat
baschet *neut.* basketball
bascheţi *m.pl.* sneakers
baterie *f.* battery
batistă *f.* handkerchief
băcănie *f.* grocery store
băiat *m.* boy
bănuială *f.* suspicion
bărbat *m.* husband
bărbieri *v.t.* to shave
bărbierit *neut.* shave
băşicuţă *f.* blister
bătrîn *adj.* old
bătrîneţe *f.* old age
băutură *f.* drink
băutură nealcoolică
    non-alcoholic drink
bea *v.t.* to drink
beat *adj.* drunk
bec *neut.* bulb
bej *adj.* beige
benzină *f.* gas
benzină fără plumb
    unleaded gas
bere *f.* beer
beton *neut.* concrete
beţiv *m.* drunk
biblie *f.* bible
bibliotecar *m.* librarian
bibliotecă *f.* library
bicicletă *f.* bicycle
biciclist *m.* cyclist
biftec *neut.* steak
bigudiuri *neut.pl.* curlers
bijuterie *f.* jewelry
bilet *neut.* ticket
bilet dus-întors round trip
    ticket
bine *adv.* well
binecuvîntare *f.* blessing
binoclu *neut.* binoculars
birou *neut.* office
biscuit *m.* biscuit
biserică *f.* church
blasfemie *f.* blasphemy

blestem *neut.* curse
bleumarin *adj.* navy blue
bliț *neut.* flash
blînd *adj.* mild; kind
bloc *neut.* block
bloc *neut.* de locuințe apartment building
bloca *v.t.* to obstruct
blugi *m.pl.* jeans
bluză *f.* blouse
boală *f.* illness
bogat *adj.* rich
boicot *neut.* boycott
boicota *v.t.* to boycott
boiler *neut.* water heater
bol *neut.* bowl
bolnav *adj.* sick; ill
bombă *f.* bomb
bomboană *f.* candy
bombăni *v.i.* to grumble
borcan *neut.* jar
bord *neut.* board (*ship*)
bord, pe on board
bordel *neut.* brothel
botez *neut.* baptism
boteza *v.t.* to baptize
braț *neut.* arm
bravo well done
brățară *f.* bracelet
brichetă *f.* lighter
brici *neut.* razor
brînză *f.* cheese
britanic *adj.* British
briză *f.* breeze
broderie *f.* embroidery
broșă *f.* brooch
brusc *adv.* suddenly
brutărie *f.* bakery
bucată *f.* piece
buchet *neut.* bunch
buclă *f.* curl of hair
bucurie *f.* joy
bucuros *adj.* glad
bucătar *m.* cook
bucătărie *f.* kitchen
bucățică *f.* bit
bujie *f.* sparkplug
bumbac *neut.* cotton
bun *adj.* good

bun, cel mai best
bun, mai better
bunic *m.* grandfather
bunică *f.* grandmother
bunici *m.pl.* grandparents
bunuri *neut.pl.* goods
bun-venit welcome
bursă *f.* grant
busolă *f.* compass
buză *f.* lip
buzunar *neut.* pocket


# C

cabaret *neut.* cabaret
cabină *f.* cabin
cablu *neut.* cable
cadavru *neut.* corpse
cadou *neut.* present
cadru *neut.* frame
cădea *v.i.* to fall
cafea *f.* coffee
cafea instant instant coffee
cafea neagră black coffee
cafenea *f.* café
cafetieră *f.* coffee pot
caiet *neut.* notebook
caisă *f.* peach
cal *m.* horse
calculator *neut.* calculator; computer
cald *adj.* warm
cale *f.* ferată railroad
calitate *f.* quality
calm *adj.* still
calorie *f.* calorie
cameră *f.* room
cameră de probă fitting room
cameră de zi living room
camion *neut.* truck
camping *neut.* camping
cămașă *f.* shirt
cămin *neut.* home
Canada *f.* Canada
canadian *n. adj.* Canadian
canapea pat *f.* sofa-bed
cancer *neut.* cancer
candelabru *neut.* chandelier

canotaj *neut.* rowing
cantitate *f.* quantity
cap *neut.* head
capabil *adj.* capable
capac *neut.* cover
capacitate *f.* capacity
capelă *f.* chapel
capital *neut.* capital
capitală *f.* capital
capitol *neut.* chapter
capră *f.* goat
capricios *adj.* moody
capriciu *neut.* whim
caracter *neut.* character
carantină *f.* quarantine
carburant *m.* fuel
cardiac *adj.* cardiac
cardiolog *m.* cardiologist
care *pron.* which
carne *f.* meat
carne de miel lamb
carne de pasăre chicken
carne de porc pork
carte *f.* book; card
carte de credit credit card
carte de telefon telephone
  book
carte poştală postcard
cartof *m.* potato
cartofi prăjiţi french fries
casă *f.* home; house; cash
  register
casă de bilete box office
cascadă *f.* waterfall
casetă *f.* cassette
casetă audio audiocassette
casetă video videocassette
casetofon *neut.* tape recorder
casier *m.* cashier
castan *m.* chestnut
castel *neut.* castle
castravete *m.* cucumber
catedrală *f.* cathedral
catolic *m. adj.* Catholic
caz *neut.* case
caz, în acest in that case
caz, în orice by all means
casino *neut.* casino
că *prep.* that

călări *v.i.* to ride
călători *v.i.* to travel
călătorie *f.* trip; voyage
călătorie cu maşina ride
  (*in a car*)
călătorie cu vaporul boat trip
călcîi *neut.* heel
călugăr *m.* monk
călugăriţă *f.* nun
căprioară *f.* deer
căpşună *f.* strawberry
căra *v.t.* to carry
cărare *f.* path
căsători *v.r.* to marry
căsătorie *f.* marriage
către *prep.* toward
căuta *v.t.* to look for; to seek
ce *pron.* what
ceai *neut.* tea
ceainic *neut.* kettle
ceapă *f.* onion
cearşaf *neut.* bedsheet
ceartă *f.* quarrel
ceas *neut.* watch
ceaşcă *f.* cup
cec *neut.* check (*bank*)
central *adj.* central
centru *neut.* center
centrul oraşului downtown
ceramică *f.* ceramics
cercel *m.* earring
cere *v.t.* to request
cereală *f.* cereal
cerere *f.* request; application
certifica *v.t.* to certify
cetăţean *m.* citizen
ceţos *adj.* hazy
chei *neut.* wharf
cheie *f.* key
chel *adj.* bald
chelner *m.* waiter
chelneriţă *f.* waitress
cheltui *v.t.* to spend
cheltuială *f.* expense
chema *v.t.* to call
chemare *f.* call
chestiona *v.t.* to quiz
chiar *adv.* even
chibrit *neut.* match (*fire*)

chibzui *v.i.* to consider
chibzuit *adj.* wise
chiloţi *m.pl.* de damă panties
chioşc *neut.* kiosk
chioşc de ziare newsstand
chirie *f.* rent
chirurg *m.* surgeon
chiuvetă *f.* sink
cicatrice *f.* scar
ciclism *neut.* cycling
cifră *f.* digit
cilindru *neut.* cylinder
cimitir *neut.* cemetery
cîmp *neut.* field
cinci *num.* five
cine *pron.* who
cineast *m.* filmmaker
cîine *m.* dog
cinema *neut.* cinema; movie
    theater
cineva *pron.* somebody;
    someone
cinstit *adj.* honest; fair
cînta *v.t.* to sing
cîntar *neut.* scale
cîntăreţ *m.* singer
cîntări *v.i.* to weigh
cioban *m.* shepherd
ciocan *neut.* hammer
ciocni *v.i.* to collide; to clink
    (*glasses*) for a toast
ciocnire *f.* collision; clash
ciocolată *f.* chocolate
ciorap *m.* stocking
circulaţie *f.* traffic
cireaşă *f.* cherry
cîrlig *neut.* de rufe clothes
    pin/peg
cîrnat *m.* sausage
cistită *f.* cystitis
cîştig *neut.* gain
cîştiga *v.t.* to earn; to win
cît *adv.* how much
cîteva *pron.* some
citi *v.t.* to read
cîţiva *pron.* some
ciuda, în in spite of
ciudat *adj.* bizarre, weird
ciupercă *f.* mushroom

civic *adj.* civic
civilizaţie *f.* civilization
cizela *v.t.* to chisel
clădi *v.t.* to build
clădire *f.* building
clopot *neut.* bell
clopotniţă *f.* belfry
clar *adj.* clear
clarifica *v.t.* to clarify
clasa turist economy class
clasă *f.* class
claviatură *f.* keyboard
cler *neut.* clergy
cleşte *m.* tongs
client *m.* customer
climă *f.* climate
clipă *f.* instant
clovn *m.* clown
club *neut.* club
club de noapte nightclub
coace *v.t.* to bake
coafeză *f.* hairdresser
coafor *m.* hairdresser
coajă *f.* peel
coapsă *f.* thigh
coase *v.t.* to sew
coastă *f.* coast; rib
coborî *v.t.*, *v.i.* to climb down
coborîre *f.* descent
cochilie *f.* shell
cod *neut.* poştal zip code
codru *m.* forest
coerenţă *f.* coherence
cofetărie *f.* a place for selling
    and consuming gourmet
    desserts and refreshments
coji *v.t.* to peel
colaborare *f.* collaboration
colecţie *f.* collection
coleg *m.* de muncă co-worker
colegiu *neut.* college
colier *neut.* necklace
coloana *f.* vertebrală spine
colivie *f.* cage
colţ *neut.* corner
comanda *v.t.* to order
comandă *f.* order
combinezon *neut.* slip or
    petticoat

comedie *f.* comedy
comentariu *neut.* comment
comercial *adj.* commercial
comic *adj.* comic
comitet *neut.* committee
compact *adj.* compact
companie *f.* company
compara *v.t.* to compare
compartiment *neut.*
   compartment
complet *adj.* complete
complice *m.* accomplice
compliment *neut.*
   compliment
comunica *v.t.* to communicate
comunitate *f.* community
comutator *neut.* switch
concedia *v.t.* to lay off
concediu *neut.* vacation; leave
concert *neut.* concert
concesie *f.* concession
concluzie *f.* conclusion
condiment *neut.* spice
condimentat *adj.* spicy; hot
condiție *f.* condition
condoleanțe *f.pl.* condolences
condom *neut.* condom
conducător *m.* leader
conduce *v.t.* to drive; to lead
conducere *f.* pe dreapta drive
   on the right hand side
confirma *v.t.* to confirm
confirmare *f.* confirmation
conform cu according to
confortabil *adj.* comfortable
congela *v.t.* to freeze
congelator *neut.* freezer
coniac *neut.* brandy
conopidă *f.* cauliflower
consecință *f.* consequence
conserva *v.t.* to can
consiliu *neut.* council, board
consolare *f.* comfort
constipație *f.* constipation
conștient *adj.* conscious
conștiență *f.* consciousness
conștiință *f.* conscience
consul *m.* consul
consulat *neut.* consulate

consultant *m.* consultant
consumator *m.* consumer
cont *neut.* account
cont bancar bank account
conta *v.i.* to matter
contabil *m.* accountant
contact *neut.* contact
context *neut.* context
contingent *adj.* contingent
continua *v.t.* to continue
contor *neut.* electric
   electricity meter
contract *neut.* contract
contradicție *f.* contradiction
contribuție *f.* contribution
contuzie *f.* bruise
conține *v.t.* to contain
conținut *neut.* contents
convinge *v.t.* to convince
convorbire *f.* (telefonică)
   telephone call
convorbire interurbană
   long-distance call
copac *m.* tree
copertă *f.* cover
copie *f.* copy
copil *m.* child
copilaș *m.* baby
copleși *v.t.* to overwhelm
copt *adj.* ripe
cor *neut.* choir
coral *m.* coral
corecta *v.t.* to correct
corespunde *v.i.* to correspond
corespunzător *adj.* suitable
coridor *neut.* hall
corp *neut.* body
cortină *f.* curtain
corupție *f.* corruption
cosmetice *f.pl.* cosmetics
cost *neut.* cost; price
costa *v.i.* to cost
costum *neut.* suit
costum de baie swimsuit
cot *neut.* elbow
cotidian *neut., adj.* daily
cotlet *neut.* de porc pork chop
crampă *f.* cramp
cravată *f.* tie (*clothing*)

crăciun *neut.* Christmas
crea *v.t.* to create
crede *v.t.* to think; to believe
credință *f.* faith
credincios *adj.* faithful
credit *neut.* credit
creer *neut.* brain
creion *neut.* pencil
cremă *f.* cream
cremă de ras shaving cream
cremă hidratantă moisturizer
  (*cream*)
crește *v.t.* to bring up; to raise;
  to grow
creștere *f.* upbringing
creștin *m.* Christian
cretă *f.* chalk
crimă *f.* crime
criminal *m.* criminal
cristal *neut.* crystal
criteriu *neut.* criterion
critic *m.* critic
critică *f.* criticism
croazieră *f.* cruise
cronic *adj.* chronic
crosă *f.* club
cruce *f.* cross
cu *prep.* with
cucui *neut.* bump
cuib *neut.* nest
culoar *neut.* hall
culoare *f.* color
cultură *f.* culture
cumpăra *v.t.* to buy
cumpărător *m.* buyer
cumplit *adj.* excruciating
cumva *adv.* somehow
cunoaște *v.t.* to know; *v.r.* to
  meet
cunoscut *adj.* known
cununie *f.* wedding
cupru *neut.* copper
curaj *neut.* courage
curat *adj.* clean
cură *f.* cure
curăța *v.t.* to clean
curăța chimic to dry clean
curățătorie *f.* dry cleaner
curățenie *f.* cleaning

curbă *f.* curve
curcan *m.* turkey
curea *f.* belt
cureaua ventilatorului
  fan belt
curent *adj.* draft; current
curînd *adv.* soon
curios *adj.* curious
cursă *f.* flight
cursă charter charter flight
cutie *f.* box
cutie de chibrituri box of
  matches
cutie de tinichea can
cuțit *neut.* knife
cuvînt *neut.* word

# D

da *adv.* yes
da *v.i.* to give
da prioritate to yield
dacă *conj.* if
dans *neut.* dance
dansa *v.i.*, *v.t.* to dance
dată *f.* date
datorie *f.* debt; duty
deal *neut.* hill
deasupra *adv.* above; over
debarca *v.i.* to land
debușeu *neut.* outlet
decapotabil *adj.* convertible
de ce *adv.* why
declara *v.t.* to declare
declarație *f.* vamală customs
  declaration
decongela *v.t.* to defrost
decont *neut.* deduction
deconta *v.t.* to discount
dedesubt *adv.* beneath
defect *neut.* defect; fault
deficit *neut.* deficit
defileu *neut.* gorge
deget *neut.* finger
deja *adv.* already
dejun *neut.* lunch
dejun, micul breakfast
dejunul, a lua to have lunch

de la *prep.* from
delicat *adj.* delicate
delicatese *f.pl.* delicatessen
delicateţe *f.* delicacy
delicious *adj.* delicious;
    yummy
delincvent *adj.* delinquent
democraţie *f.* democracy
demodat *adj.* old-fashioned
demon *m.* devil
demonstraţie *f.* demonstration
dentist *m.* dentist
denunţa *v.t.* to denounce
deodată *adv.* at once,
    suddenly
deodorant *neut.* deodorant
departe *adv.* far
depozit *neut.* warehouse
depresiune *f.* nervoasă
    depression
depune *v.t.* to deposit
depunere *f.* deposit
deranja *v.t.* to trouble
descărca *v.t.* to unload; to
    discharge
descărcare *f.* discharge
deschide *v.t.* to open
deschidere *f.* opening
descoperi *v.t.* to discover
descuia *v.t.* to unlock
desert *neut.* dessert
deşert *neut.* desert
desfiinţa *v.t.* to eliminate
desigur *adv.* of course
deşi *prep.* although
despărţi *v.t.* to divide
deştept *adj.* clever
destinatar *m.* addressee
destinaţie *f.* destination
destinde *v.r.* to relax
destul *adv.* enough
deşuruba *v.t.* to unscrew
detaliu *neut.* detail
detergent *m.* detergent
detergent de vase
    dishwashing detergent
deveni *v.i.* to become
devora *v.t.* to devour

devreme *adv.* early
dezavantaj *neut.* handicap
dezavantaja *v.t.* to handicap
dezbatere *f.* dispute
dezbrăca *v.r.* to undress
dezgust *neut.* disgust
dezgusta *v.t.* to disgust
dezgustător *adj.* disgusting
dezinfectant *neut.* disinfectant
dezlega *v.t.* to untie
dezordine *f.* disorder;
    untidiness
dezvolta *v.t.*, *v.r.* to develop
dezvoltare *f.* development
diabet *neut.* diabetes
dialect *neut.* dialect
diamant *neut.* diamond
diaree *f.* diarrhea
dicţionar *neut.* dictionary
diesel *adj.* diesel
diferenţă *f.* difference
diferit *adj.* different
dificil *adj.* difficult
dificultate *f.* difficulty
difuza *v.t.* to broadcast
digera *v.t.* to digest
digestie *f.* digestion
digital *adj.* digital
dimineaţa *adv.* in the
    morning
dimineaţă *f.* morning
dimineaţă, azi this morning
diminua *v.t.* to diminish
din *prep.* from; of
diplomat *m.* diplomat
direct *adj.* direct; straight
director *m.* director
direcţie *f.* direction
direcţie, semnal de
    directional signal
disc *neut.* disk
disc compact compact disc,
    CD
discotecă *f.* disco
discurs *neut.* speech
discuta *v.t.* to discuss; to talk
discuţie *f.* talk
disloca *v.t.* to dislocate

dispărea *v.i.* to disappear
dispoziție *f.* mood
dispoziție bună good mood
dispoziție proastă bad mood
disprețui *v.t.* to despise
distra *v.r.* to have fun
distractiv *adj.* funny
distracție *f.* fun; entertainment
distribui *v.t.* to distribute
district *neut.* district
distrugere *f.* destruction
divinitate *f.* god
divorț *neut.* divorce
divorța *v.i.* to divorce
dizolva *v.t.* to dissolve
doamnă *f.* lady
Doamne *excl.* Lord
doar *adv.* barely
dobîndă *f.* interest (*finance*)
doctor *m.* doctor
doctorie *f.* drug
doi *num.* two
dolar *m.* dollar
doliu *neut.* mourning
domnișoară *f.* miss (Ms.)
domnul mister (Mr.)
dop *neut.* plug
dori *v.i.* to wish
dorință *f.* wish
dormi *v.i.* to sleep
dormitor *neut.* bedroom
dovadă *f.* proof; evidence
dovedi *v.t.* to prove
dovleac *m.* pumpkin
dozaj *neut.* dosage
drac *m.* devil
dragoste *f.* love
drăguț *adj.* pretty
dramă *f.* drama
drapel *neut.* flag
drept *adj.* right
dreptate *f.* justice
dreptate, a avea to be right
drum *neut.* way; road
dubios *adj.* dubious
dublu *adj.* double
duce *v.t.* to carry
dulap *neut.* cupboard

dulce *adj.* sweet
dulciuri *neut.pl.* candy
dulgher *m.* carpenter
duminică *f.* Sunday
dumneata *pron.* you
dumneavoastră *pron.* you
   (*formal*)
Dumnezeu *m.* God
după *prep.* after
dur *adj.* tough
dura *v.i.* to last
durea *v.r.* to ache
durere *f.* ache; pain
dureros *adj.* painful
duș *neut.* shower (*bath*)
dușman *m.* enemy
duzină *f.* dozen

# E

ea *pron.* she
echilibru *neut.* balance
echipament *neut.* equipment
echipă *f.* team
economie *f.* economy
ediție *f.* edition
educa *v.t.* to educate, to train
egal *adj.* equal
egala *v.t.* to equal
ei *pron.* they
elastic *adj.* elastic
ele *pron.* they
electric *adj.* electric
electrician *m.* electrician
electricitate *f.* electricity
electronic *adj.* electronic
elegant *adj.* elegant
eleganță *f.* elegance
elibera *v.t.* to liberate
email *neut.* enamel
emigrant *m.* emigrant
emisiune *f.* broadcast
emoție *f.* emotion
emoționant *adj.* exciting
energie *f.* energy
entuziasm *neut.* enthusiasm
episcop *m.* bishop

episcopie *f.* diocese
epuiza *v.r.* to exhaust, to run out
escroc *m.* con man; cheat
esențial *adj.* essential
esofag *neut.* throat
eșarfă *f.* scarf
etaj *neut.* floor
etaj, la upstairs
etanș *adj.* watertight
etern *adj.* eternal
etichetă *f.* label
eu *pron.* I
Europa *f.* Europe
european *n;.adj.* European
evada *v.i.* to escape
evadare *f.* escape
eveniment *neut.* event
evita *v.t.* to avoid
evoluție *f.* evolution
evreiesc *adj.* Jewish
evreu *m.* Jew
exact *adj.* exact
exagera *v.t.* to exaggerate
exagerat *adj.* exaggerated;
    overdone
examen *neut.* examination
excepție *f.* exception
excepțional *adj.* exceptional
exclude *v.t.* to exclude
excursie *f.* trip
excursie de o zi day trip
exclamație *f.* exclamation
exemplu *neut.* example
exemplu, de for example
exercițiu *neut.* exercise
exersa *v.t.* to practice
experiență *f.* experience
experiment *neut.* experiment
expira *v.i.* to expire
expirare, dată de expiration
    date
export *neut.* export
expres *adj.* express
expresie *f.* expression; phrase
expunere *f.* account; exposé;
    lecture
exterior *neut.* exterior
extra *adj.* extra
extrem *adv.* extremely

# F

fabrică *f.* factory
face *v.t.* to make; to do
face cumpărături to go
    shopping
facultate *f.* faculty
falcă *f.* jaw
faleză *f.* cliff
faliment *neut.* bankruptcy
fals *adj.* false
familiaritate *f.* familiarity
familie *f.* family
familie, nume de family name
fantasmă *f.* apparition
fantezie *f.* fancy
far *neut.* headlight
farfurie *f.* plate
farfurioară *f.* saucer
farmacie *f.* pharmacy
farmacist *m.* pharmacist
farmec *neut.* charm
fasole *f.* beans
fată *f.* girl
fațadă *f.* façade
față *f.* face
față, în in front
faună *f.* fauna
favoare *f.* favor
fax *neut.* fax
făină *f.* flour
febră *f.* temperature
februarie *m.* February
fel *neut.* kind
fel (de mîncare) course; dish
    (*food*)
felicita *v.t.* to congratulate
felicitări *f.pl.* congratulations
felie *f.* slice
femeie *f.* woman
femelă *f.* female
feminin *adj.* feminine
ferăstrău *neut.* saw
fereastră *f.* window
fericire *f.* happiness
fericit *adj.* happy
ferm *adj.* firm
fermă *f.* farm
fermă de lapte dairy farm

**fermecător** *adj.* fascinating
**fermier** *m.* farmer
**fermoar** *neut.* zipper
**fertil** *adj.* fertile
**festival** *neut.* festival
**fi** *v.aux.* to be
**ficat** *m.* liver
**fie...fie** *conj.* either...or
**fiecare** *adj.* every; *pron.*
  everybody
**fier** *neut.* iron
**fier de călcat** iron (*clothing*)
**fierar** *m.* blacksmith
**fierbe** *v.i.* to boil
**fierbere** *f.* boiling; excitement
**fierbinte** *adj.* hot
**fiică** *f.* daughter
**filantropie** *f.* charity
**fildeș** *neut.* ivory
**film** *neut.* film; movie
**filtru** *neut.* filter
**fin** *adj.* fine
**finanța** *v.t.* to finance
**finanțe** *f.pl.* finance(s)
**fîntînă** *f.* fountain
**fir** *neut.* thread
**firesc, în mod** normally
**firește** *adv.* naturally
**firmă** *f.* business firm
**fiu** *m.* son
**fix** *adj.* set
**fixa** *v.t.* to fix
**flacără** *f.* flame
**flămînd** *adj.* hungry
**flecăreală** *f.* chatter
**floare** *f.* flower
**floră** *f.* flora
**fluture** *m.* butterfly
**fluviu** *neut.* river
**foaier** *neut.* lobby
**foame** *f.* hunger
**foarte** *adv.* very
**foarte mult(ă)** very much
**foarte mulți** very many
**fobie** *f.* phobia
**foc** *neut.* fire
**folos** *neut.* use
**folosi** *v.t.* to use
**folositor** *adj.* useful

**formă** *f.* form, shape
**formular** *neut.* form
**forță** *f.* force
**fost** *adj.* former
**fotbal** *neut.* soccer
**foto, aparat** camera
**fotocopia** *v.t.* to xerox
**fotocopiat, aparat de**
  photocopier
**fotografia** *v.t.* to take pictures
**fotografie** *f.* photograph;
  picture
**fotoliu** *neut.* armchair
**fraged** *adj.* tender
**frămînta** *v.t.* to knead
**francez** *n. adj.* French
**freca** *v.t.* to rub
**frecție** *f.* rub
**frecvent** *adj.* frequent
**frică** *f.* fear
**frig** *neut.* cold
**frig, a-i fi** to be cold
**frige** *v.t.* to fry; to roast
**frigider** *neut.* refrigerator
**frînă** *f.* brake
**frînghie** *f.* rope
**friptură** *f.* roast
**frizer** *m.* hairdresser
**frizerie** *f.* barber shop
**frontieră** *f.* border; frontier
**fruct** *neut.* fruit
**frumos** *adj.* beautiful
**frumusețe** *f.* beauty
**frunte** *f.* forehead
**frunză** *f.* leaf
**fular** *neut.* scarf
**fulgi** *m.pl.* **de porumb** cereal
**fum** *neut.* smoke
**fuma** *v.t.* to smoke
**fumător** *m.* smoker
**funcție** *f.* function
**funcționar** *m.* office worker
**fund** *neut.* bottom
**fundație** *f.* foundation
**fura** *v.t.* to steal
**furculiță** *f.* fork
**furie** *f.* anger; rage
**furios** *adj.* angry
**furnică** *f.* ant

furniza *v.t.* to supply, to
   deliver
furt *neut.* theft
furtună *f.* storm
fustă *f.* skirt

# G

galben *adj.* yellow
galerie *f.* gallery
galerie de artă art gallery
găleată *f.* bucket
galon *neut.* gallon
garaj *neut.* garage
garanta *v.t.* to guarantee
garanţie *f.* guarantee
gară *f.* railway station
garderobă *f.* wardrobe
gargară, a face to gargle
găsi *v.t.* to find
găti *v.t.* to cook
geamăn(ă) *m., f.* twin
gelozie *f.* jealousy
gem *neut.* jam
genera *v.t.* to generate
generos *adj.* generous
genunchi *m.* knee
german *n. adj.* German
Germania *f.* Germany
gheată *f.* boot
gheaţă *f.* ice
ghici *v.t.* to guess
ghid *m.* guide
ghinion *neut.* mishap
ghişeu *neut.* window (*through
   which business is
   transacted*)
gînd *neut.* thought
gîndi *v.i.* to think
ginecolog *m.* gynecologist
gît *neut.* neck
glandă *f.* gland
gleznă *f.* ankle
glob *neut.* globe
glumă *f.* joke
glumi *v.i.* to joke; to be
   kidding
gol *adj.* empty

golf *neut.* golf
grabă *f.* hurry
grad *neut.* degree
grafic *neut.* timetable,
   schedule
gram *neut.* gram
gramatică *f.* grammar
grandios *adj.* great
gras *adj.* fat
gratuit *adj.* free (*of charge*)
graţie *f.* grace(fulness)
gravidă *adj.* pregnant
grăbi *v.r.* to hurry up
grădină *f.* garden
grădină botanică botanical
   garden
grădină zoologică zoo
grătar *neut.* grill
greaţă *f.* nausea
greşeală *f.* mistake
greşeală, a face o to make a
   mistake
greşi *v.i.* to be wrong
greşit *adj., adv.* wrong
greu *adj.* difficult; *adv.* hard
greutate *f.* weight
gri *adj.* grey
grijă *f.* care
grijă, fără carefree
gripă *f.* flu; influenza
gros *adj.* thick
grozav *adj.* great, terrific
grup *neut.* group
grupă *f.* group
grupă sangvină blood group
gumă *f.* de mestecat chewing
   gum
gunoi *neut.* garbage
gură *f.* mouth
gust *neut.* taste
gusta *v.t.* to taste
gustare *f.* snack
gustos *adj.* savory
guverna *v.t.* to govern

# H

haină *f.* coat
handicap *neut.* handicap

hartă f. map
hepatită f. hepatitis
hîrtie f. paper
hîrtie igienică bath tissue
hoinăreală f. stroll
holeră f. cholera
hotărî v.t. to decide
hotărîre f. decision
hotel neut. hotel
hoţ m. thief
hrană f. food
hrană pentru sugari baby
    food
hrăni v.t. to feed

# I

ianuarie m. January
iarăşi adv. again
iarbă f. grass
iarnă f. winter
iată interj. there
iaurt neut. yogurt
iaz neut. pond
icter neut. jaundice
idee f. idea
ieftin adj. cheap; affordable
iepure m. rabbit
ieri adv. yesterday
ierta v.t. to forgive
iertare f. forgiveness
ieşi v.i. to go out
ieşire f. exit
igienă f. hygiene
Iisus Hristos Jesus Christ
ilustra v.t. to illustrate
iluzie f. illusion
imagina v.t. to figure out
imediat adv. immediately
imn neut. hymn
imperiu neut. empire
important adj. important
importanţă f. importance
imposibil adj. impossible
impozit neut. tax
impresie f. impression
impresiona v.t. to impress
impresionant adj. impressive

inaugurare f. inauguration
incomod adj. inconvenient
inconştient adj. unconscious
independenţă f.
    independence
indice neut. index
indigestie f. indigestion
individual adj. individual
inel neut. ring
infecţie f. infection
infirm adj. crippled
infirmieră f. nurse
inflamare f. inflammation
influenţă f. influence
informa v.t. to inform
informaţii f.pl. information
informaţii, ghişeu de
    information desk
inginer m. engineer
inimă f. heart
iniţiativă f. initiative
injecţie f. injection
insectă f. bug, insect
insignă f. badge
insista v.i. to insist
insolaţie f. sunstroke
insomnie f. insomnia
instalaţie f. installation
instinct neut. instinct
institut neut. institute
instrucţiune f. instruction
instrui v.t. to train
instrument neut. instrument
insulă f. island
insulta v.t. to insult
intenţie f. intention
interes neut. interest
interesa v.t. to interest
interesant adj. interesting
interior neut. interior
interior, în indoor
internaţional adj.
    international
internist m. internist
interpret m. interpreter
interviu neut. interview
intestine neut.pl. bowels
intim adj. intimate
intra v.i. to enter

intrare f. entrance; entry
intrare, taxă de entrance fee
intrare, viză de entry visa
inutil adj. useless
învăţător m. teacher
inventa v.t. to invent
invidia v.t. to envy
invidie f. envy
invitaţie f. invitation
iod neut. iodine
ipocrit m. hypocrite
ipocrizie f. hypocrisy
ipotecă f. mortgage
iritaţie f. itch; rash
Irlanda f. Ireland
irlandez n. adj. Irish
isteţ adj. clever; smart
istorie f. history
istovi v.r. to overwork
istovit adj. exhausted
iubi v.t. to love
iubire f. love
iubit(ă) adj. beloved; m., f.
   lover
izbi v.t. to run into
izbucni v.i. to burst
izbucnire f. outburst

# Î

îmbrăca v.t. to dress; v.r. to
   get dressed
îmbrăcăminte f. clothes
îmbrăţişa v.t. to hug; to
   embrace
îmbrăţişare f. hug
împărtăşi v.t. to share
împleti v.t. to knit
împodobi v.t. to decorate
împotriva prep. against
împrejur adv. around
împrejurimi f.pl. environs
împreună adv. together
împrumut neut. loan
împrumut, a lua cu to
   borrow
împrumuta v.t., v.i. to lend
în prep. in; into

în jos adv. down(wards)
înainte adv. forward; prep.
   before
înapoi adv. backward; prep.
   behind
înalt adj. tall; high
înălţime f. height
înăuntru adv. within
încasa v.t. to cash
încă adv. still; yet
încălzi v.t. to heat
încălzire f. heating
încălzire centrală central
   heating
începe v.t. to begin; to start
început neut. beginning
încerca v.t. to try
încet adj., adv. slow
încetini v.i. to slow down
încheiere f. conclusion, end
încheietura f. mîinii wrist
închide v.t. to shut; to close
încînta v.t. to delight
încîntare f. delight
încîntător adj. charming
închiria v.t. to hire; to rent
închis adj. closed
încredere f. confidence; trust
încrezut adj. conceited, cocky
încuia v.t. to lock
încurca v.t. to entangle; to
   hamper; to confuse
încurcat adj. confused
încurcătură f. confusion
îndatorire f. duty
îndepărtat adj. distant
îndeplini v.t. to do
îndoi v.r. to doubt
îndoială f. doubt
îndrăgi v.t. to like
îndrăgosti v.r. to fall in love
îndragostit(ă) adj. in love
îndruma v.t. to direct; to
   guide
îndura v.t., v.i. to suffer
îneca v.r. to drown
înfăşura v.t. to wrap
înfăţişa v.t. to depict, to
   describe

înger *m.* angel
înghețată *f.* ice cream
înghiți *v.t.* to swallow
îngriji *v.t.* to take care of, to nurse
îngrijorare *f.* worry
îngropa *v.t.* to bury
îngust *adj.* narrow
înjura *v.t., v.i.* to swear; to abuse
înjurătură *f.* curse
înmormîntare *f.* funeral
înnorat *adj.* cloudy
înota *v.i.* to swim
înotător *m.* swimmer
înrăutăți *v.r.* to deteriorate
înregistrare *f.* registration
înregistrare, fișă de registration form
înrudit *adj.* related
însărcina *v.t.* to commission, to charge
însărcinată *adj.* expecting (*pregnant*)
însemna *v.t., v.i.* to mean
însetat *adj.* thirsty
însoțitor *m.* companion
înșela *v.t.* to cheat
întîlni *v.t.* to meet
întîlnire *f.* appointment
întîmpla *v.r.* to happen
întîmplare *f.* chance
întîmplare, la at random
întinde *v.t.* to spread
întins *adj.* stretched; vast
întîrzia *v.i.* to be late
întîrziat *adj.* late
întîrziere *f.* delay
întoarce *v.t.* to turn
întotdeauna *adv.* always
între *prep.* between
întreba *v.t.* to ask
întrebare *f.* question
întrerupe *v.t.* to cut off
întrerupere (curent) *f.* power outage
întreg *adj.* whole
întunecat *adj.* dark; overcast
întuneric *neut.* dark

înțelege *v.t.* to understand
înțeles, de understandable
înțepa *v.t.* to sting
înțepătură *f.* sting
învăța *v.t.* to learn
învățat *adj.* learned, erudite

## J

jachetă *f.* jacket; coat
jaluzea *f.* blind
japonez *n., adj.* Japanese
Japonia *f.* Japan
jeep *neut.* jeep
joc *neut.* game
joc electronic electronic game
joi *f.* Thursday
jos *adj.* low; *adv.* downstairs
jos, mai ~ de below
jubileu *neut.* jubilee, celebration
jucărie *f.* toy
jumătate *f.* half
jura *v.t.* to swear
jurămînt *neut.* oath
just *adj.* correct
justiție *f.* justice

## K

kilogram *neut.* kilo(gram)
kilometraj *neut.* mileage
kilometraj nelimitat unlimited mileage
kilometru *m.* kilometer

## L

la *prep.* at
lac *neut.* lake
lacăt *neut.* lock
lacrimă *f.* tear (drop)
lamă *f.* blade
lampă *f.* lamp
lanț *neut.* chain
lapte *neut.* milk

larg *adj.* wide
laş *m.* coward
latură *f.* side
laudă *f.* praise
laxativ *neut.* laxative
lămîie *f.* lemon
lăptărie *f.* dairy
lățime *f.* breadth
lăuda *v.t.* to praise
leagăn *neut.* cradle
lectură *f.* reading
lecție *f.* lesson
lega *v.t.* to tie
legal *adj.* lawful
legăna *v.t.* to lull to sleep
legătură *f.* connection
lege *f.* law
legitimație *f.* ID card
legumă *f.* vegetable
leneș *adj.* lazy
lenjerie *f.* de corp underwear
lentilă *f.* lens
liber *adj.* free
libertate *f.* freedom
librărie *f.* bookstore
lighean *neut.* basin
limbă *f.* language; tongue
limpede *adj.* plain
lînă *f.* wool
lînă pură virgin wool
lingură *f.* spoon
linguriță *f.* teaspoon
linie *f.* line
linie de metrou metro line,
   subway
liniște *f.* silence
liniștit *adj.* quiet
listă *f.* list
listă de vinuri wine list
literatură *f.* literature
litoral *neut.* seacoast
litru *m.* liter
livră *f.* pound
loc *neut.* place
locui *v.i.* to live
locuință *f.* lodging
locuitor *m.* inhabitant
logodit, a fi to be engaged
logodnă *f.* engagement

logodnic(ă) *m., f.* fiancé(e)
lor *pron.* their
loțiune *f.* lotion
loțiune după ras after-shave
   lotion
lovi *v.t.* to strike
lovitură *f.* blow
lua (pasager) *v.t.* to pick up;
   to take (*a passenger*)
luci *v.i.* to shine
lucra *v.t.* to work
lucru *neut.* thing
lume *f.* world; people
lumina soarelui sunshine
lumină *f.* light
lumînare *f.* candle
lună *f.* month; moon
lung *adj.* long
luni *f.* Monday
lup *m.* wolf
lupta *v.t., v.i.* to fight
luptă *f.* fight
lux *neut.* luxury
luxos *adj.* luxurious

# M

machiaj *neut.* make-up
magazin *neut.* shop; store
magazin cu autoservire
   supermarket
magazin de antichități
   antique shop
magazin de artizanat
   craft shop
magazin de bijuterii
   jewelry shop
magazin universal
   department store
mamă *f.* mother
mandat *neut.* mandate
maniere *f.pl.* manners
manta *f.* de ploaie raincoat
marcă *f.* brand
mare *f.* sea; *adj.* big
mare, rău de seasickness
margarină *f.* margarine
maron *adj.* brown

martie *m.* March
marți *f.* Tuesday
martor *m.* witness
masa (principală) *f.* dinner
masaj *neut.* massage
masă *f.* table
masă (de prînz, etc.) meal
mască *f.* mask
mascul *m., adj.* male
masculin *adj.* masculine
mașină *f.* machine
mașină de închiriat rental car
mașină de spălat washing
   machine
mașină de spălat vase
   dishwasher
material *neut.* fabric; material
matur *adj.* mature
maxilar *neut.* jaw
mazăre *f.* pea
măgar *m.* donkey
mănăstire *f.* convent;
   monastery
mănușă *f.* glove
măr *neut.* apple
măreț *adj.* magnificent
mări *v.t.* to enlarge
mărime *f.* size
mărturisi *v.t.* to confess
măslină *f.* olive
măsura *v.t.* to measure
măsură *f.* size
mătase *f.* silk
mătura *v.t.* to sweep
mătură *f.* broom
mătușă *f.* aunt
mea *pron.* my
mecanic *m.* mechanic
meci *neut.* match (*sports*)
medalie *f.* medal
medicament *neut.* medicine
medie *f.* average
mediu *neut.* environment
mei *pron.* my
mele *pron.* my
membru *m.* member
meniu *neut.* menu
menstruație *f.* period
   (*menstrual*)

menționa *v.t.* to mention
mențiune *f.* mention
mereu *adv.* again and again
merge *v.i.* to go
merge la cumpărături to go
   shopping
mesaj *neut.* message
mesteca *v.t.* to chew
mestecat, gumă de chewing
   gum
meșteșugar *m.* craftsman
metrou *neut.* subway
meu *pron.* my
mic *adj.* small
microbist *m.* fan (*sports*)
microunde *f.pl.* microwave
miel *m.* lamb
miere *f.* honey
miere, lună de honeymoon
migrenă *f.* headache
mijloc *neut.* middle
mijlocul, în in the middle
milă *f.* pity
milă, a-i fi to pity
milion *neut.* million
mină *f.* mine; pit
minciună *f.* lie
miner *m.* miner
minge *f.* ball
minor *m., adj.* minor
minte *f.* mind
minți *v.i.* to lie
minunat *adj.* wonderful
minune *f.* marvel
minut *neut.* minute
miracol *neut.* miracle
mire *m.* bridegroom
mireasă *f.* bride
miros *neut.* smell
mirosi *v.t., v.i.* to smell
mîine *adv.* tomorrow
mînă *f.* hand
mînca *v.t.* to eat; to dine
mînca prea mult to overeat
mîncare *f.* food
mînecă *f.* sleeve
mîner *neut.* handle
mînui *v.t.* to handle
mișca *v.i.* to move

mişcare *f.* movement
moale *adj.* soft
moarte *f.* death
moaşă *f.* midwife
mobilă *f.* furniture
mod *neut.* manner
modă *f.* fashion
modă, la fashionable
model *neut.* model; pattern
modern *adj.* modern
moment *neut.* moment
moment, un just a moment
monedă *f.* coin
monstru *m.* monster
monument *neut.* monument
morcov *m.* carrot
mormînt *neut.* grave
mort *adj.* dead
moşteni *v.t.* to inherit
mostră *f.* sample
motiv *neut.* reason, motive
motor *neut.* engine
mov *adj.* purple
muchie *f.* edge
mult *adj., adv.* much
mult, mai more
mult, din ce în ce mai more
  and more
mult, prea too much
multe *adj.* many
mulţi *adj.* many
mulţime *f.* crowd
mulţumesc thank you
mulţumi *v.i.* to thank
muncă *f.* work
munci *v.i.* to work
muncitor *m.* worker
munte *m.* mountain
murdar *adj.* dirty
muri *v.i.* to pass away
muşca *v.t.* to bite
muşcătură *f.* bite
muşchi *m.* muscle
mustaţă *f.* moustache
muştar *neut.* mustard
muzeu *neut.* museum
muzical *adj.* musical
muzică *f.* music
muzică country country
  music

# N

nap *m.* turnip
nas *neut.* nose
nasture *m.* button
naş *m.* godfather
naşă *f.* godmother
naşte *v.t.* to give birth; *v.r.* to
  be born
naştere *f.* birth
naştere, a da to give birth
naştere, zi de birthday
natură *f.* nature
naţionalitate *f.* nationality
naţiune *f.* nation
navă *f.* ship
nebunie *f.* madness
necaz *neut.* trouble
necăji *v.t.* to anger; to bother
necesar *adj.* necessary
necesita *v.t.* to need
nefericit *adj.* unhappy
nefumător *adj.* non-smoking
nega *v.t.* to deny
neghiob *adj.* foolish
neglija *v.t.* to neglect
neglijare *f.* neglect
negru *adj.* black
neîngrijit *adj.* untidy
neînţelegere *f.*
  misunderstanding
nelinişte *f.* anxiety
nemulţumire *f.* complaint
nenorocos *adj.* unlucky
neplăcut *adj.* unpleasant
nepoată *f.* niece
nepot *m.* nephew
nerv *m.* nerve
nesociabil *adj.* unsociable
neted *adj.* flat
neurolog *m.* neurologist
neutru *adj.* neuter; neutral
nevoie *f.* need
nevralgie *f.* toothache
nici măcar not even
niciodată *adv.* never
nici unul *pron.* none
nimeni *pron.* nobody
nimic *pron.* nothing

ninge *v.imp.* to snow
nisip *neut.* sand
nisipos *adj.* sandy
nivel *neut.* level
noapte *f.* night
noapte, peste overnight
nod *neut.* knot
noi *pron.* we
nor *m.* cloud
nord *adv.* north
noroc *neut.* luck
norocos *adj.* lucky
noroi *neut.* mud
nostru *pron.* our
notar *m.* notary
noţiune *f.* concept
nou *adj.* new
Noua Zeelandă *f.*
  New Zealand
nouă *num.* nine
nu *adv.* no; not
nu încă not yet
numai *adv.* only
număr *neut.* number
număra *v.t.* to count
nume *neut.* name
nume de fată maiden name
nuntă *f.* wedding

# O

oaie *f.* sheep
oală *f.* pot
oală de gătit cooking pot;
  saucepan
oarecum *adv.* rather
obicei *neut.* custom
obicei, de usually
obiect *neut.* object
obiect antic antique
obiecta *v.i.* to object
obişnui *v.r.* to get used to
obosi *v.i.* to be tired
obosit *adj.* tired
obscen *adj.* obscene
observa *v.t.* to notice
observatory *m.* observer
obstacol *neut.* obstacle

obţine *v.t.* to obtain
ochelari *m.pl.* glasses
ochi *m.* eye
ocol *neut.* detour
ocupat *adj.* busy
ocupaţie *f.* occupation
odată *adv.* once
odihnă *f.* rest
odihni *v.r.* to rest
odinioară *adv.* formerly
oferi *v.t., v.i.* to offer
ofertă *f.* offer
oficiu *neut.* poştal post office
oftalmolog *m.*
  ophthalmologist
oglindă *f.* mirror
oglindi *v.t.* to mirror, to reflect
olărit *neut.* pottery (*making of*)
om *m.* man
om de ştiinţă scientist
omenire *f.* mankind
omletă *f.* omelet
omorî *v.t.* to kill
opări *v.t., v.i.* to scald
operă *f.* opera
operator *m.* operator
operaţie *f.* operation
opinie *f.* opinion
opiu *neut.* opium
opri *v.t.* to stop
oprire *f.* stop
opt *num.* eight
optician *m.* optician
opus *adj.* opposite
orar *neut.* schedule
oraş *neut.* town; city
oră *f.* hour
oră de vîrf rush hour
orb *adj.* blind
orbi *v.t.* to blind
orchestră *f.* orchestra
ordonat *adj.* tidy
orez *neut.* rice
orfan *m.* orphan
organe *neut.pl.* genitale
  genitals
organizare *f.* organization
oricare *pron.* any
orice *pron.* anything

oricine *pron.* anyone
oricum *adv.* however
origine *f.* origin
ornitologie *f.* ornithology
ortodox *m. adj.* Orthodox
ortografia *v.t.* to spell
os *neut.* bone
otravă *f.* poison
otrăvi *v.t.* to poison
oţel *neut.* steel
oţet *neut.* vinegar
ou *neut.* egg

# P

pace *f.* peace
pachet *neut.* pack; parcel
pagubă *f.* damage
pahar *neut.* glass
pahar de apă drinking glass
palat *neut.* palace
palpitaţie *f.* palpitation
pană *f.* breakdown
pantaloni *m.pl.* pants
pantof *m.* shoe
papetărie *f.* stationer's shop
papă *m.* pope
papuc *m.* slipper
paradă *f.* parade
paradis *neut.* paradise
pară *f.* pear
parbriz *neut.* windshield
parc *neut.* park
parca *v.t.* to park
parcaj *neut.* parking lot
parcare *f.* parking lot
parcometru *neut.* parking
    meter
parfum *neut.* perfume
parlament *neut.* parliament
parte *f.* side
partea dreaptă right side
particular *adj.* private
partid *neut.* party
partid politic political party
pasager *m.* passenger
pasăre *f.* bird
pasiune *f.* hobby

pastă *f.* de dinţi toothpaste
paste făinoase pasta
pastilă *f.* pill
paşaport *neut.* passport
pat *neut.* bed
pată *f.* stain
patina *v.i.* to skate
patină *f.* skate
patiserie *f.* pastry
patriarh *m.* patriarch
patron *m.* boss; employer
patru *num.* four
pază *f.* guard; watch
paznic *m.* guardian
păcăli *v.t.* to fool
păcat *neut.* sin
păcătui *v.i.* to sin
pădure *f.* forest, woods
pălărie *f.* hat
pămînt *neut.* land
păr *m.* hair
părăsi *v.t.* to leave
păstra *v.t.* to keep
păstrăv *m.* trout
păta *v.t.* to stain
pătrat *neut., adj.* square
pătrunjel *m.* parsley
pătură *f.* blanket
păzi *v.t.* to mind; to watch
pe *prep.* on; upon
pedeapsă *f.* penalty
pediatru *m.* pediatrician
peluză *f.* lawn
penel *neut.* paintbrush
penicilină *f.* penicillin
penis *neut.* penis
pensulă *f.* paintbrush
pentru *prep.* for
pentru a in order to
pentru că because
pentru puţin you're welcome
pepene *m.* melon
perdea *f.* curtain
perfecţiona *v.t.* to improve
peria *v.t.* to brush
perie *f.* brush
perie de curăţat scrubbing
    brush
periuţă *f.* de dinţi toothbrush

perlă f. pearl
permanent neut. perm(anent)
    (hairstyling); adj.
    permanent
permis neut. permit
permis de conducere driver's
    license
permisiune f. leave
permite v.t., v.i. to permit;
    to allow
pernă f. pillow
peron neut. platform
persecuta v.t. to persecute
persoană f. person
persoană cu handicap
    disabled person
peruzea f. turquoise
pescuit neut. fishing
pescuit, a merge la to go
    fishing
peste prep. over
pește m. fish
peșteră f. cave
petrecere f. party
piatră f. stone
piață f. market
piață neagră black market
picătură f. drop
picior m. foot; leg
picta v.t. to paint
pictor m. painter
pictură f. painting
picura v.i. to drip
piele f. leather; skin
piept neut. chest
pieptene neut. comb
pierde v.t. to lose; to miss
    (a train)
piersică f. peach
piesă f. piece; part; play
    (theater)
piesă de schimb (spare) part
pieton m. pedestrian
pijama f. pajamas
pilă f. file (tool)
pilot m. pilot
pilulă f. pill
piper neut. pepper
piscină f. pool

pisică f. cat
pizza f. pizza
pișcot neut. cookie
pîine f. bread
pîine prăjită toast
pînă la prep. until; till
pînză f. cloth
pînză f. de in linen cloth
pîrîu neut. stream
plafon neut. ceiling
plajă f. beach
plan neut. plan
planta v.t. to plant
plantă f. plant
plat adj. flat
plată f. pay(ment)
platină f. platinum
plăcea v.t., v.i. to please
plăcere f. pleasure
plăcintă f. pie
plăcut adj. pleasant
plămîn m. lung
plănui v.t. to plan
plăti v.t. to pay
pleca v.i. to leave; to go away
plecare f. departure
plecăciune f. bow
plecăciune, a face o to bow
plic neut. envelope
plicticos adj. boring
plicticos, om a bore
plictisi v.t. to bore
plimba v.r. to walk
plimbare f. walk
plin adj. full
plînge v.t. to weep; to cry
ploaie f. rain
plombă f. filling (dental)
plonja v.i. to dive
plonjon neut. dive
ploua v.imp. to rain
pneumonie f. pneumonia
poartă f. gate
poate adv. maybe; perhaps
pod neut. bridge
podea f. floor
podgorie f. vineyard
poftă f. appetite
polen neut. pollen

**politeţe** *f.* politeness
**politicos** *adj.* polite
**poliţie** *f.* police
**poliţie, circa de** police precinct (station)
**poliţist** *m.* policeman
**polua** *v.t.* to pollute
**pompieri** *m.pl.* **serviciu de** fire station
**pop, muzică** pop music
**popular** *adj.* popular; folk
**porc** *m.* pig
**porc, carne de** pork
**poreclă** *f.* nickname
**port** *neut.* harbor; port
**portbagaj** *neut.* trunk of a car
**porţelan** *neut.* porcelain
**portocală** *f.* orange
**portocaliu** *adj.* orange
**portofel** *neut.* wallet
**porumb** *m.* corn
**porumb, floricele de** popcorn
**porumbel** *m.* pigeon
**posibil** *adj.* possible
**posibil, a fi** may; to be possible
**post** *neut.* **liber** vacancy
**poşetă** *f.* handbag
**poştă** *f.* post office
**potpuriu** *neut.* medley
**potrivi** *v.r.* to fit; to match
**potrivit** *adj.* suitable
**poveste** *f.* story
**povesti** *v.t.* to tell
**poză** *f.* snapshot, picture, photo
**practica** *v.t.* to practice
**practică** *f.* practice
**praf** *neut.* dust
**praz** *m.* leek
**prăbuşi** *v.r.* to collapse
**prăbuşire** *f.* collapse
**prăji** *v.t.* to fry
**prăjitor** *neut.* **de pîine** toaster
**prăjitură** *f.* cake; pastry
**prea** *adv.* too
**prea mult** too much
**precis** *adj.* precise

**preda** *v.t.* to teach; to deliver (*a message*)
**predare** *f.* delivery; teaching
**prefera** *v.t.* to prefer
**preferinţă** *f.* preference
**prefix** *neut.* area/dialing code
**pregăti** *v.t.* to prepare
**pregătit** *adj.* ready
**preîntîmpina** *v.t.* to prevent
**prelua** *v.t.* to take over
**premiu** *neut.* award; prize
**preot** *m.* priest
**presă** *f.* press
**prescrie** *v.t., v.i.* to prescribe
**presupune** *v.t.* to suppose
**preşedinte** *m.* president
**pretenţie** *f.* claim; pretension
**pretinde** *v.t.* to require; to claim
**pretutindeni** *adv.* everywhere
**preţ** *neut.* price
**preţios** *adj.* valuable
**prevedea** *v.t.* to foresee
**prevenire** *f.* prevention
**prezent** *adj.* present
**prezenta** *v.t.* to introduce; to present
**prezervativ** *neut.* condom
**pricepe** *v.t.* to figure out; to understand
**pricepere** *f.* ability
**pricina, din** on account of, because
**pricinui** *v.t., v.i.* to cause
**prieten** *m.* friend
**prietenă** *f.* girlfriend
**prietenie** *f.* friendship
**prilej** *neut.* occasion
**prilej favorabil** opportunity
**prilejui** *v.t.* to occasion
**primar** *m.* mayor
**primejdie** *f.* danger
**primejdios** *adj.* dangerous
**primi** *v.t.* to receive
**prin** *prep.* through
**principal** *adj.* main; principal
**prinde** *v.t.* to catch
**prindere** *f.* catch
**printre** *prep.* among

privat *adj.* private
privelişte *f.* view; landscape
privi *v.i.* to look at
privire *f.* look, glance
priză *f.* outlet (*electric*)
prînz *neut.* lunch
proaspăt *adj.* fresh
proba *v.t.* to try on
probabil *adj.* probable
problemă *f.* problem
proceda *v.i.* to proceed
proces *neut.* trial
procesiune *f.* procession
produce *v.t.* to produce
producţie *f.* production
produs *neut.* product; produce
proeminent *adj.* prominent
profesie *f.* profession
profesor *m.* teacher
profit *neut.* profit
profita *v.i.* to benefit by
profitabil *adj.* profitable
profund *adj.* profound
prognoză *f.* forecast
prognoză meteo weather
    forecast
program *neut.* schedule;
    program
progres *neut.* progress
proiect *neut.* project
promisiune *f.* promise
promite *v.t.* to promise
promotor *m.* promoter
promova *v.t.* to promote
pronume *neut.* pronoun
pronunţa *v.t.* to pronounce
pronunţie *f.* pronunciation
proprietar *m.* landlord
proprietăreasă *f.* landlady
proprietate *f.* property
propriu *adj.* personal
propune *v.t.* to propose
prosop *neut.* towel
prosop de baie bath towel
prospeţime *f.* freshness
prost *adj.* ignorant; foolish
prostată *f.* prostate
prostie *f.* stupidity
proteja *v.t.* to protect

protecţie *f.* protection
proverb *neut.* proverb
provoca *v.t.* to challenge
provocare *f.* challenge
prudent *adj.* cautious
prună *f.* plum
prunc *m.* baby
psihiatru *m.* psychiatrist
public *neut., adj.* public
publicitate *f.* advertisement,
    publicity
pudră *f.* powder
pudră de talc talcum powder
pui *m.* chicken
pulover *neut.* sweater
puls *neut.* pulse
pulveriza *v.t.* to pulverize, to
    spray
pulverizator *neut.* atomizer,
    sprayer
punct *neut.* point; period
punctual *adj.* punctual
pune *v.t.* to put
pungă *f.* purse; bag
pupa *v.t.* to kiss
pur *adj.* pure
purta *v.t.* to wear; to carry
purtare *f.* behavior
pustii *v.t.* to devastate
pustiu *neut.* desert
putea *v.t.* to be able
putere *f.* power; strength
puternic *adj.* strong
puţin *adv.* little
puţin, cel at least
puţini *adj.* few


# R

rachetă *f.* rocket; racket
    (*sports*)
rade *v.r.* to shave
radiator *neut.* radiator
radio *neut.* radio
radio, staţie de broadcasting
    station
ramă *f.* frame
ramă de tablou picture frame

ramursa *v.t.* to refund
rambursare *f.* refund
rană *f.* injury; wound
rapid *adj.* fast; quick
raport *neut.* report
rar *adj.* rare
rață *f.* duck
rație *f.* ration
rațiune *f.* reason
rază *f.* ray
razoar *neut.* shaver
răbdare *f.* patience
răceală *f.* cold
rădăcină *f.* root
rămîne *v.i.* to remain
răni *v.t.* to injure; to hurt
răsări *v.i.* to rise
răsărit *neut.* east
răscruce *f.* crossroad
răsfoi *v.t.* to leaf through
răspîndi *v.r.* to spread
răspîndit *adj.* widespread
răspunde *v.i.* to answer; to
  reply
răspundere *f.* responsibility
răspuns *neut.* answer; reply
răsturna *v.t.* to overturn
răsuci *v.t.* to twist
rătăci *v.r.* to lose one's way
rău *adj.* bad
război *neut.* war
real *adj.* real
realitate *f.* reality
rece *adj.* cold
recent *adj.* recent
reciproc *adj.* reciprocal
recîştiga *v.t.* to regain
reclamă *f.* advertisement
recomanda *v.t.* to recommend
recomandată *f.* registered
  letter
recunoaşte *v.t.* to recognize
recunoscător *adj.* grateful;
  thankful
redacta *v.t.* to write out; to
  edit
reduce *v.t.* to reduce
redus *adj.* reduced

reface *v.t.* to remake, to
  restore
referitor (la) concerning
reflecta *v.i.* to reflect
refugiu *neut.* refuge
refuza *v.t.* to refuse
regim (alimentar) *neut.* diet
regulat *adj.* regular
relatare *f.* account; narration
relație *f.* relation
religie *f.* religion
remediu *neut.* remedy
remorca *v.t.* to tow
renunța *v.i.* to give up
repara *v.t.* to repair
reparație *f.* repair
repede *adv.* quick; fast
repeta *v.t.* to repeat
republică *f.* republic
reputație *f.* reputation
respect *neut.* respect
respecta *v.t.* to respect
respira *v.i.* to breathe
respirație *f.* breath
restaurant *neut.* restaurant
reşedință *f.* residence
retrage *v.t.* to withdraw
rețetă *f.* prescription
reumatism *neut.* rheumatism
reuşit *adj.* successful
revolta *v.r.* to revolt
revoltă *f.* revolt
revedere, la good-bye
reveni *v.i.* to return
revenire *f.* comeback
revistă *f.* review; magazine
rezerva *v.t.* to reserve
rezervare *f.* reservation
rezultat *neut.* effect; result
ridica *v.t.* to pick up
ridicare *f.* rise; growth
rinichi *m.* kidney
risc *neut.* risk
risca *v.t.* to risk
risipi *v.t.* to scatter
rîde *v.i.* to laugh
rînd *neut.* line; row
rîs *neut.* laughter
rîu *neut.* river

roată f. wheel
roată de rezervă spare tire
rochie f. dress
roşie f. tomato
roşu adj. red
rotire f. twist
rotund adj. round
rouă f. dew
roz adj. pink
rubin neut. ruby
rudă f. relative
rugină f. rust
rugini v.i. to rust
ruj neut. de buze lipstick
rupe v.t. to tear; to break
ruptură f. break; tear
ruşine f. shame
ruşine, a-i fi to be ashamed
rută f. route

# S

sac neut. bag
sac de voiaj handbag
safir neut. sapphire
salam neut. salami
salariat m. employee
salariu neut. salary
salată f. salad; lettuce
salon neut. de coafură beauty
  salon
saltea f. mattress
salut neut. welcome
saluta v.t. to greet; to
  welcome
salva v.t. to save
salvare f. ambulance
sandviş neut. sandwich
sarcină f. load; task,
  assignment
sare f. salt
sarma f. stuffed cabbage or
  grape leaves
sat neut. village
satisface v.t. to satisfy
satisfăcător adj. satisfying
sau conj. or
savura v.t. to enjoy; to relish

săgeată f. arrow
sălbatic adj. savage; wild
sămînţă f. seed
sănătate f. health
sănătos adj. healthy
săptămînal adj. weekly
săptămînă f. week
săptămînă de lucru work
  week
săpun neut. soap
săra v.t. to salt
sărac adj. poor
sărat adj. salted
sărăcie f. poverty
sărbătoare f. celebration
sărbători v.t. to celebrate
sărbătorire f. celebration
sări v.t. to jump
săritură f. jump
sărut neut. kiss
săruta v.t. to kiss
sărut mîna respectful
  greeting for women, clergy
  and elders (literally,
  "I kiss your hand")
sătean m. villager, peasant
sătesc adj. village, rural
săvîrşi v.t. to perform; to
  commit
scandal neut. scandal
scară f. ladder; scale; stairs
scaun neut. chair
scădea v.t. to reduce; to
  diminish
scăpa v.i. to escape; v.t. to
  drop
scenă f. scene; stage
scenă, pe on the stage
schimb neut. change;
  exchange
schimb, curs de exchange
  rate
schimb valutar currency
  exchange
schimba v.t. to change; v.r. to
  change clothes
schimba bani to change
  money
schimbare f. change

schimbător *adj.* changeable
schiţa *v.t.* to outline; to sketch
schiţă *f.* design; draft
scîndură *f.* plank
scînteie *f.* spark
scîrţii *v.i.* to creak
scoate *v.t.* to take out
scop *neut.* goal; purpose
Scoţia *f.* Scotland
scoţian *n., adj.* Scottish
scrie *v.t.* to write
scriitor *m.* writer
scris *neut.* writing
scrisoare *f.* letter
scrumieră *f.* ashtray
scuar *neut.* square
scufunda *v.r.* to sink
scula *v.r.* to wake up
sculpta *v.t.* to sculpt
sculptor *m.* sculptor
sculptură *f.* sculpture
scump *adj.* expensive
scund *adj.* short
scurge *v.t.* to strain
scurt *adj.* short
scurta *v.t.* to shorten
scutece *neut.pl.* diapers
scutit de taxă duty free
scuza *v.t.* to excuse
scuzabil *adj.* excusable
scuzaţi excuse me, sorry
scuză *f.* excuse
seamă *f.* account; importance
seama, a ţine ~ de to take
  into consideration
seară *f.* evening
seară, haine de evening dress
sec *adj.* dry
secol *neut.* century
secretar(ă) *m., f.* secretary
secţiune *f.* section
secundă *f.* second
sedativ *neut., adj.* sedative
seducător *adj.* seductive
selecta *v.t.* to select
selecţiona *v.t.* to select
semafor *neut.* traffic signal
semăna *v.i.* to look like
semn *neut.* sign

semnal *neut.* signal
semnal de direcţie directional
  signal
semnificaţie *f.* sense, meaning
senin *adj.* clear
sentiment *neut.* sentiment
separa *v.t.* to separate
separate *adj.* separate
septembrie *m.* September
serie *f.* series
serios *adj.* serious
seriozitate *f.* seriousness
servi *v.t., v.i.* to serve
serviciu *neut.* service;
  work; job
servietă *f.* briefcase
sete *f.* thirst
sete, a-i fi to be thirsty
sezon *neut.* season
sfat *neut.* advice
sfătui *v.t.* to advise
sfeclă *f.* beet
sferă *f.* sphere
sfert *neut.* quarter
sfîrşi *v.t.* to finish
sfîrşit *neut.* end, ending
sfîrşit de săptămînă weekend
sfîşia *v.t.* to tear
sfoară *f.* string
sforţare *f.* effort
sida *f.* AIDS
sigur *adj.* sure; certain
siguranţă *f.* safety; fuse
siguranţă, tablou de fuse box
sili *v.t.* to force
simpatic *adj.* nice
simplu *adj.* simple
simţ *neut.* sense
simţi *v.t.* to feel
simţitor *adj.* sensitive
sincer *adj.* sincere
sindicat *neut.* union
sînge *neut.* blood
sîngera *v.i.* to bleed
singur *adj.* alone
sintetic *adj.* synthetic
sîmbătă *f.* Saturday
sîn *m.* bosom, breast, chest
sirop *neut.* syrup

sirop de tuse cough syrup
situație *f.* situation; condition
ski nautic *neut.* water ski
slab *adj.* thin
slăbi *v.i.* to lose weight
slujbă *f.* job
smalț *neut.* enamel
smarald *neut.* emerald
smoching *neut.* dinner jacket
smuci *v.t.* to jerk
smulge *v.t.* to tear off
snob *m.* snob
soacră *f.* mother-in-law
soare *m.* sun
sobă *f.* stove
societate *f.* society
socoteală *f.* count; calculation
socoti *v.t.* to calculate; to
    count
sofa *f.* sofa
soia *f.* soy
sold *neut.* balance; clearance
    sale
soldat *m.* soldier
solid *adj.* solid
somn *neut.* sleep
somnifer *neut.* sleeping pill
somon *m.* salmon
soră *f.* sister
sos *neut.* sauce
sosi *v.i.* to arrive
sosire *f.* arrival
soț *m.* husband; spouse
soție *f.* wife; spouse
spanac *neut.* spinach
sparanghel *neut.* asparagus
sparge *v.t.* to break
spargere *f.* burglary
spate *neut.* back
spațiu *neut.* space
special *adj.* special
spăla *v.t.* to wash
spălătorie *f.* laundromat
specialist *m.* expert
specializa *v.r.* to specialize
specie *f.* species
specific *adj.* specific
specimen *neut.* specimen

spectacol *neut.* performance;
    show
spectator *m.* spectator
speculă *f.* speculation
spera *v.t.* to hope
speria *v.t.* to frighten
spirit *n.* spirit; wit (*humor*)
spiritual *adj.* spiritual; witty
spital *neut.* hospital
splendoare *f.* splendor
sponsor *m.* sponsor
spontan *adj.* spontaneous
spori *v.t.*, *v.i.* to grow
sporire *f.* increase
sport *neut.* sport
sportiv *adj.* sports,
    sportsman-like
sprai *neut.* spray
spre *prep.* toward; to
sprijin *neut.* support
sprijini *v.t.* to support
spune *v.t.* to say; to tell
sta *v.i.* to stand; to stay
stabili *v.t.* to establish; to set
stabilit *adj.* set
stadion *neut.* stadium
stadiu *neut.* stage
stagiune *f.* season (*theatrical*)
stare *f.* state
stat *neut.* state
Statele Unite ale Americii
    United States of America
statuie *f.* statue
stație *f.* bus/trolley stop
stație de benzină gas station
staționa *v.i.* to stand; to be
    stationed
stațiune de vacanță holiday
    resort
stațiune termală spa
stea *f.* star
steag *neut.* flag
stereo *adj.* stereo
sticlă *f.* bottle
stil *neut.* style
stilou *neut.* (fountain) pen
stimă *f.* esteem
stinge *v.t.* to put out
stîncă *f.* rock

stîng *adj.* left (*direction*)
stîngaci *adj.* clumsy
stoarce *v.t.* to squeeze
stofă *f.* material; cloth
stomac *neut.* stomach
stradă *f.* street
străbate *v.t.* to pass through
strădui *v.r.* to strive
străin *adj.* foreign; *m.*
    foreigner
străluci *v.i.* to shine
strălucit *adj.* brilliant
strălucitor *adj.* bright
strămoş *m.* ancestor
strica *v.t.* to break
striga *v.i.* to shout
strigăt *neut.* shout
strîmta *v.r.* to shrink
strînge *v.t.* to collect
strîns *adj.* tight
struguri *m.pl.* grapes
student(ă) *m.*, *f.* student
studia *v.t.* to study
studiu *neut.* study
stupefiant *neut.* dope
stupid *adj.* stupid
sub *prep.* under
subiect *neut.* subject
subsol *neut.* basement
substitui *v.t.* to substitute
suc *neut.* juice
succes *neut.* success
sud *neut.* south
suferi *v.t.* to suffer
suferinţă *f.* suffering
suficient *adj.* sufficient
sufla *v.i.* to blow
suflet *neut.* soul
sufletesc *adj.* spiritual
sufragerie *f.* dining room
suna *v.i.* to sound; to ring
sunet *neut.* sound
supă *f.* soup
supăra *v.t.* to bother; to upset
supărare *f.* trouble; anger;
    sorrow
supărat *adj.* angry; upset
super *adj.* super
superb *adj.* superb

superficial *adj.* shallow
suprasolicitare *f.* overwork
supravieţui *v.i.* to survive
suprima *v.t.* to eliminate
supune *v.t.* to conquer; *v.r.* to
    submit
surd *adj.* deaf
surprinde *v.t.* to surprise
surprinzător *adj.* unexpected
surpriză *f.* surprise
sus *adv.* up
suspiciune *f.* suspicion
susţine *v.t.* to support
sută *f.* hundred
sutien *neut.* bra

# Ş

şampanie *f.* champagne
şampon *neut.* shampoo
şansă *f.* chance
şanse egale equal
    opportunities; even odds
şapcă *f.* cap
şapte *num.* seven
şase *num.* six
şchiop *adj.* lame
şcoală *f.* school
şedea *v.t.*, *v.i.* to sit
şedere *f.* stay
şezlong *neut.* deck chair
şi *conj.* and
şifonier *neut.* wardrobe
şiret *adj.* shrewd
şlagăr *neut.* hit (*song*)
şoarece *m.* mouse
şofer *m.* driver
şort *neut.* shorts
şorţ *neut.* apron
şosea *f.* road
ştampila *v.t.* to stamp
ştampilă *f.* seal; stamp
ştergător *neut.* doormat;
    windshield wiper
şterge *v.t.* to wipe; to erase
şti *v.t.* to know
ştiinţă *f.* science

şuncă f. ham
şurubelniţă f. screwdriver

# T

tabără f. camp
tablou neut. picture
tacîmuri neut.pl. cutlery
talie f. waist
tare adj. loud; hard
tastatură f. keyboard
tată m. father
taxă f. tax; charge
taxă vamală f. duty
taxi neut. taxi
tăcut adj. silent
tăia v.t. to cut
tăia felii v.t. to slice
tăietură f. cut
tăiţei m.pl. noodles
tău pron. your
teatru neut. theater
tejghea f. counter
telecabină f. cable car
telefon neut. telephone; phone
telefon direct direct-dial
    telephone
telefon public pay phone
telefona v.i. to phone
telemobil neut. cellular phone
televizor neut. television
temperatură f. temperature
temporar adj. temporary
tendon neut. tendon
tensiune f. arterială blood
    pressure
terasă f. terrace
teren neut. ground
teribil adj. awful
termometru neut.
    thermometer
ticălos m. scoundrel
tichet neut. ticket
timbru neut. stamp
timbru poştal postage stamp
timid adj. shy; timid
timp neut. time

timp îndelungat for a long
    time
timp, între in the meantime
timp, în ~ ce while
timpuriu adj. early
tinereţe f. youth
tipări v.t. to print
tirbuşon neut. bottle opener
titlu neut. title
tîmplar m. carpenter
tînăr adj. young
tîrziu adj, adv. late
toaletă f. restroom; toilet
toaletă pentru doamne
    women's restroom
toaletă pentru bărbaţi men's
    restroom
tolera v.t. to tolerate
total adj. entire; complete
totul pron. everything
totuşi adv. nevertheless
toţi pron. everybody
trabuc neut. cigar
tracţiune pe patru roţi
    four-wheel drive
traduce v.t. to translate
traducere f. translation
trage v.t. to pull
tramvai neut. streetcar
tranchilizant neut.
    tranquilizer
transformator neut.
    transformer
transport neut. transportation
tranzacţie f. transaction
traversa v.t. to cross
trăi v.t., v.i. to live
trăznet neut. thunderbolt
trebui v.mod. must
treaz adj. awake
trece v.i. to cross; to pass; to
    go by
trecere f. crossing
trecere pietoni pedestrian
    crossing
trei num. three
tremura v.i. to tremble
tren neut. train

trezi *v.i.* to awake; *v.t.* to
    wake up
tribunal *neut.* court of justice
tricota *v.t.* to knit
tricou *neut.* T-shirt
trimite *v.t.* to send
trotuar *neut.* sidewalk
tu *pron.* you
tulbura *v.t.* to disturb
tulburare *f.* disturbance
tumoare *f.* tumor
tumult *neut.* uproar
tunel *neut.* tunnel
tuns *neut.* haircut
tur *neut.* tour
turism *neut.* tourism
turist *m.* tourist
turn *neut.* tower
tuse *f.* cough
tuşi *v.i.* to cough
tutun *neut.* tobacco

# Ţ

ţară *f.* country
ţăran *m.* peasant
ţărm *neut.* shore
ţelină *f.* celery
ţigară *f.* cigarette
ţine *v.t.* to hold
ţinută *f.* de seară formal dress
ţipa *v.i.* to scream; to shout
ţipăt *neut.* scream
ţuică *f.* plum brandy

# U

ucigaş *m.* murderer
ud *adj.* wet
uda *v.t.* to water
uda leoarcă to drench
uimitor *adj.* amazing
uita *v.t.* to forget
ulcer *neut.* ulcer
ulcior *neut.* pitcher
ulei *neut.* oil
uliţă *f.* narrow street, lane

ultim *adj.* last
ului *v.t.* to astonish
uluitor *adj.* stunning
umăr *m.* shoulder
umbră *f.* shadow
umbrelă *f.* umbrella
umed *adj.* humid
umeraş *neut.* (coat) hanger
umezeală *f.* dampness
umezi *v.t.* to dampen
umfla *v.r.* to swell
umflătură *f.* inflammation
umple *v.t.* to fill
unchi *m.* uncle
unde *adv.* where
unde, de from where
undeva *adv.* somewhere
unealtă *f.* tool
unghie *f.* nail
uni *v.t.* to join
unic *adj.* unique
unire *f.* union
unitate *f.* unit
universitate *f.* university
unsuros *adj.* greasy
unt *neut.* butter
unu *num.* one
ura *v.i.* to wish
ura bun venit to welcome
ură *f.* hatred
urări de bine good wishes
urca *v.t.* to climb
urcuş *neut.* climb
ureche *f.* ear
urgenţă *f.* emergency
uriaş *adj.* enormous
urină *f.* urine
urî *v.t.* to hate
urît *adj.* ugly
urma *v.t.* to follow
urmă *f.* trace
urmă, la *adv.* last
următor *adj.* next
urolog *m.* urologist
uscător *neut.* de păr hair
    dryer
usturoi *m.* garlic
uşă *f.* door
uşor *adj.* easy

uşura *v.t.* to relieve; to soothe
uter *neut.* uterus

# V

vacanţă *f.* vacation
vacă *f.* cow
vag *adj.* vague
vagin *neut.* vagina
vagon neut. (railroad) car
vagon restaurant dining car
val *neut.* wave
valabil *adj.* valid
vale *f.* valley
valiză *f.* suitcase
valoare *f.* value
valută *f.* currency
vamă *f.* customs
vamă, declaraţie de customs
  declaration
vanilie *f.* vanilla
vapor *neut.* ship
vară *f.* summer
varietate *f.* variety
varză *f.* cabbage
vas *neut.* boat
vată *f.* cotton
vază *f.* vase
văduv *m.* widower
văduvă *f.* widow
văl *neut.* veil
văr *m.* cousin
vechi *adj.* old
vecin *m.* neighbor
vedea *v.t.* to see
vegetarian *m.* vegetarian
vehicul *neut.* vehicle
venă *f.* vein
veni *v.i.* to come
ventilator *neut.* fan
verb *neut.* verb
verbal *adj.* verbal
verde *adj.* green
verdict *neut.* verdict
verifica *v.t.* to verify
verişoară *f.* cousin
versant *m.* slope
vesel *adj.* happy

veselă *f.* dishes
vest *neut.* west
vestiar *neut.* changing room
vestit *adj.* famous
vezică *f.* biliară bladder
viaţă *f.* life
victimă *f.* victim
video *neut.* video
videocameră *f.* camcorder
videocasetofon *neut.* video
  cassette recorder
vierme *m.* worm
viitor *neut.* future
vin *neut.* wine
vinde *v.t.* to sell
vindeca *v.t.* to cure
vineri *f.* Friday
vinovat *adj.* guilty
vioară *f.* violin
vioi *adj.* lively
viol *neut.* rape
viola *v.t.* to rape
violet *adj.* purple
virgulă *f.* comma
virtute *f.* virtue
vitamină *f.* vitamin
vite *f.pl.* cattle
viteză *f.* speed
vizavi *prep.* across
viză *f.* visa
vizita *v.t.* to visit
vizită *f.* visit
vîna *v.t.* to hunt
vînat *neut.* venison
vînătă *f.* eggplant
vînătoare *f.* hunting
vînător *m.* hunter
vînt *neut.* wind
vînzare *f.* sale
vîrf *neut.* peak
vîrstă *f.* age
vocală *f.* vowel
voce *f.* voice
voi *pron.* you
voinţă *f.* will
volei *neut.* volleyball
voltaj *neut.* voltage
volum *neut.* volume
vomita *v.i.* to throw up

vorbi *v.t.* to speak
vot *neut.* vote
vota *v.t.* to vote
vrăji *v.t.* to bewitch
vrea *v.t.* to want
vreme *f.* weather
vreme frumoasă nice weather
vreme urîtă bad weather
vulgar *adj.* vulgar
vulpe *f.* fox
vultur *m.* eagle

# Z

zahăr *neut.* sugar
zarvă *f.* uproar
zăpadă *f.* snow

zbor *neut.* flight
zbura *v.i.* to fly
zdruncina *v.t.* to jolt
zdruncinătură *f.* jolt
zebră *f.* zebra
zece *num.* ten
zel *neut.* zeal
zero *neut.* zero
zeu *m.* god
zgîrcit *adj.* stingy
zgomot *neut.* noise
zi *f.* day
ziar *neut.* newspaper
ziarist *m.* journalist
zid *neut.* wall
zmeură *f.* raspberry
zonă *f.* zone
zori *m.pl.* dawn

# ENGLISH-ROMANIAN
# DICTIONARY

## A

**abandon** *v.t.* a abandona
**abbey** *n.* mănăstire *f.*
**abdomen** *n.* abdomen *neut.*
**ability** *n.* pricepere *f.*
**able** *adj.* capabil
**aboard** *adv.* pe bord; în tren
**abolish** *v.t.* a aboli
**above** *prep.* (mai) sus;
   deasupra
**abroad** *adv.* în/din străinatate
**absence** *n.* absență *f.*
**absent** *adj.* absent
**absolute** *adj.* absolut
**abundance** *n.* abundență *f.*
**abundant** *adj.* abundent
**abuse** *n.* insultă *f.*
**academy** *n.* academie *f.*
**accent** *n.* accent *neut.*
**accept** *v.t.* a accepta
**accessory** *n.* accesoriu *neut.*
**accident** *n.* accident *neut.*
**accommodate** *v.t.* a găzdui
**accompany** *v.t.* a acompania
**accord** *n.* acord *neut.*
**account** *n.* cont *neut.*
**accurate** *adj.* exact
**accuse** *v.t.* a acuza
**ache** *n.* durere *f.*
**acid** *n.* acid *neut.*
**acknowledge** *v.t.* a recunoaşte
**acquaintance** *n.* cunostință *f.*
**acquisition** *n.* achiziție *f.*
**across** *adv.* în curmeziș; *prep.*
   peste
**act** *n.* acțiune *f.*; *v.i.* a acționa
**active** *adj.* activ
**activity** *n.* activitate *f.*
**actuality** *n.* realitate *f.*
**acupuncture** *n.* acupunctură *f.*
**acupuncturist** *n.* specialist *m.*
   in acupunctură

**adapt** *v.t.* a adapta
**adaptation** *n.* adaptare *f.*
**adaptor** *n.* adaptor *neut.*
**add** *v.t.* a adăuga
**addict** *n.* consumator (*drug*)
**address** *n.* adresă *f.*
**adequate** *adj.* potrivit
**adhesive** *n.* adeziv *neut.*
**adjust** *v.t.* a aranja
**administration** *n.*
   administrație *f.*
**admission** *n.* admitere *f.*
**admit** *v.t.* a accepta
**adopt** *v.t.* a adopta
**adoption** *n.* adopțiune *f.*
**advantage** *n.* avantaj *neut.*
**adventure** *n.* aventură *f.*
**advertise** *v.t.* a face reclamă
   pentru
**advertisement** *n.* reclamă *f.*;
   publicitate *f.*
**advice** *n.* sfaturi *neut.pl.*
**advisable** *adj.* recomandabil
**adviser** *n.* consilier *m.*
**affair** *n.* afacere *f.*; treabă *f.*
**affidavit** *n.* declarație *f.* sub
   (prestare de) jurământ
**affiliation** *n.* afiliere *f.*
**affluence** *n.* afluență *f.*
**afford** *v.t.* a-și permite
**afraid** *adj.* speriat
**after** *adv.* după aceea; *prep.*
   după
**afternoon** *n.* după amiază *f.*
**afterward** *adv.* după aceea
**again** *adv.* iarăşi
**against** *prep.* împotrivă
**age** *n.* vîrstă *f.*
**aged** *adj.* bătrîn
**agency** *n.* agenție *f.*
**agent** *n.* operator *m.*; agent *m.*
**aggression** *n.* agresiune *f.*
**agree** *v.t., v.i.* a fi de acord

**agreeable** *adj.* plăcut
**agreement** *n.* acord *neut.*
**agricultural** *adj.* agricol
**agriculture** *n.* agricultură *f.*
**agronomist** *n.* agronom *m.*
**AIDS** *n.* sida *f.*
**aim** *n.* ţel *neut.*
**air** *n.* aer *neut.*
**aircraft** *n.* avion *neut.*
**airmail** *n.* poşta *f.* aeriană
**airplane** *n.* avion *neut.*
**airport** *n.* aeroport *neut.*
**alarm clock** *n.* (ceas)
    deşteptător *neut.*
**alcohol** *n.* alcool *neut.*
**alcoholic** *n.* alcoolic *m.*
**alive** *adj.* viu
**all** *det.* tot; *pron.* toţi, toată
    lumea
**allergic** *adj.* alergic
**allergy** *n.* alergie *f.*
**allow** *v.t.* a permite
**almost** *adv.* aproape
**alphabet** *n.* alfabet *neut.*
**already** *adv.* deja
**also** *adv.* de asemenea
**although** *conj.* deşi
**always** *adv.* întotdeauna
**amateur** *n.* amator *m.*
**amazing** *adj.* uimitor
**ambassador** *n.* ambasador *m.*
**ambulance** *n.* salvare *f.*
**America** *n.* America *f.*
**American** *n., adj.* american
**amount** *n.* cantitate *f.*
**amusement** *n.* distracţie *f.*
**ancestor** *n.* strămoş *m.*
**ancient** *adj.* antic
**and** *conj.* şi
**anesthetic** *n.* anestetic *neut.*
**anesthesiologist** *n.* anestezist *m.*
**angel** *n.* înger *m.*
**anger** *n.* furie *f.*; *v.t.* a supăra
**angry** *adj.* supărat; **to get ~** a
    se supăra
**animal** *n.* animal *neut.*
**ankle** *n.* gleznă *f.*
**announce** *v.t.* a anunţa
**announcement** *n.* anunţ *neut.*

**annoy** *v.t.* a enerva
**another** *det.* alt(a); *pron.* un
    altul, o alta
**answer** *n.* răspuns *neut.*; *v.i.* a
    răspunde
**ant** *n.* furnică *f.*
**antibiotic** *n.* antibiotic *neut.*
**antique** *n.* obiect *neut.* antic
**antique shop** *n.* magazin
    *neut.* de antichităţi
**anxiety** *n.* nelinişte *f.*;
    anxietate *f.*
**any** *det.* orice; oricare; *pron.*
    oricare
**anyone** *pron.* oricine
**anything** *pron.* orice
**apartment** *n.* apartament *neut.*
**aperitif** *n.* aperitiv *neut.*
**apologize** *v.r.* a se scuza
**apparatus** *n.* aparat *neut.*
**appear** *v.i.* a apărea
**appendicitis** *n.* apendicita *f.*
**appendix** *n.* apendice *neut.*
**appetite** *n.* poftă *f.*
**appetizer** *n.* gustare *f.*;
    aperitiv *neut.*
**applause** *n.* aplauze *f. pl.*
**apple** *n.* măr *neut.*
**application** *n.* cerere *f.*
**appointment** *n.* întîlnire *f.*
**approach** *v.i.* a se apropia
**April** *n.* aprilie *n.*
**apron** *n.* şorţ *neut.*
**approve** *v.t.* a aproba
**architect** *n.* arhitect *m.*
**architecture** *n.* arhitectură *f.*
**area** *n.* suprafaţă *f.*
**Argentina** *n.* Argentina *f.*
**arm** *n.* braţ *neut.*
**armchair** *n.* fotoliu *neut.*
**around** *adv.* (de jur) împrejur
**arrange** *v.t., v.r.* a (se) aranja
**arrest, to be under ~** a fi sub
    arest/arestat
**arrival** *n.* sosire *f.*
**arrive** *v.i.* a sosi
**arrogant** *adj.* trufaş
**arrow** *n.* săgeată *f.*
**art** *n.* artă *f.*

art gallery *n.* galerie *f.* de artă
arteriosclerosis *n.* ateroscleroză *f.*
artery *n.* arteră *f.*
arthritis *n.* artrită *f.*
artificial *adj.* artificial
artist *n.* artist *m.*
ashtray *n.* scrumieră *f.*
ask *v.t., v.i.* a întreba
asleep *adj.* adormit
asparagus *n.* sparanghel *m.*
aspirin *n.* aspirină *f.*
assemble *v.t.* a aduna
associate *n.* asociat *m.*; *v.t., v.r.* a (se) asocia
assurance *n.* asigurare *f.*
asthma *n.* astmă *f.*
astonish *v.t.* a ului
astray *adv.* in lumea largă
at *prep.* la
at least cel puţin
athlete *n.* atlet *m.*
athletics *n.* sport *neut.*
atmosphere *n.* atmosferă *f.*
attach *v.t.* a ataşa
attack *n.* atac *neut.*; *v.t.* a ataca
attempt *n.* încercare *f.*; *v.t.* a atenta
attendant *n.* ajutor *neut.*
attentive *adj.* atent
attitude *n.* atitudine *f.*
ATM *n.* bancomat *neut.*
attract *v.t.* a atrage
attraction *n.* atracţie *f.*
attractive *adj.* atrăgător
August *n.* august *m.*
aunt *n.* mătuşă *f.*
Australia *n.* Australia *f.*
Australian *n., adj.* australian
author *n.* scriitor *m.*
authority *n.* autoritate *f.*
automatic *adj.* automat
average *n.* medie *f.*; *adj.* mediu
avoid *v.t.* a evita
awake *adj.* treaz; *v.t., v.r.* a (se) trezi
award *n.* premiu *neut.*; *v.t.* a acorda

away *adv.* departe
awful *adj.* teribil

# B

baby *n.* copilaş *m.*
baby food *n.* hrană *f.* pentru sugari
back *n.* spate *neut.*; *v.t.* a sprijini
backward *adv.* înapoi
bad *n.* rău *neut.*; *adj.* rău
badge *n.* insignă *f.*
bag *n.* sac *neut.*
baggage *n.* bagaj *neut.*
bake *v.t., v.i.* a (se) coace
bakery *n.* brutărie *f.*
balance balanţă *f.*; *v.t.* a echilibra
balcony *n.* balcon *neut.*
bald *adj.* chel
ball *n.* minge *f.*
balloon *n.* balon *neut.*
banana *n.* banană *f.*
band *n.* orchestră *f.*
bandage *n.* bandaj *neut.*
bank *n.* bancă *f.*
bank account *n.* cont *neut.* bancar
banker *n.* bancher *m.*
bankruptcy *n.* faliment *neut.*
baptize *v.t.* a boteza
baptism *n.* botez *neut.*
bar *n.* bar *neut.*
barber *n.* frizer *m.*
barber shop *n.* frizerie *f.*
barely *adv.* abia, doar
baseball *n.* baseball *neut.*
basement *n.* subsol *neut.*
basin *n.* lighean *neut.*
basket *n.* coş *neut.*
basketball *n.* baschet *neut.*
bath *n.* baie *f.*
bath, to take a ~ a face o baie
bathrobe *n.* halat *neut.* de baie
bathroom (odaie) de baie *f.*
bathtub (cadă de) baie *f.*
bath tissue *n.* hîrtie *f.* igienică

bath towel *n.* prosop *neut.* de baie
bathe *v.t., v.r.* a (se) scălda
battery *n.* baterie *f.*
be *v.aux.* a fi
beans *n.* fasole *f.*
beard *n.* barbă *f.*
beautiful *adj.* frumos
beauty *n.* frumusețe *f.*
beauty salon *n.* salon *neut.* de coafură
because *prep.* pentru că
become *v.i.* a deveni
bed *n.* pat *neut.*
bedding *n.* așternut *neut.*
bedroom *n.* dormitor *neut.*
bee *n.* albină *f.*
beef *n.* carne *f.* de vacă
beer *n.* bere *f.*
beet *n.* sfeclă *f.*
before *prep.* înainte
begin *v.t., v.i.* a începe
beginning *n.* început *neut.*
behavior *n.* purtare *f.*
behind *adv.* în urmă; *n.* spate *neut.*
beige *adj.* bej
belfry *n.* clopotniță *f.*
believe *v.t., v.i.* a crede
bell *n.* clopot *neut.*
belong *v.i.* a aparține
beloved *adj.* iubit(ă)
below *adv.* mai jos
belt *n.* curea *f.*
bench *n.* bancă *f.*
beneath *adv.* dedesubt
berth *n.* cușetă *f.*
beside *prep.* alături de
best *adj.* cel mai bun, cea mai bună
better *adj.* mai bun; superior
between *prep.* între
beverage *n.* băutură *f.*
Bible *n.* biblie *f.*
bicycle *n.* bicicletă *f.*
big *adj.* mare
bill *n.* notă *f.* de plată ; bancnotă *f.*
binoculars *n.* binoclu *neut.*

bird *n.* pasăre *f.*
birth *n.* naștere *f.*
birthday *n.* zi *f.* de naștere
birth, to give ~ a da naștere
biscuit *n.* pișcot *neut.*
bishop *n.* episcop *m.*
bit *n.* bucățică *f.*
bite *n.* mușcătură *f.*; înțepătură *f.*; *v.t.* a mușca
bitter *adj.* amar
bizarre *adj.* ciudat
black *adj.* negru
black coffee *n.* cafea *f.* neagră
black market *n.* piață *f.* neagră
blacksmith *n.* fierar *m.*
bladder *n.* vezica *f.* urinară
blade *n.* lamă *f.*
blanket *n.* pătură *f.*
blasphemy *n.* blasfemie *f.*
bleed *v.i.* a sîngera
blessing *n.* binecuvîntare *f.*
blind *n.* jaluzea *f.*; *adj.* orb
blister *n.* bășicuță *f.*
block (city) *n.* cvartal *neut.*; *v.t.* a bloca
blood *n.* sînge *neut.*
blood pressure *n.* tensiune *f.* arterială
blouse *n.* bluză *f.*
blow *n.* lovitură *f.*; *v.i.* a sufla
blue *adj.* albastru
bluff *v.t.* a păcăli
board *n.* bord *neut.*
board, on *adv.* pe bord
boat *n.* vas *neut.*
boat trip *n.* plimbare *f.* cu vaporul
body *n.* corp *neut.*
boil *v.t., v.i.* a fierbe
boiling water *n.* fierbere *f.*
bomb *n.* bombă *f.*
bone *n.* os *neut.*
book *n.* carte *f.*; *v.t.* a rezerva (*tickets, etc.*)
bookcover *n.* copertă de carte *f.*
bookstore *n.* librărie *f.*
boot *n.* gheată *f.*

border *n.* frontieră *f.*; *v.t.* a se
învecina (cu)
bore *n.* om *m.* plicticos; *v.t.* a
plictisi
boring *adj.* plicticos
born, to be ~ a se naşte
borrow *v.t.* a lua cu împrumut
botanical garden *n.* grădină *f.*
botanică
bother *n.* necaz *neut.*; *v.t.* a
necăji
bottle *n.* sticlă *f.*
bottle opener *n.* tirbuşon *neut.*
bottom *n.* fund *neut.*; *adj.*
ultimul
bounce *v.i.* a sări
bow *n.* plecăciune *f.*; *v.i.* a
face o plecăciune
bowel *n.* intestin *neut.*
bowl *n.* castronaş *neut.*
box *n.* cutie *f.*
box-office *n.* casă *f.* de bilete
box of matches *n.* cutie *f.* de
chibrituri
boy *n.* băiat *m.*
boyfriend *n.* prieten *m.*
boycott *n.* boicot *neut.*; *v.t.* a
boicota
bra *n.* sutien *neut.*
bracelet *n.* brăţară *f.*
brain *n.* creer *neut.*
brake *n.* frînă *f.*
bread *n.* pîine *f.*
breadth *n.* lăţime *f.*
break *n.* ruptură *f.*; *v.t.* a sparge
breakdown *n.* pană *f.*
breakfast *n.* micul dejun; to
have ~ a lua micul dejun
breathe *v.t.*, *v.i.* a respira
breathtaking care iţi taie
respiraţia
breeze *n.* briză *f.*
bride *n.* mireasă *f.*
bridegroom *n.* mire *m.*
bridge *n.* pod *neut.*
briefcase *n.* servietă *f.*
briefs *n.* chiloţi *m.pl.*
(*underwear*)
bright *adj.* strălucitor

brilliant *adj.* strălucit
bring *v.t.* a aduce
bring up *v.t.* a creşte
Britain *n.* Marea Britanie *f.*
British *n.*, *adj.* britanic
broad *adj.* larg
broadcast *n.* emisiune *f.*; *v.t.* a
difuza
broadcasting station *n.* staţie
*f.* de radio
brochure *n.* broşură *f.*
brooch *n.* broşă *f.*
broom *n.* mătură *f.*
bronze *n.* bronz *neut.*
brothel *n.* bordel *neut.*
brother *n.* frate *m.*
brown *adj.* maron
browse *v.t.* a răsfoi
bruise *n.* contuzie *f.*; *v.t.* a
se lovi
brush *n.* perie *f.*; *v.t.* a peria
bucket *n.* găleată *f.*
bug *n.* insectă *f.*
build *v.t.* a clădi
building *n.* clădire *f.*
bulb *n.* bec *neut.* electric
bump *n.* cucui *neut.*; *v.t.* a
ciocni
bunch *n.* mănunchi *neut.*
burger *n.* hamburgher *m.*
burglary *n.* spargere *f.*
burn *n.* arsură *f.*; *v.t.*, *v.i.* a arde
burning *n.* arsură *f.*
burst *n.* izbucnire *f.*; *v.i.* a
izbucni
bury *v.t.* a îngropa
bus *n.* autobuz *neut.*
bus route *n.* linie *f.* de autobuz
bus station *n.* autogară *f.*
bus stop *n.* staţie *f.* de autobuz
business *n.* companie *f.* de
afaceri
business, on in interes de
afaceri
business person *n.* om *m.* de
afaceri
business trip *n.* călătorie *f.* de
afaceri
busy *adj.* ocupat

but *conj.* dar
butcher *n.* măcelarie *f.*
butter *n.* unt *neut.*
butterfly *n.* fluture *m.*
button *n.* nasture *m.*
buy *v.t.* a cumpăra
buyer *n.* cumpărător *m.*
bye-bye *interj.* la revedere

# C

cabaret *n.* cabaret *neut.*
cabbage *n.* varză *f.*
cabin *n.* cabină *f.*
cable *n.* cablu *neut.*
cable car *n.* telecabină *f.*
café *n.* cafenea *f.*
cage *n.* cuşcă *f.*
cake *n.* prăjitură *f.*, tort *neut.*
calculator *n.* calculator *neut.*
call *n.* chemare *f.*; *v.t.* a chema
call back a chema din nou (la
    telefon)
calorie *n.* calorie *f.*
camcorder *n.* videocameră *f.*,
    cameră de luat vederi
camera *n.* aparat *neut.* de
    fotografiat
camp *n.* tabără *f.*
camping *n.* camping *neut.*
can *n.* cutie *f.* de tinichea;
    *v.mod.* a putea
Canada *n.* Canada *f.*
Canadian *n.*, *adj.* canadian
cancel *v.t.* a anula
cancellation *n.* anulare *f.*
cancer *n.* cancer *neut.*
candle *n.* lumînare *f.*
candy *n.* bomboane *f.pl.*
cap *n.* şapcă *f.*
capacity *n.* capacitate *f.*
capital *n.* capital *neut.*;
    capitală *f.*
caprice *n.* capriciu *neut.*
car *n.* automobil *neut.*
car part piesă *f.* (de schimb)
    auto

car rental *n.* birou *neut.* de
    închiriat de maşini
card *n.* carte *f.*; legitimaţie *f.*
    (*ID*)
cardiac *adj.* cardiac
cardiologist *n.* cardiolog *m.*
care *n.* grijă *f.*
carefree *adj.* fără griji
careful *adj.* atent
carpenter *n.* dulgher *m.*
carpet *n.* covor *neut.*
carrot *n.* morcov *m.*
carry *v.t.* a duce
case *n.* caz *neut.*
case, in that ~ în acest caz
cash *n.* bani *m.pl.* gheaţă;
    *v.t.* a încasa
cashier *n.* casier *m.*
cash register *n.* maşină *f.*
    de casă
casino *n.* cazinou *neut.*
cassette *n.* casetă *f.*
castle *n.* castel *neut.*
cat *n.* pisică *f.*
catch *n.* prindere *f.*; *v.t.* a
    prinde
cathedral *n.* catedrală *f.*
Catholic *n.* catolic *m.*
cattle *n.* vite *f.pl.*
cauliflower *n.* conopidă *f.*
cause *n.* motiv *neut.*; cauză
    *fem.*; *v.t.* a pricinui
cave *n.* peşteră *f.*
compact disc, CD *n.* disc
    *neut.* compact
celebration *n.* sărbătorire *f.*
ceiling *n.* plafon *neut.*
celery *n.* ţelină *f.*
cemetery *n.* cimitir *neut.*
center *n.* centru *neut.*
central *adj.* central
central heating *n.* încălzire *f.*
    centrală
century *n.* secol *m.*
ceramics *n.* ceramică *f.*
cereal *n.* cereală *f.*
certain *adj.* sigur
certificate *n.* certificat *neut.*
certify *v.t.* a atesta
chain *n.* lanţ *neut.*

chair *n.* scaun *neut.*
chalk *n.* cretă *f.*
challenge *n.* provocare *f.*; *v.t.*
　a provoca
champagne *n.* şampanie *f.*
chance *n.* întîmplare *f.*; şansă *f.*
chandelier *n.* candelabru *neut.*
change *n.* schimbare *f.*; *v.t.* a
　schimba
change, to ~ clothes a se
　schimba
change, to ~ money a
　schimba bani
changeable *adj.* schimbător
changing rooms *n.* vestiar
　*neut.*
chapel *n.* capelă *f.*
chapter *n.* capitol *neut.*
character *n.* caracter *neut.*
charge *n.* taxă *f.*; (buy with
　credit card) a cumpăra cu
　carte de credit
charity *n.* filantropie *f.*
charm *n.* farmec *neut.*; *v.t.* a
　vrăji
charming *adj.* încîntător
charter flight *n.* cursă *f.*
　charter
chatter *n.* flecăreală *f.*; *v.i.* a
　trăncăni
cheap *adj.* ieftin
cheat *n.* escroc *m.*; *v.t.* a înşela
check *n.* verificare *f.*; *v.t.* a
　verifica
cheese *n.* brînză *f.*
cherry *n.* cireaşă *f.*
chess *n.* joc *neut.* de şah
chest *n.* piept *neut.*
chestnut *n.* castan *m.*
chewing gum *n.* gumă *f.* de
　mestecat
chicken *n.* pui *m.*
child *n.* copil *m.*
chisel *n.* daltă *f.*; *v.t.* a cizela
chips *n.* cartofi *m.pl.* prăjiţi
　(*potato*)
chocolate *n.* ciocolată *f.*
choice *n.* alegere *f.*
choir *n.* cor *neut.*

cholera *n.* holeră *f.*
choose *v.t.* a alege
chop *n.*cotlet *neut.* (*pork*)
Christian *n.* creştin *m.*
Christmas *n.* crăciun *neut.*
Christmas card *n.* felicitare *f.*
　de crăciun
chronic *adj.* cronic
church *n.* biserică *f.*
cigar *n.* trabuc *neut.*
cigarette *n.* ţigară *f.*
cinema *n.* cinema(tograf) *neut.*
circulation *n.* circulaţie *f.*
circumstance *n.* împrejurare *f.*
citizen *n.* cetăţean *m.*
city *n.* oraş *neut.*
civic *adj.* civic
civilization *n.* civilizaţie *f.*
claim *n.* pretenţie *f.*; *v.t.* a
　pretinde
clarify *v.t.*, *v.i.* a (se) clarifica
clash *n.* ciocnire *f.*; *v.t.*, *v.i.* a
　(se) ciocni
class *n.* clasă *f.*
clean *adj.* curat; *v.t.* a curăţa
cleaning *n.* curăţenie *f.*
clear *adj.* clar
clear up *v.t.* a lămuri
clergy *n.* cler *neut.*
clever *adj.* deştept
client *n.* client *m.*
cliff *n.* faleză *f.*
climate *n.* climă *f.*
climb *n.* urcuş *neut.*; *v.t.* a urca
clock *n.* orologiu *neut.*
cloister *n.* mănăstire *f.*
close *v.t.* a închide
closed *adj.* închis
clothes *n.* haine *f.pl.*
clothes hanger *n.* umeraş
　*neut.* de haine
clothes pin *n.* cîrlig *neut.* de
　rufe
clothing *n.* îmbrăcăminte *f.*
cloudy *adj.* înnorat
clown *n.* clovn *m.*
club *n.* club *neut.*
clumsy *adj.* stîngaci
coast *n.* coastă *f.*

coat *n.* haină *f.*
cobweb *n.* pînză *f.* de păianjen
cockpit *n.* carlingă *f.*
cocky *adj.* încrezut
code *n.* prefix *neut.* (*area*)
coffee *n.* cafea *f.*
coffeehouse *n.* cafenea *f.*
coffeepot *n.* cafetieră *f.*
coherence *n.* coerență *f.*
coin *n.* monedă *f.*
cold *n.* frig *neut.*; răceală *f.*;
   *adj.* rece
collapse *n.* prăbușire *f.*; *v.i.* a
   se prăbuși
collect *v.* a strînge *tr*
collection *n.* colecție *f.*
college *n.* colegiu *neut.*
collision *n.* ciocnire *f.*
color *n.* culoare *f.*
color film *n.* film *neut.* color
comb *n.* pieptene *m.*
come *v.i.* a veni
come back *v.i.* a reveni
comedy *n.* comedie *f.*
comfort *n.* alinare *f.*
comfortable *adj.* confortabil
comic *adj.* comic
comma *n.* virgulă *f.*
comment *n.* comentariu *neut.*;
   *v.t.* a face comentarii
commercial *adj.* comercial; *n.*
   reclamă *f.* publicitară
commission *n.* autorizație *f.*
committee *n.* comitet *neut.*
compact *adj.* compact
compact disc *n.* disc *neut.*
   compact
communicate *v.t.* a comunica
community *n.* comunitate *f.*
companion *n.* însoțitor *m.*
company *n.* companie *f.*
compare *v.t.* a compara
compartment *n.*
   compartiment *neut.*
compass *n.* busolă *f.*
complaint *n.* nemulțumire *f.*
complete *adj.* complet
completely *adv.* total

compliment *n.* compliment
   *neut.*
computer *n.* calculator *neut.*
concept *n.* noțiune *f.*
concerning referitor la
concession *n.* concesie *f.*
conclusion *n.* concluzie *f.*
concrete *adj.* concret; *n.*
   beton *neut.*
concert *n.* concert *neut.*
condition *n.* stare *f.*
condolence *n.* condoleanțe *f.pl.*
condom *n.* prezervativ *neut.*
conductor *n.* dirijor *m.*
conference *n.* conferință *f.*
confess *v.t.* a mărturisi
confidence *n.* încredere *f.*
confirm *v.t.* a confirma
confirmation *n.* confirmare *f.*
conflict *n.* conflict *neut.*
confuse *v.t.* a încurca
confused *adj.* încurcat
confusion *n.* dezordine *f.*
congratulate *v.t.*, *v.i.* a (se)
   felicita
congratulations *n.*
   felicitări *f.pl.*
connection *n.* legătură *f.*
conscience *n.* conștiință *f.*
   morală
conscious *adj.* conștient
consciousness *n.* conștiență *f.*
consequence *n.* consecință *f.*
consider *v.t.* a chibzui
constipation *n.* constipație *f.*
consul *n.* consul *m.*
consulate *n.* consulat *neut.*
consultant *n.* consultant *m.*
consumer *n.* consummator *m.*
contact *n.* contact *neut.*; *v.t.* a
   lua legatura cu
contain *v.t.* a conține
content(s) *n.* conținut *neut.*
context *n.* context *neut.*
continue *v.t.* a continua
contraceptive *n.*
   anticoncepțional *neut.*
contract *n.* contract *neut.*; *v.t.*
   a contracta

**contradict** *v.t.* a contrazice
**contradiction** *n.* contradicţie *f.*
**contribution** *n.* contribuţie *f.*
**convent** *n.* mănăstire *f.* de
  maici
**convenient** *adj.* corespunzător
**convertible (car)** *n.* maşină *f.*
  decapotabilă
**convince** *v.t.* a convinge
**cook** *n.* bucătar *m.*; *v.t.* a găti
**cookie** *n.* pişcot *neut.*
**cooking pot** *n.* oală *f.* de gătit
**copper** *n.* cupru *neut.*
**copy** *n.* copie *f.*; *v.t.* a copia
**coral** *n.* coral *m.*
**corkscrew** *n.* tirbuşon *neut.*
**corn** *n.* porumb *m.*
**corner** *n.* colţ *neut.*
**corpse** *n.* cadavru *neut.*
**corpulent** *adj.* gras
**correct** *adj.* corect; *v.t.* a
  corecta
**correspond** *v.i.* a coresponda
**corruption** *n.* corupţie *f.*
**cosmetics** *n.* cosmetice *f.pl.*
**cost** *n.* cost *neut.*; *v.t.* a costa
**costume** *n.* costum *neut.*
**cotton** *n.* bumbac *neut.*
**cotton wool** *n.* vată *f.*
**cough** *n.* tuse *f.*; *v.i.* a tuşi
**cough syrup** *n.* sirop *neut.* de
  tuse
**count** *n.* socoteală *f.*; *v.t.* a
  socoti
**counter** *n.* tejghea *f.*
**country** *n.* ţară *f.*
**country music** *n.* muzică *f.* country
**countryside** *n.* la ţară *f.*
**couple** *n.* pereche *f.*
**courage** *n.* curaj *neut.*
**course** *n.* fel *neut.* de mincare
**course, of** desigur
**court of justice** *n.* tribunal
  *neut.*
**cousin** *n.* văr *m.*; verişoară *f.*
**cover** *n.* capac *neut.*; *v.t.* a
  acoperi
**cow** *n.* vacă *f.*

**coward** *n.* laş *m.*
**cradle** *n.* leagăn *neut.*
**craft shop** *n.* magazin *neut.*
  de artizanat
**craftsman** *n.* meşteşugar *m.*
**cramp** *n.* crampă *f.*
**crash** *n.* prăbuşire *f.*; *v.i.* a se
  prăbuşi
**crazy** *adj.* nebun
**creak** *v.i.* a scîrţîi
**cream** *n.* cremă *f.*
**create** *v.t.* a crea
**creative** *n.* creator *m.*
**credit** *n.* credit *neut.*
**credit card** *n.* carte *f.* de
  credit
**crime** *n.* crimă *f.*
**criminal** *n.* criminal *m.*
**crippled** *adj.* infirm
**crisis** *n.* criză *f.*
**criterion** *n.* criteriu *neut.*
**critical** *adj.* critic
**criticism** *n.* critică *f.*
**cross** *v.t.* a traversa; *n.* cruce *f.*
**crossing** *n.* trecere *f.*
**crossroad** *n.* răscruce *f.*
**crowd** *n.* mulţime *f.*
**crowded** *adj.* aglomerat
**crucifix** *n.* crucifix *neut.*
**cruel** *adj.* crud
**cruise** *n.* croazieră *f.*
**crystal** *n.* cristal *neut.*
**cucumber** *n.* castravete *m.*
**culprit** *n.* vinovat *m.*
**culture** *n.* cultură *f.*
**cup** *n.* ceaşcă *f.*
**cupboard** *n.* dulap *neut.*
**cure** *n.* cură *f.*
**curious** *adj.* curios
**curl of hair** *n.* buclă *f.*
**curlers** *n.* bigudiuri *neut.pl.*
**currency** *n.* monedă *f.*;
  valută *f.*
**currency exchange office** *n.*
  birou *neut.* de schimb
  valutar
**current** *adj.* curent
**curse** *n.* înjurătură *f.*; *v.t.* a
  înjura

curtain *n.* perdea *f.*
customs *n.* vamă *f.*
customs declaration *n.*
    declarație *f.* de vamă
cut *n.* reducere *f.*; tuns *neut.*;
    *v.t.* a tăia
cutlery *n.* tacîmuri *neut.pl.*
cycling *n.* ciclism *neut.*
cyclist *n.* biciclist *m.*
cylinder *n.* cilindru *m.*
cystitis *n.* cistită *f.*

# D

daily *n.* ziar (*newspaper*)
    *neut.* cotidian; *adj.* zilnic
dairy *n.* lăptărie *f.*
dairy farm *n.* fermă *f.* de
    lapte
damage *n.* pagubă *f.*; *v.t.* a
    strica
damp *adj.* umed
dampness *n.* umezeală *f.*
dance *n.* dans *neut.*; *v.t.*, *v.i.* a
    dansa
danger *n.* primejdie *f.*; pericol
    *neut.*
dangerous *adj.* primejdios;
    periculos
dark *n.* întuneric *neut.*; *adj.*
    întunecat
date *n.* dată *f.*; *v.t.* a data
daughter *n.* fiică *f.*
dawn *n.* zori *pl.* ; *v.i.* a se face
    ziuă
day *n.* zi *f.*
day trip *n.* excursie *f.* de o zi
dead *adj.* mort
deaf *adj.* surd
deal *n.* afacere *f.*
deal, to ~ with a se ocupa de
dear *adj.* scump
death *n.* moarte *f.*
debt *n.* datorie *f.*
decade *n.* deceniu *neut.*
deceive *v.t.* a înșela
decide *v.t.*, *v.i.* a (se) hotărî
decision *n.* hotărîre *f.*

deck chair *n.* șezlong *neut.*
declaration *n.* declarație *f.*
declare *v.t.* a declara
decorate *v.t.* a împodobi
deduct *v.t.* a scădea
deer *n.* cerb *m.*; căprioară *f.*
defect *n.* defect *neut.*
defense *n.* apărare *f.*
defend *v.t.* a apăra
defrost *v.t.* a decongela
deficit *n.* deficit *neut.*
degree *n.* grad *neut.*
delay *n.* întîrziere *f.*; *v.t.* a
    întîrzia
delicacy *n.* delicatețe *f.*
delicate *adj.* delicat
delicatessen *n.* delicatese *f.pl.*
delicious *adj.* delicious
delight *n.* încîntare *f.*; *v.t.* a
    încînta
delightful *adj.* încîntător
deliver *v.t.* a furniza
delivery *n.* predare *f.*
democracy *n.* democrație *f.*
demonstration *n.*
    demonstrație *f.*
denounce *v.t.* a acuza
dentist *n.* dentist *m.*
deny *v.t.* a refuza
deodorant *n.* deodorant *neut.*
depart *v.i.* a pleca
department store *n.* magazin
    *neut.* universal
departure *n.* plecare *f.*
deposit *n.* depunere *f.*; *v.t.* a
    depune
depression *n.* depresiune *f.*
    nervoasă
descent *n.* coborîre *f.*
describe *v.t.* a înfățișa
desert *n.* pustiu *neut.*
design *n.* desen *neut.*; *v.t.* a
    schița
despise *v.t.* a disprețui
dessert *n.* desert *neut.*
destination *n.* destinație *f.*
destroy *v.t.* a nimici
destruction *n.* distrugere *f.*
detail *n.* amănunt *neut.*

detergent *n.* detergent *neut.*

deteriorate *v.i.* a (se) înrăutăți

detour *n.* ocol *neut.*

devastate *v.t.* a pustii

devastation *n.* distrugere *f.*

develop *v.t.* a dezvolta

development *n.* dezvoltare *f.*

devil *n.* drac *m.*

devour *v.t.* a devora

dew *n.* rouă *f.*

diabetes *n.* diabet *neut.* zaharat

dialect *n.* dialect *neut.*

diamond *n.* diamant *neut.*

diapers *n.* scutece *neut.pl.*

diarrhea *n.* diaree *f.*

dictionary *n.* dicționar *neut.*

die *v.i.* a muri

diesel *n.* diesel *neut.*

diet *n.* regim *neut.*

difference *n.* deosebire *f.*

different *adj.* diferit

difficult *adj.* dificil

digest *v.t.* a digera

digestion *n.* digestie *f.*

digit *n.* cifră *f.* sau număr pînă la nouă

digital *adj.* digital

diminish *v.t.* a diminua

dine *v.i.* a mînca (prînzul sau cina)

dining car *n.* vagon *neut.* restaurant

dining room *n.* sufragerie *f.*

dinner *n.* masa *f.* principală a zilei

dinner jacket *n.* smoching *neut.*

diocese *n.* episcopie *f.*

diplomat *n.* diplomat *m.*

direct *adj.* direct

direct-dial telephone telefon direct

direction *n.* direcție *f.*

directional signal *n.* semnal *m.* de direcție

director *n.* director *m.*

dirty *adj.* murdar; *v.t.* a murdări

disabled (person) *n.* persoană *f.* cu handicap

disagree *v.i.* a nu fi de accord

disappear *v.i.* a dispărea

disc *n.* disc *neut.*

discharge *n.* descărcare *f.*; *v.t.* a descărca

disco(teque) *n.* discotecă *f.*

discount *n.* reducere *f.* de prețuri

discover *v.t.* a descoperi

disgrace *n.* rușine *f.*; *v.t.* a dezonora

disgust *n.* dezgust *neut.*; *v.t.* a dezgusta

disgusting *adj.* dezgustător

dish *n.* (fel de) mîncare (*food*) *f.*; farfurie (*plate*) *f.*

dishwasher *n.* mașină *f.* de spălat vase

dishwashing detergent *n.* detergent *neut.* de vase

disinfectant *n.* dezinfectant *neut.*

dislocate *v.t.* a disloca

disorder *n.* dezordine *f.*

display *n.* expoziție *f.*; *v.t.* a expune

disposable *adj.* de unică folosința

dispute *n.* dispută *f.*; *v.t.* a contesta

dissolve *v.t.* a dizolva

distant *adj.* îndepărtat

distilled water *n.* apă *f.* distilată

distress *n.* necaz *neut.*; *v.t.* a necăji

distribute *v.t.* a distribui

district *n.* regiune *f.*; district *neut.*

disturb *v.t.* a tulbura

disturbance *n.* tulburare *f.*

dive *n.* plonjon *neut.*; *v.i.* a plonja

diversion *n.* abatere *f.*

divide *v.t.* a despărți

divorce *n.* divorț *neut.*; *v.i.* a divorța

dizziness *n.* ameţeală *f.*
dizzy *adj.* ameţit
do *v.t.* a îndeplini; a face
doctor *n.* doctor *m.*
dog *n.* cîine *m.*
dollar *n.* dolar *m.*
donkey *n.* măgar *m.*
door *n.* uşă *f.*
dope *n.* stupefiant *neut.*; *v.t.* a
  dopa
dosage *n.* dozaj *neut.*
dot *n.* punct *neut.*
double *adj.* dublu
double bed pat dublu
double room cameră cu două
  paturi
doubt *n.* îndoială *f.*; *v.i.* a se
  îndoi
doubtful *adj.* neîncrezător
dough *n.* aluat *neut.*
down(wards) *adv.* în jos
downstairs *adv.* jos; la parter
downtown *adj.* în centru
dozen *n.* duzină *f.*
draft *n.* schiţă *f.*; *v.t.* a schiţa
drama *n.* dramă *f.*
dream *n.* vis *neut.*; *v.t.* a visa
drench *v.t.* a uda leoarcă
dress *n.* rochie *f.*; *v.i.* a
  îmbrăca
dressed, to get ~ a se îmbrăca
drink *n.* băutură *f.*; *v.t.* a bea
drinking glass *n.* pahar *neut.*
  de apă
drinking water *n.* apă *f.*
  potabilă
drive *n.* plimbare *f.* cu un
  vehicul; *v.t.* a conduce
  maşina
driver *n.* şofer *m.*
drop *n.* picătură *f.*
drown *v.t.*, *v.i.* a (se) îneca
drug *n.* doctorie *f.*; *v.t.* a droga
drunk *n.* beţiv *m.*; *adj.* beat
dry *adj.* uscat; *v.t.*, *v.i.* a (se)
  usca
dry-clean *v.t.* a curăţa chimic
dry cleaner's *n.* curăţătorie *f.*
  chimică

dubious *adj.* dubios
duck *n.* raţă *f.*
due *n.* datorie *f.*; *adj.* scadent
during *prep.* în timpul
dust *n.* praf *neut.*; *v.t.* a
  scutura de praf
duty *n.* taxă (vamală) *f.*
duty-free *adj.* scutit de taxe
  vamale

# E

each *pron.* fiecare (în parte)
eagle *n.* vultur *m.*
ear *n.* ureche *f.*
ear drops *n.* picături *f.pl.*
  pentru urechi
early *adj.* timpuriu; *adv.*
  devreme
earn *v.t.* a cîştiga
earring *n.* cercel *m.*
east *n.* răsărit *neut.*; *adj.* de
  răsărit; *adv.* spre răsărit
easy *adj.* uşor
eat *v.t.* a mînca
economist *n.* economist *m.*
economy *n.* economie *f.*
economy class *n.* clasa *f.*
  turist
edge *n.* muchie *f.*
edifice *n.* clădire *f.*
edition *n.* ediţie *f.*
effect *n.* rezultat *neut.*
effort *n.* sforţare *f.*
egg *n.* ou *neut.*
eggplant *n.* vînătă *f.*
eight *num.* opt
either ... or fie ... fie
elastic *adj.* elastic
elbow *n.* cot *neut.*
election *n.* alegere *f.*
electric *adj.* electric
electric shaver *n.* aparat *neut.*
  de ras electric
electrician *n.* electrician *m.*
electricity *n.* electricitate *f.*
electricity meter *n.* contor
  *neut.* electric

electronic game *n.* joc *neut.*
electronic
elegant *adj.* elegant
elevator *n.* lift *neut.*,; ascensor
*neut.*
eliminate *v.t.* a desfiinţa
else, something ~ altceva
embarkation point *n.* punct
*neut.* de îmbarcare
embarrassment *n.*
încurcătură *f.*
embassy *n.* ambasadă *f.*
embrace *n.* îmbrăţişare *f.*; *v.t.*
a îmbrăţişa
embroidery *n.* broderie *f.*
emerald *n.* smarald *neut.*
emergency *n.* urgenţă *f.*
emigrant *n.* emigrant *m.*
emotion *n.* emoţie *f.*
empire *n.* imperiu *neut.*
employee *n.* salariat *m.*
employer *n.* patron *m.*
empty *adj.* gol
enamel *n.* email *neut.*
enchant *v.t.* a vrăji
end *n.* sfîrşit *neut.*; *v.t.*, *v.i.* a
(se) sfîrşi
enemy *n.* duşman *m.*
energy *n.* energie *f.*
engaged, to be ~ a fi logodit
engagement *n.* logodnă *f.*
engine *n.* motor *neut.*
engineer *n.* inginer *m.*
England *n.* Anglia *f.*
English *n.*, *adj.* englez
English-speaking vorbitor *m.*
de limba engleză
enjoy *v.t.* a-i plăcea
enlarge *v.t.* a mări
enormous *adj.* uriaş
enough *adv.* destul
enter *v.i.* a intra
entertainment *n.* distracţie *f.*
entire *adj.* tot, toată
entirely *adv.* total
entrance *n.* intrare *f.*
entrance fee *n.* taxă *f.* de
intrare
entry *n.* intrare *f.*

entry visa *n.* viză *f.* de intrare
envelope *n.* plic *neut.*
environment *n.* mediu *neut.*
envy *n.* invidie *f.*; *v.t.* a invidia
equal *adj.* egal; *v.t.* a egala
equilibrium *n.* echilibru *neut.*
equipment *n.* echipament
*neut.*
error *n.* greşeală *f.*
escape *n.* scăpare *f.*; *v.i.* a
scăpa
essential *adj.* esenţial
esteem *n.* stimă *f.*
eternal *adj.* etern
Europe *n.* Europa *f.*
European *n.*, *adj.* european
eve, on the ~ of în ajunul
even *adj.* neted; *adv.* chiar
evening *n.* seară *f.*
evening dress *n.* haine *f.pl.* de
seară
evening, in the ~ seara
even odds *n.* şanse *f.pl.* egale
event *n.* eveniment *neut.*
every *det.* fiecare
everybody *pron.* toată lumea;
toţi
everyone *pron.* fiecare
everything *pron.* totul
everywhere *adv.* pretutindeni
evidence *n.* dovadă *f.*
evil *adj.* malefic
evolution *n.* evoluţie *f.*
exaggerate *v.t.*, *v.i.* a exagera
examination *n.* examen *neut.*
example *n.* exemplu *neut.*
example, for ~ de exemplu
except *prep.* în afară de
exception *n.* excepţie *f.*
exceptional *adj.* excepţional
excess baggage *n.* bagaj *neut.*
excedentar
exchange *n.* schimb *neut.*; *v.t.*
a schimba
exchange rate *n.* curs *neut.* de
schimb
exciting *adj.* emoţionant
exclamation *n.* exclamaţie *f.*
exclude *v.t.* a exclude

**excruciating** *adj.* cumplit
**excursion** *n.* excursie *f.*
**excuse** *n.* scuză *f.*; *v.t.* a scuza
**exercise** *n.* exercițiu *neut.*; *v.t.*
   a exercita
**exhausted** *adj.* epuizat
**exhibition** *n.* expoziție *f.*
**exit** *n.* ieșire *f.*; *v.i.* a ieși
**expect** *v.t.* a se aștepta la
**expenditure** *n.* cheltuială *f.*
**expense** *n.* cheltuială *f.*
**experience** *n.* experiență *f.*;
   *v.t.* a simți
**experiment** *n.* probă *f.*; experiență *f.*; *v.i.* a experimenta
**expert** *n.* specialist *m.*
**expiration date** *n.* dată *f.* de
   expirare
**expire** *v.i.* a expira
**export(ation)** *n.* export *neut.*
**exposure** *n.* expunere *f.*
**express** *adj.* expres
**express mail** *n.* (scrisoare) *f.*
   expres
**extra** *adj.* extra, suplimentar
**extremely** *adv.* extrem
**eye** *n.* ochi *m.*
**eyeglasses** *n.* ochelari *m.pl.*

# F

**fable** *n.* fabulă *f.*
**fabric** *n.* material *neut.*
**façade** *n.* fațadă *f.*
**face** *n.* față *f.*
**facility** *n.* instalație *f.*
**factory** *n.* fabrică *f.*
**faculty** *n.* facultate *f.*
**fair** *adj.* cinstit
**faith** *n.* credință *f.*
**faithful** *adj.* credincios
**fall** *v.i.* a cădea
**false** *adj.* fals
**familiarity** *n.* familiaritate *f.*
**family** *n.* familie *f.*
**family name** *n.* nume *n.* de
   familie
**famous** *adj.* vestit

**fan** *n.* ventilator *neut.*;
   microbist *m.* (*sport*)
**fanbelt** *n.* cureaua *f.*
   ventilatorului
**fancy** *n.* fantezie *f.*
**fantasy** *n.* iluzie *f.*
**far** *adv.* departe
**fare** *n.* costul *neut.* unei
   călătorii
**farm** *n.* fermă *f.*
**farmer** *n.* fermier *m.*
**fascinating** *adj.* fermecător
**fashion** *n.* modă *f.*; *v.t.* a
   modela
**fashionable** *adj.* la modă, in
   vogă
**fast** *adj, adv.* repede, iute
**fat** *adj.* gras
**father** *n.* tată *m.*
**fault** *n.* defect *neut.*
**fauna** *n.* faună *f.*
**favor** *n.* favoare *f.*
**fax** *n.* fax *neut.*
**fear** *n.* frică *f.*; *v.t.* a se teme
**feast** *n.* sărbătoare *f.*
**February** *n.* februarie *m.*
**feeble** *adj.* slab
**feed** *v.t.* a hrăni
**feel** *v.t., v.i.* a simți
**feeling** *n.* sentiment *neut.*
**female** *n.* femelă *f.*; *adj.*
   feminin
**fertile** *adj.* fertil
**festival** *n.* festival *neut.*
**fever** *n.* temperatură *f.*
**few** *pron.* puțini, nu mulți
**fiancé** *n.* logodnic *m.*
**fiancée** *n.* logodnică *f.*
**field** *n.* cîmp *m.*
**fight** *n.* luptă *f.*; *v.i.* a (se) lupta
**file** *n.* pilă *f.*
**fill** *v.t.* a umple
**filling** (dental) *n.* plombă *f.*
**film** *n.* film *neut.*
**filmmaker** *n.* cineast *m.*
**filter** *n.* filtru *neut.*
**filthy** *adj.* murdar
**finance** *v.t.* a finanța

**finances** *n.* situaţie *f.*
 financiară
**find** *v.t.* a găsi
**fine** *adj.* excelent; *n.* amendă
 *f.*; *v.t.* a amenda
**finger** *n.* deget *neut.*
**finish** *v.t.* a sfîrşi; *n.* încheiere *f.*
**fire** *n.* incendiu *neut.*
**fire station** *n.* serviciu *n.* de
 pompieri
**firm** *adj.* ferm
**first** *adj.* prim, întîi
**fish** *n.* peşte *m.*
**fishing** *n.* pescuit *neut.*
**fishing, to go** ~ a merge la
 pescuit
**fit** *v.i.* a se potrivi
**fitting room** *n.* cameră *f.* de
 probă
**fix** *v.t.* a fixa
**flag** *n.* steag *neut.*
**flame** *n.* flacără *f.*
**flash** *n.* bliţ *neut.*
**flat** *adj.* plat
**flight** *n.* zbor *neut.*
**floor** *n.* podea *f.*
**flora** *n.* floră *f.*
**flour** *n.* făină *f.*
**flower** *n.* floare *f.*
**flu** *n.* gripă *f.*
**fluent** *adj.* fluent
**fly** *v.i.* a zbura
**folk art** *n.* artă *f.* populară
**folk music** *n.* muzică *f.*
 populară
**follow** *v.t.* a urma
**food** *n.* hrană *f.*
**fool** *n.* neghiob *m.*; *v.t.* a păcăli
**foolish** *adj.* neghiob
**foot** *n.* picior *neut.*
**football** *n.* fotbal *neut.*
**footpath** *n.* cărare *f.*
**for** *prep.* pentru
**force** *n.* forţă *f.*
**forecast** *n.* prognoză *f.*; *v.t.* a
 prevedea
**forehead** *n.* frunte *f.*
**foreign** *adj.* străin
**foreigner** *n.* străin *m.*

**forest** *n.* pădure *f.*; codru *m.*
**forget** *v.t.* a uita
**forgive** *v.t.* a ierta
**forgiveness** *n.* iertare *f.*
**fork** *n.* furculiţă *f.*
**form** *n.* formular *neut.*
**formal dress** *n.* ţinută *f.* de
 seară
**former** *adj.* fost, trecut
**formerly** *adv.* odinioară
**forward** *adv.* înainte; *adj.*
 din faţă
**forwarding address** *n.* adresă
 *f.* de reexpediere
**foundation** *n.* fundaţie *f.*
**fountain** *n.* fîntînă *f.* arteziană
**four-wheel drive** *n.* tracţiune
 *f.* pe patru roţi
**fragrance** *n.* parfum *neut.*
**frame** *n.* cadru *neut.*
**free** *adj.* liber; *v.t.* a elibera
**free of charge** gratuit
**freedom** *n.* libertate *f.*
**freezer** *n.* congelator *neut.*
**frequent** *adj.* frecvent
**fresh** *adj.* proaspăt
**Friday** *n.* vineri *f.*
**friend** *n.* prieten *m.*
**friendship** *n.* prietenie *f.*
**fries** *n.* cartofi *m.pl.* prăjiţi
**frightening** *adj.* înfricoşător
**frog** *n.* broască *f.*
**from** *prep.* de la, din
**front, in** *adv.* în faţă
**frontier** *n.* frontieră *f.*
**frozen** *adj.* congelat
**fruit** *n.* fruct *neut.*
**fry** *v.t.* a prăji
**frying pan** *n.* tigaie *f.*
**fuel** *n.* carburant *m.*
**full** *adj.* plin
**fun** *n.* distracţie *f.*
**fun, to have** ~ a se distra/amuza
**function** *n.* funcţie *f.*; *v.i.* a
 funcţiona
**funeral** *n.* înmormîntare *f.*
**funny** *adj.* amuzant, distractiv
**furniture** *n.* mobilă *f.*,
 mobilier *neut.*

fuse *n.* siguranţă *f.*
fuse box *n.* tablou *neut.* de
    siguranţă
future *n.* viitor *neut.*

# G

gain *n.* cîştig *neut.*; *v.t.* a
    ciştiga
gallon *n.* galon *neut.*
game *n.* joc *neut.*
garage *n.* garaj *neut.*
garbage *n.* gunoi *neut.*
garden *n.* grădină *f.*
gargle *v.i.* a face gargară
garlic *n.* usturoi *m.*
gas *n.* benzină *f.*
gas station *n.* staţie *f.* de
    benzină
gate *n.* poartă *f.*
gather *v.t.* a strînge
gauze *n.* tifon *neut.*
generate *v.t.* a genera
generous *adj.* generos
genitals *n.pl.* organe *neut.pl.*
    genitale
genuine *adj.* veritabil
German *n.*, *adj.* german
Germany *n.* Germania *f.*
get *v.t.* a obţine
get by *v.i.* a trece (pe lîngă)
gift *n.* cadou *neut.*
girl *n.* fată *f.*
girlfriend *n.* prietenă *f.*
give *v.t.* a da
give way a da prioritate
glad *adj.* bucuros
gland *n.* glandă *f.*
glass *n.* sticlă *f.*; pahar *neut.*
glasses *n.* ochelari *neut.pl.*
glassware *n.* sticlărie *f.*
globe *n.* glob *neut.*
glove *n.* mănuşă *f.*
go *v.i.* a merge, a umbla
go away *v.i.* a pleca
go for a walk a face o
    plimbare

go out *v.i.* a ieşi (afară)
go shopping a merge la
    cumpărături
go up *v.t.* a urca
goat *n.* capră *f.*
God *n.* Dumnezeu *m.*
god *n.* zeu *m.*
godfather *n.* naş *m.*
godmother *n.* naşă *f.*
gold *n.* aur *neut.*
golf *n.* golf *neut.*
good *adj.* bun
good-bye la revedere
good luck! noroc!
goods *n.* bunuri *neut.pl.*
good wishes urări de bine
gorge *n.* defileu *neut.*
govern *v.t.*, *v.i.* a guverna
government *n.* guvern *neut.*
grace *n.* graţie *f.*
gram *n.* gram *neut.*
grammar *n.* gramatică *f.*
grandfather *n.* bunic *m.*
grandmother *n.* bunică *f.*
grandparents *n.* bunici *m.pl.*
grant *n.* bursă *f.*; *v.t.* a acorda
grapes *n.* struguri *m.pl.*
grass *n.* iarbă *f.*
grateful *adj.* recunoscător
gratis *adj.*, *adv.* gratis, gratuit
gray *adj.* gri, cenuşiu
greasy *adj.* unsuros
great *adj.* măreţ, grandios
great! grozav!
Greece *n.* Grecia *f.*
Greek *n.*, *adj.* grec
green *adj.* verde
greet *v.t.* a saluta
grey *adj.* gri
grief *n.* supărare *f.*
grill *n.* grătar *neut.*; *v.t.* a frige
    la/pe grătar
grocery store *n.* băcănie *f.*
group *n.* grup *neut.*
grow *v.t.*, *v.i.* a creşte
grown-up *n.* adult *m.*
grumble *v.i.* a bombăni
guarantee *n.* garanţie *f.*
guard *n.* gardă *f.*; *v.t.* a păzi

guess n. bănuială f.; v.t. a ghici
guide n. ghid m.; v.t. a
    îndruma
guidebook n. ghid neut.
guilty adj. vinovat
guilty person n. persoană f.
    culpabilă
gum n. gumă f. de mestecat
gun n. armă f. de foc

# H

hair n. păr m.
haircut n. tuns neut.
hairdresser coafor m.;
    coafeză f.; frizer m.
hair dryer n. uscător neut.
    de păr
half n. jumătate f.
hall n. coridor neut.
halt v.t., v.i. a opri
ham n. şuncă f.
hammer n. ciocan neut.; v.t. a
    ciocăni
hand n. mînă f.
handbag n. sac m. de voiaj
handicap n. handicap neut.
handicrafts n. artizanat neut.
handkerchief n. batistă f.
hand luggage n. bagaj neut.
    de mînă
handle n. mîner neut.
hanger n. umeraş neut.
happen v.i. a se întîmpla
happiness n. fericire f.
happy adj. fericit
harbor n. port neut.
hard adj. tare; adv. greu
hardly adv. abia (dacă, de)
hardship n. dificultate f.
harsh adj. aspru
hat n. pălărie f.
hate v.t. a urî; n. ură f.
hatred n. ură f.
haughty adj. arogant
have v.t., v.aux. a avea
hazy adj. ceţos

head n. cap neut.; v.i. a merge
    (spre)
headache n. migrenă f.
heading, to be (in a direction)
    a merge spre
headlight n. far neut. (auto)
heal v.t., v.i. a vindeca
health n. sănătate f.
healthy adj. sănătos
hear v.t., v.i. a auzi
heart n. inimă f.
heating n. încălzire f.
heavy adj. greu
height n. înălţime f.
hello alo!, da!, hei!
help n. ajutor neut.; v.t. a ajuta
hepatitis n. hepatită f.
here adv. aici
hi interj. bună!, salut!
high adj. înalt
hike n. plimbare f.; v.i. a face
    o plimbare
hill n. deal neut.
hire v.t. a închiria
history n. istorie f.
hit (song) n. şlagăr neut.
hobby n. pasiune f.
hold v.t. a ţine
holiday resort n. staţiune f. de
    vacanţă
home n. cămin neut., casă f.
honeymoon n. luna f. de
    miere
horse n. cal m.
hospital n. spital neut.
hot adj. fierbinte
hot dog n. hot dog m.
hotel n. hotel neut.
hour n. oră f.
house n. casă f.
how adv. cum, în ce fel
however conj. oricum; adv.
    oricît de mult
humid adj. umed
humor n. dispoziţie f.
hunger n. foame f.
hungry adj. flămînd
hunt v.t. a vîna
hunter n. vînător m.

hunting *n.* vînătoare *f.*
hurry *n.* grabă *f.*
hurry up *v.i.* a se grăbi
hurt *v.t.* a răni; *n.* rană *f.*
husband *n.* soț *m.*
hygiene *n.* igienă *f.*
hymn *n.* imn *neut.*
hypocrisy *n.* ipocrizie *f.*

# I

ice *n.* gheață *f.*
ice cream *n.* înghețată *f.*
idea *n.* idee *f.*
if *conj.* dacă, de
ill *adj.* bolnav
illness *n.* boală *f.*
illusion *n.* iluzie *f.*
illustrate *v.t.* a ilustra
imagine *v.t.* a(-și) imagina
immediately *adv.* imediat
important *adj.* important
impossible *adj.* imposibil
impress *v.t.* a impresiona
impression *n.* impresie *f.*
impressive *adj.* impresionant
improve *v.t.* a perfecționa
in *prep.* în; la; înăuntrul
inauguration *n.* inaugurare *f.*
inconvenient *adj.* incomod
increase *v.t.* a spori; *n.*
   sporire *f.*
independence *n.*
   independență *f.*
index *n.* indice *m.*
indigestion *n.* indigestie *f.*
individual *n.* om *m.*; *adj.*
   individual
indoor *adj.* in interior
infection *n.* infecție *f.*
inflammation *n.* inflamare *f.*
influence *n.* influență *f.*
influenza *n.* gripă *f.*
inform *v.t.* a informa
informal *adj.* obișnuit
information *n.* informații *f.pl.*

information desk *n.* ghișeu
   *neut.* de informații
inhabitant *n.* locuitor *m.*
inherit *v.t.* a moșteni
initiative *n.* inițiativă *f.*
injection *n.* injecție *f.*
injure *v.t.* a răni
injury *n.* rană *f.*
inquire *v.i.* a se interesa
insect *n.* insectă *f.*
inside *adv.* înăuntru
insist *v.i.* a insista
installation *n.* instalație *f.*
instance, for de exemplu
instant *n.* clipă *f.*
instant coffee cafea instant
instead (of) *adv.* în schimb;
   mai degrabă
instinct *n.* instinct *neut.*
institute *n.* institut *neut.*
instrument *n.* instrument
   *neut.*
insurance *n.* asigurare *f.*
insurance certificate *n.* poliță
   *f.* de asigurare
intention *n.* intenție *f.*
interest *n.* interes *neut.*
interesting *adj.* interesant
international *adj.*
   internațional
internist *n.* internist *m.*
interpreter *n.* interpret *m.*
interview *n.* interviu *neut.*
intestine *n.* intestin *neut.*
intimate *adj.* intim
into *prep.* în; spre; cu
invent *v.t.* a inventa
investigation *n.* cercetare *f.*
invitation *n.* invitație *f.*
invite *v.t.* a invita
iodine *n.* iod *neut.*
Ireland *n.* Irlanda *f.*
Irish *n., adj.* irlandez
iron *n.* fier *neut.* de călcat; *v.t.*
   a călca (*clothes*)
island *n.* insulă *f.*
Italy *n.* Italia *f.*
Italian *n., adj.* Italian
itch *n.* iritație *f.*
ivory *n.* fildeș *neut.*

# J

jacket n. jachetă f.
jam n. gem neut.; v.t. a bloca
January n. ianuarie m.
Japan n. Japonia f.
Japanese n., adj. japonez
jar n. borcan neut.
jaundice n. icter neut.
jaw n. maxilar neut.
jealousy n. gelozie f.
jeans n. blugi m.pl.
jeep n. jeep neut.
jelly n. gem neut.
Jesus Christ Iisus Hristos
Jew n. evreu m.
jewelry n. bijuterii f.pl.
jewelry shop n. magazin n. de
  bijuterii
job n. slujbă f.
jogging n. jogging neut.
join v.t., v.i. a (se) uni
joint n. articulație f.
joke n. glumă f.; v.i. a glumi
jolt n. zdruncinătura f.; v.i. a
  zdruncina
journalist n. ziarist m.
journey n. călătorie f.
jubilee n. jubileu neut. de 50
  de ani
jug n. ulcior neut.
juice n. suc neut.
jump n. săritură f.; v.i. a sări
jumper n. rochie f. de casă
justice n. justiție f.

# K

keep v.t. a păstra
ketchup n. sos neut. picant
kettle n. ceainic neut.
key n. cheie f.
keyboard n. tastatură f.
kidney n. rinichi m.
kill v.t. a omorî
kilo(gram) n. kilogram neut.
kilometer n. kilometru m.
kind n. fel neut.; adj. blînd

kindhearted adj. bun (la
  inimă)
kiosk n. chioşc neut.
kiss n. sărut neut.; v.t. a săruta
kitchen n. bucătărie f.
knead v.t. a frămînta
knee n. genunchi m.
knife n. cuțit neut.
knit v.t., v.i. a tricota
knot n. nod neut.
know v.t., v.i. a cunoaşte
known adj. cunoscut

# L

label n. etichetă f.; v.t. a
  eticheta
ladder n. scară f. mobilă
ladies restroom n. toaletă f.
  pentru doamne
lake n. lac neut.
lamb n. miel m.
lame adj. şchiop
lamp n. lampă f.
land n. pămînt neut.; v.i.
  debarca; a ateriza
landlady n. proprietăreasă f.
landlord n. proprietar m.
lane n. uliță f.
language n. limbă f.
large adj. întins
last adj. ultim; v.i. a dura
late adj., adv. tîrziu
late, to be a întîrzia
laugh n. rîs neut.; v.i. a rîde
laughter n. rîs neut.
laundromat n. spălătorie f.
  automată
law n. lege f.
lawful adj. legal
lawyer n. avocat m.
laxative n. laxativ neut.
lay off v.t. a concedia
lazy adj. leneş
lead v.t. a conduce
lead n. plumb neut.
lead-free adj. fără plumb
leader n. conducător m.

leaf *n.* frunză *f.*
leaflet *n.* manifest *neut.*
learn *v.t., v.i.* a învăţa
learned *adj.* învăţat
leather *n.* piele (lucrată) *f.*
leave *n.* permisiune *f.; v.i.* a
  părăsi
leek *n.* praz *m.*
left *n.* stînga *f.; adj.* din stînga
left-handed *adj.* stîngaci
leg *n.* picior *neut.*
legal *adj.* legal
lemon *n.* lămîie *f.*
lend *v.t.* a da cu împrumut
lens *n.* lentilă *f.*
lesson *n.* lecţie *f.*
let *v.t.* a închiria
letter *n.* scrisoare *f.*
level *n.* nivel *neut.*
liberate *v.t.* a elibera
librarian *n.* bibliotecar *m.*
library *n.* bibliotecă *f.*
license *n.* autorizaţie *f.*
license, driver's *n.* permis
  *neut.* de conducere
lie *n.* minciună *f.; v.i.* a minţi
life *n.* viaţă *f.*
lift *v.t.* a ridica; *n.* ridicare *f.*
light *n.* lumină *f.; v.i.* a lumina
lighter *n.* brichetă *f.*
lightning *n.* fulger *neut.*
like *adj.* asemănător; *v.t.* a
  îndrăgi; *prep.* ca
line *n.* rînd *neut.,* coadă *f.*
linen *n.* pînză *f.* de in
lip *n.* buză *f.*
lipstick *n.* ruj *neut.* de buze
list *n.* listă *f.*
listener *n.* ascultător *m.*
liter *n.* litru *m.*
literature *n.* literatură *f.*
little *adj.* mic; *adv.* puţin
live *v.i., v.t.* a trăi
live (broadcast) *n.*
  transmisiune *f.* în direct
lively *adj.* vioi
liver *n.* ficat *m.*
living room *n.* cameră *f.* de zi
loan *n.* împrumut *neut.*

lobby (hotel, etc.) *n.* foaier
  *neut.*
locality *n.* aşezare *f.*
lock *n.* lacăt *neut.; v.t., v.i.* a
  încuia
lodging *n.* locuinţă *f.*
long *adj.* lung
long-distance call *n.*
  convorbire *f.* interurbană
look *n.* privire *f.; v.i.* a privi
look for *v.i.* a căuta
look forward to a aştepta cu
  nerăbdare
loose (clothing) *adj.* larg
Lord *excl.* Doamne
lose *v.t.* a pierde
loud *adj., adv.* tare
love *n.* dragoste *f.; v.t., v.i.*
  a iubi
lover *n.* îndrăgostit *m.*
low *adj.* jos; *adv.* (în partea
  de) jos
low-fat (food) *adj.* slab
lower *adj.* inferior
luck *n.* noroc *neut.*
lucky *adj.* norocos
luggage *n.* bagaj *neut.*
lunch *n.* dejun *neut.,* masa *f.*
  de prînz; *v.i.* a lua dejunul
lung *n.* plămîn *m.*
luxurious *adj.* luxos
luxury *n.* lux *neut.*

# M

machine *n.* maşină *f.*
machine, washing *n.* maşină *f.*
  de spălat
madness *n.* nebunie *f.*
magazine *n.* revistă *f.* ilustrată
magnificent *adj.* măreţ,
  minunat
maiden name *n.* nume *neut.*
  de fată
mail *n.* corespondenţă *f.*
main *adj.* principal
make (brand) *n.* marcă *f.; v.t.*
  a face

**make-up** *n.* machiaj *neut.*;
  fard *neut.*
**male** *n.* mascul *m.*; *adj.*
  masculin
**man** *n.* om *m.*; bărbat *m.*
**man, young** *n.* tînăr *m.*
**manager** *n.* director *m.*
**mandate** *n.* mandat *neut.*; *v.t.*
  a delega
**mankind** *n.* omenire *f.*
**manner** *n.* mod *neut.*
**manners** *n.* maniere *f.pl.*
**many** *adj., pron.* mulți, multe
**many, how** cîți, cîte
**map** *n.* hartă *f.*
**March** *n.* martie *m.*
**margarine** *n.* margarină *f.*
**market** *n.* piață *f.*; *v.t., v.i.* a
  vinde
**marriage** *n.* căsătorie *f.*
**marry** *v.t.* a căsători; *v.i.* a se
  căsători
**marvel** *n.* minune *f.*; *v.i.* a se
  minuna
**masculine** *adj.* masculin
**mask** *n.* mască *f.*
**mass** *n.* mulțime *f.*
**massage** *n.* masaj *neut.*
**match** *n.* meci *neut.*; *v.t.* a se
  potrivi cu
**material** *n.* material *neut.*
**matter** *n.* subiect *neut.*; *v.i.* a
  conta
**mattress** *n.* saltea *f.*
**mature** *adj.* matur
**may** *v.mod.* a avea voie, a
  putea; a fi posibil
**maybe** *adv.* poate
**mayor** *n.* primar *m.*
**meal** *n.* masă *f.* (de prînz etc)
**mean** *v.i.* a însemna
**means** *n.* mijloace *neut.pl.*
**means, by all** în orice caz
**meantime, in the** între timp
**measure** *n.* măsură *f.*; *v.t.* a
  măsura
**measurement** *n.* măsură *f.*
**meat** *n.* carne *f.*
**medal** *n.* medalie *f.*

**medicine** *n.* medicament *neut.*
**medium** *n.* mediu *neut.*; *adj.*
  mediu
**medley** *n.* potpuriu *neut.*
**meet** *v.t., v.i.* a (se) întîlni, a
  (se) cunoaște
**melon** *n.* pepene *m.*
**member** *n.* membru *m.*
**mention** *n.* mențiune *f.*; *v.t.*,
  *v.i.* a menționa
**menu** *n.* meniu *neut.*
**message** *n.* mesaj *neut.*
**meter** *n.* metru *m.*; contor *neut.*
**microwave** *n.* cuptor *neut.* cu
  microunde
**middle, in the** în mijlocul
**midwife** *n.* moașă *f.*
**mild** *adj.* blînd
**milk** *n.* lapte *neut.*
**million** *n.* milion *neut.*
**mind** *n.* minte *f.*; *v.t.* a păzi;
  *v.i.* a obiecta la
**mine** *n.* mină *f.*
**mineral water** *n.* apă *f.*
  minerală
**minor** *n, adj.* minor
**minute** *n.* minut *neut.*
**miracle** *n.* miracol *neut.*
**mirror** *n.* oglindă *f.*
**mishap** *n.* ghinion *neut.*
**miss (Ms.)** domnișoară
**miss** *v.t.* a pierde; *v.i.* a-și greși
  ținta
**missing, to be** a fi dat dispărut
**mistake** *n.* greșeală *f.*; *v.i.* a
  greși
**mister (Mr.)** domnul
**misunderstanding** *n.*
  neînțelegere *f.*
**mix** *v.t., v.i.* a (se) amesteca
**mixture** *n.* amestec *neut.*
**model** *n.* model *neut.*; *adj.*
  model
**modern** *adj.* modern
**moisturizer** *n.* cremă *f.*
  hidratantă (*cream*)
**moment** *n.* moment *neut.*
**monastery** *n.* mănăstire *f.*
**Monday** *n.* luni *f.*

money *n.* bani *m.pl.*
money, to change a schimba
    bani
monk *n.* călugăr *m.*
monster *n.* monstru *m.*
month *n.* lună *f.*
monument *n.* monument
    *neut.*
moody *adj.* capricios
moon *n.* lună *f.*
more *adj.* mai mult/mulți;
    *adv.* mai mult
more and more din ce în ce
    mai mult
morning *n.* dimineață *f.*
morning, in the dimineața
morning, this azi dimineață
mortgage *n.* ipotecă *f.*; *v.t.* a
    ipoteca
most *adj.* cei mai mulți; *adv.*
    foarte
mother *n.* mamă *f.*
mother-in-law *n.* soacră *f.*
motion *n.* mișcare *f.*; *v.i.* a
    face semn (cuiva)
motor *n.* motor *neut.*
motorboat *n.* barcă *f.* cu
    motor
mountain *n.* munte *m.*
mourning *n.* doliu *neut.*
mouse *n.* șoarece *m.*
moustache *n.* mustață *f.*
mouth *n.* gură *f.*
move *n.* mișcare *f.*; *v.i.* a
    mișca
movement *n.* mișcare *f.*
movie *n.* film *neut.*
movie theater *n.* cinema *neut.*
much *adj., adv.* mult
much, how cît
much, too prea mult(a)
mud *n.* noroi *neut.*
mugging *n.* atac *neut.* asupra
    unei personae
murderer *n.* ucigaș *m.*
muscle *n.* mușchi *m.*
museum *n.* muzeu *neut.*
mushroom *n.* ciupercă *f.*
music *n.* muzică *f.*

musical *n.* comedie *f.*
    muzicală; *adj.* muzical
must *v.mod.* a trebui; *n.* nece-
    sitate *f.*
mustard *n.* muștar *neut.*

# N

nail *n.* unghie *f.*
naked *adj.* gol
name *n.* nume *neut.*; *v.t.* a
    numi
napkin *n.* șervețel *neut.*
narrow *adj.* îngust
nation *n.* națiune *f.*
nationality *n.* naționalitate *f.*
native *n.* localnic *m.*; *adj.*
    autohton
naturally *adv.* firește, în mod
    natural
nature *n.* natură *f.*
nausea *n.* greață *f.*
navy blue *adj.* bleumarin
near *adj.* apropiat; *adv.*
    aproape; *v.i.* a se apropia
nearly *adv.* aproape, cît pe-aci
necessary *adj.* necesar
neck *n.* gît *neut.*
necklace *n.* colier *neut.*
need *n.* nevoie *f.*; *v.i.* a
    necesita
needle *n.* ac *neut.*
neglect *n.* neglijare *f.*; *v.i.* a
    neglija
neighbor *n.* vecin *m.*
nephew *n.* nepot *m.*
nerve *n.* nerv *m.*
nest *n.* cuib *neut.*
neurologist *n.* neurolog *m.*
neuter *adj.* neutru
never *adv.* niciodată
nevertheless *adv.* totuși
new *adj.* nou
newspaper *n.* ziar *neut.*
newsstand *n.* chioșc *neut.*
    de ziare
New Zealand *n.* Noua
    Zeelandă *f.*

next *adj.* următorul
nice *adj.* frumos
nickname *n.* poreclă *f.*
niece *n.* nepoată *f.*
night *n.* noapte *f.*
night-club *n.* local *neut.* de
   noapte
no *adj.* nici un/o; *adv.* nu
nobody *pron.* nimeni
noise *n.* zgomot *neut.*
non-alcoholic *adj.* (băutură)
   fără alcool
non-smoking *adj.* pentru
   nefumători
none *pron.* nici unul; nimic
noodles *n.pl.* tăiței *m.pl.*
normally *adv.* în mod firesc
north *n.* nord *neut.*; *adj.*
   nordic
nose *n.* nas *neut.*
not *adv.* nu
not even nici măcar
not yet nu încă
notary *n.* notar *m.*
notebook *n.* caiet *neut.*
nothing *pron.* nimic; *adv.*
   deloc
notice *n.* anunț *neut.*; *v.t.* a
   observa
noun *n.* substantiv *neut.*
now *adv.* acum
number *n.* număr *neut.*; *v.t.*,
   *v.i.* a număra
nun *n.* călugăriță *f.*
nurse *n.* infirmieră *f.*, soră
   medicală; *v.t.* a îngriji

# O

oak *n.* stejar *m.*
oath *n.* jurămînt *neut.*
obey *v.t.*, *v.i.* a asculta
object *n.* obiect *neut.*; *v.t.*, *v.i.*
   a obiecta
obscene *adj.* obscen
observe *v.t.* a respecta
observer *n.* observator *m.*
obstacle *n.* obstacol *neut.*

obstruct *v.t.* a bloca
obtain *v.t.* a obține
occasion *n.* prilej *neut.*; *v.i.* a
   prilejui
occupation *n.* ocupație *f.*
of *prep.* al, a, ai, ale; de; din
offer *n.* ofertă *f.*; *v.t.* a oferi
office *n.* birou *neut.*
office worker *n.* funcționar *m.*
often *adv.* adesea
oil *n.* ulei *neut.*
okay *excl.* bine!; bun!; în
   regulă!; s-a făcut!
old *adj.* vechi
olive *n.* măslină *f.*
omelet *n.* omletă *f.*
on *adv.* înainte; *prep.* pe
once *adv.* odată; *conj.* îndată ce
once, at deodată
one *pron.* cineva; *num.* unu
onion *n.* ceapă *f.*
only *adj.* singur; *adv.* numai
open *v.t.*, *v.i.* a deschide
opening *n.* deschidere *f.*
opera *n.* operă *f.*
operation *n.* operație *f.*
operator *n.* operator *m.*
ophthalmologist *n.*
   oftalmolog *m.*
opinion *n.* opinie *f.*
opium *n.* opiu *neut.*
opportunity *n.* prilej *neut.*
   favorabil; șansă *f.*
opposite *adj.* opus
oppression *n.* asuprire *f.*
optician *n.* optician *m.*
or *conj.* sau
orange *n.* portocală *f.*; *adj.*
   portocaliu
orchestra *n.* orchestră *f.*
order *n.* comandă *f.*; *v.t.*, *v.i.* a
   comanda
organization *n.* organizare *f.*
origin *n.* origine *f.*
ornithology *n.* ornitologie *f.*
orphan *n.* orfan *m.*
other *adj.* alt; *pron.* (un) altul
our *adj.* nostru
out *adv.* afară; pe sfîrșite

outlet *n.* debuşeu *neut.*
outside *n.* exterior *neut.*; *adj.*
    exterior; *adv.* afară
over *adj.* încheiat; *adv.*
    deasupra, peste
overcast *adj.* întunecat
overdone *adj.* exagerat; fript
    prea tare
overeat *v.i.* a mînca prea mult
overnight *adj.* peste noapte
over there *adv.* acolo
overwhelm *v.i.* a copleşi
overwork *n.* suprasolicitare *f.*;
    *v.i.* a (se) istovi
own *adj.* propriu


# P

pack *n.* pachet *neut.*; *v.t.*, *v.i.* a
    împacheta
package *n.* pachet *neut.*
pain *n.* durere *f.*
paint *n.* culoare *f.*; *v.i.* a picta
paintbrush *n.* pensulă *f.*,
    penel *neut.*
painter *n.* pictor *m.*
painting *n.* pictură *f.*
pair *n.* pereche *f.*
pajamas *n.* pijama *f.*
palace *n.* palat *neut.*
palpitation *n.* palpitaţie *f.*
panties *n.* chiloţi *m.pl.* de
    damă
pants *n.* pantaloni *m.pl.*
paper *n.* hîrtie *f.*
parade *n.* paradă *f.*; *v.i.* a trece
    in revistă
paradise *n.* paradis *neut.*
parcel *n.* pachet *neut.*
parent *n.* părinte *m.*
park *n.* parc *neut.*; *v.t.*, *v.i.* a
    parca
parking lot *n.* parcaj *neut.*,
    parcare *f.*
parking meter *n.* parcometru
    *neut.*
parliament *n.* parlament *neut.*
parsley *n.* pătrunjel *m.*

part *n.* piesă *f.* de schimb
party *n.* partid (politics) *neut.*;
    petrecere (social) *f.*
pass *n.* trecere *f.*; *v.i.* a trece
passenger *n.* pasager *m.*
passport *n.* paşaport *neut.*
pasta *n.* paste *f.pl.* făinoase
pastime *n.* distracţie *f.*
pastry *n.* patiserie *f.*
patience *n.* răbdare *f.*
pattern *n.* model *neut.*
pay *n.* plată *f.*; *v.t.*, *v.i.* a plăti
pay phone *n.* telefon *neut.*
    public
payment *n.* plată *f.*
pea *n.* mazăre *f.*
peace *n.* pace *f.*
peach *n.* piersică *f.*
peak *n.* vîrf *neut.* de munte
pear *n.* pară *f.*
pearl *n.* perlă *f.*
peasant *n.* ţăran *m.*
pedestrian crossing *n.* trecere
    *f.* pietoni
pediatrician *n.* pediatru *m.*
peel *n.* coajă *f.*; *v.t.* a coji ; *v.i.*
    a se coji
pen *n.* stilou *neut.*
penalty *n.* pedeapsă *f.*
pencil *n.* creion *neut.*
penicillin *n.* penicilină *f.*
penis *n.* penis *neut.*
people *n.* lume *f.*, oameni *m.pl.*
pepper *n.* piper *neut.*; ardei *m.*
performance *n.* spectacol
    *neut.*
perfume *n.* parfum *neut.*
perhaps *adv.* (se prea) poate
period *n.* menstruaţie *f.*
    (*menstrual*)
permanent *n.* permanent
    *neut.* (*hairstyle*); *adj.*
    permanent
permission *n.* permisiune *f.*
permit *n.* permis *neut.*; *v.t.* a
    permite
persecute *v.t.* a persecuta
person *n.* persoană *f.*
pet *n.* animal de casă *neut.*

pharmacist *n.* farmacist *m.*
pharmacy *n.* farmacie *f.*
phobia *n.* fobie *f.*
phone *n.* telefon *neut.*; *v.i.* a telefona
photo *n.* fotografie *f.*
photocopier *n.* aparat *neut.* de fotocopiat
phrase *n.* expresie *f.*
pick up *v.t.* a ridica (*object*); a lua (*passenger*)
picture *n.* tablou *neut.*
picture frame *n.* ramă *f.* de tablou
pie *n.* plăcintă *f.*
piece *n.* bucată *f.*
pig *n.* porc *m.*
pigeon *n.* porumbel *m.*
pill *n.* pilulă *f.*
pillow *n.* pernă *f.*
pilot *n.* pilot *m.*
pink *adj.* roz
pitcher *n.* ulcior *neut.*
pity *n.* milă *f.*; *v.t.* a-i fi milă de
pizza *n.* pizza *f.*
place *n.* loc *neut.*; *v.t.* a pune
plain *adj.* limpede
plan *n.* plan *neut.*; *v.i.* a plănui
plank *n.* scîndură *f.*
plant *n.* plantă *f.*; *v.t.* a planta
plate *n.* farfurie *f.*
platinum *n.* platină *f.*
platform *n.* peron *neut.*
play *n.* piesă *f.*; *v.t.*, *v.i.* a interpreta
pleasant *adj.* plăcut
please *v.t.* a mulțumi; *v.i.* a plăcea
pleasure *n.* plăcere *f.*
plug *n.* dop *neut.*; *v.i.* a astupa
plum *n.* prună *f.*
plum brandy *n.* țuică *f.*
plumber *n.* instalator *m.*
pneumonia *n.* pneumonie *f.*
pocket *n.* buzunar *neut.*
point *n.* punct *neut.*; *v.t.* a indica
poison *n.* otravă *f.*; *v.t.* a otrăvi
police *n.* poliție *f.*
policeman *n.* polițist *m.*

police station *n.* circa *f.* de poliție
polite *adj.* politicos
political party *n.* partid *neut.* politic
pollen *n.* polen *neut.*
pollute *v.t.*, *v.i.* a polua
pond *n.* iaz *neut.*
pool *n.* piscină *f.*
poor *adj.* sărac
popcorn *n.* floricele *f.pl.* de porumb
pope *n.* papă *m.*
pop music *n.* muzică *f.* pop
popular *adj.* de succes
porcelain *n.* porțelan *neut.*
pork *n.* carne *f.* de porc
portion *n.* parte *f.*
possible *adj.* posibil
postage stamp *n.* timbru *neut.* poștal
postcard *n.* carte *f.* poștală
post office *n.* oficiu *neut.* poștal
pot *n.* oală *f.*
potato *n.* cartof *m.*
pottery *n.* olărit *neut.*
poultry *n.* păsări *f.pl.* de curte
pound (weight) *n.* livră *f.*, funt *neut.*
poverty *n.* sărăcie *f.*
powder *n.* pudră *f.*
practice *n.* practică *f.*; *v.t.*, *v.i.* a practica
praise *n.* laudă *f.*; *v.t.* a lăuda
precise *adj.* precis
prefer *v.t.* a prefera
pregnant *adj.* gravidă
prepare *v.t.*, *v.i.* a pregăti
prescribe *v.t.* a prescrie
prescription *n.* rețetă *f.*
present *adj.* prezent; *n.* cadou *neut.*; *v.t.*, *v.i.* a prezenta
preserve *v.t.* a păstra
press *v.t.* a apăsa
pretend *v.t.*, *v.i.* a invoca, a pretexta
pretty *adj.* drăguț
prevent *v.t.* a preîntimpina

**prevention** *n.* prevenire *f.*
**price** *n.* preţ *neut.*
**priest** *n.* preot *m.*
**primary** *adj.* esenţial
**principal** *adj.* principal
**print** *v.t.*, *v.i.* a tipări; *n.*
   publicaţie *f.*
**private** *adj.* privat, particular
**prize** *n.* premiu *neut.*
**probable** *adj.* probabil
**procession** *n.* procesiune *f.*
**product** *n.* produs *neut.*
**profession** *n.* profesie *f.*
**profit** *n.* profit *neut.*; *v.t.* a fi
   de folos (cuiva)
**progress** *n.* progres *neut.*
**prohibit** *v.t.* a interzice
**prominent** *adj.* proeminent
**promise** *n.* promisiune *f.*; *v.t.*
   a promite
**pronunciation** *n.* pronunţie *f.*
**proof** *n.* dovadă *f.*
**property** *n.* proprietate *f.*
**prostate** *n.* prostată *f.*
**protect** *v.t.* a proteja
**proverb** *n.* proverb *neut.*
**provide** *v.t.*, *v.i.* a aproviziona
**prudent** *adj.* prudent
**psychiatrist** *n.* psihiatru *m.*
**public** *adj.* public; *n.* public
   *neut.*
**pull** *v.t.* a trage
**pullover** *n.* pulovăr *neut.*
**pulse** *n.* puls *neut.*
**pumpkin** *n.* dovleac *m.*
**punctual** *adj.* punctual
**puncture** *n.* pană *f.*
**punishment** *n.* pedeapsă *f.*
**pure** *adj.* pur
**purple** *adj.* violet
**purpose** *n.* scop *neut.*
**purse** *n.* portofel *neut.*
**put** *v.t.* a pune

# Q

**quality** *n.* calitate *f.*
**quantity** *n.* cantitate *f.*

**quarantine** *n.* carantină *f.*
**quarrel** *n.* ceartă *f.*; *v.i.* a se
   certa
**quarter** *n.* sfert *neut.*
**question** *n.* întrebare *f.*; *v.t.* a
   întreba
**quick** *adj.* rapid; *adv.* iute,
   repede
**quiet** *adj.* liniştit

# R

**rabbit** *n.* iepure *m.*
**race** *n.* cursă *f.*
**racket** *n.* rachetă *f.*
**radiator** *n.* radiator *neut.*
**radio** *n.* radio *neut.*
**rage** *n.* furie *f.*
**railroad** *n.* cale *f.* ferată
**rain** *n.* ploaie *f.*; *v.imp.* a ploua
**raincoat** *n.* manta *f.* de ploaie
**raise** *v.t.* a ridica; *n.* urcare *f.*
**random, at** la întâmplare
**rape** *v.t.* a viola; *n.* viol *neut.*
**rare** *adj.* rar; (fript) în sînge
   (meat)
**rash** *n.* iritaţie *f.*
**raspberry** *n.* zmeură *f.*
**rather** *adv.* mai bine/curînd
**ration** *n.* raţie *f.*; *v.t.* a
   distribui
**ravioli** *n.* ravioli *neut.pl.*
**razor** *n.* brici *neut.*; aparat
   *neut.* de ras
**reach** *v.i.* a ajunge
**read** *v.t.*, *v.i.* a citi
**reading** *n.* lectură *f.*
**ready** *adj.* pregătit, disponibil
**real** *adj.* real, existent
**reason** *n.* raţiune *f.*
**receipt** *n.* chitanţă *f.*
**receive** *v.t.* a primi
**recent** *adj.* recent
**recognize** *v.t.*, *v.i.* a recunoaşte
**recommend** *v.t.* a recomanda
**record** *v.t.* a înregistra; *n.*
   dosar *neut.*
**red** *adj.* roşu

refreshment *n.* aperitiv *neut.*
refrigerator *n.* frigider *neut.*
refund *n.* rambursare *f.*; *v.t.*,
   *v.i.* a rambursa
refuse *v.t.*, *v.i.* a refuza
registered mail *n.* scrisoare *f.*
   recomandată
registration form *n.* fişă *f.* de
   inregistrare
regular *adj.* regulat
reimburse *v.t.*, *v.i.* a rambursa
relative *n.* rudă *f.*
relax *v.i.* a (se) destinde
relieve *v.i.* a uşura
religion *n.* religie *f.*
remedy *n.* remediu *neut.*
remember *v.i.* a-şi aminti
remind *v.t.* a aminti
renounce *v.t.* a renunţa
rent *n.* chirie *f.*; *v.t.* a închiria
rental car *n.* maşină *f.* de
   închiriat
repair *v.t.*, *v.i.* a repara; *n.*
   reparaţie *f.*
repeat *v.t.*, *v.i.* a repeta
reply *n.* răspuns *neut.*; *v.i.* a
   răspunde
report *n.* ştire *f.*; *v.i.* a raporta
republic *n.* republică *f.*
reputation *n.* reputaţie *f.*
request *n.* cerere *f.*; *v.t.*, *v.i.*
   a cere
resemblance *n.* asemănare *f.*
reservation *n.* rezervare *f.*
reserve *v.t.* a rezerva
residence *n.* reşedinţă *f.*
respect *n.* respect *neut.*; *v.t.* a
   respecta
rest *n.* odihnă *f.*; *v.i.* a se
   odihni
restaurant *n.* restaurant *neut.*
restroom *n.* closet *neut.*,
   toaletă *f.*
return *v.i.* a reveni
review *n.* revistă *f.*
revolt *n.* revoltă *f.*; *v.i.* a se
   revolta
rheumatism *n.* reumatism
   *neut.*

rib *n.* coastă *f.*
rice *n.* orez *neut.*
rich *adj.* bogat
ride *n.* călătorie *f.* cu maşina
right *adj.* drept
right, to be a avea dreptate
right-hand drive *n.*
   conducere *f.* pe dreapta
ring *n.* inel *neut.*
ripe *adj.* copt
rise *v.i.* a se urca; *n.* ridicare *f.*
risk *n.* risc *neut.*
river *n.* rîu *neut.*
road *n.* drum *neut.*
roast *v.t.* a frige; *n.* friptură *f.*
roastbeef *n.* friptură *f.* de vită
robbery *n.* furt *neut.*
rock *n.* stîncă *f.*
roof *n.* acoperiş *neut.*
room *n.* cameră *f.*
root *n.* rădăcină *f.*
rope *n.* frînghie *f.*
rough *adj.* aspru; *adv.* dur
round *adj.* rotund; *v.t.* a
   rotunji
round-trip ticket *n.* bilet
   *neut.* dus-întors
row *n.* rînd *neut.*; *v.i.* a vîsli
rowing *n.* canotaj *neut.*
rub *v.t.* a freca; *n.* frecţie *f.*
run *v.i.* a fugi
run, to ~ into a se izbi de
run, to ~ out (*fuel*) a nu mai
   avea
rush hour *n.* oră *f.* de vîrf
rust *n.* rugină *f.*; *v.i.* a rugini

# S

safe *adj.* sigur
safety *n.* siguranţă *f.*
salad *n.* salată *f.*
salami *n.* salam *neut.*
salary *n.* salariu *neut.*
sale *n.* vînzare *f.*; sold *neut.*
salmon *n.* somon *m.*
saloon *n.* bar *neut.*
salt *n.* sare *f.*; *v.t.*, *v.i.* a săra

same *adj.* identic; *adv.* la fel
sample *n.* mostră *f.*; *v.t.* a
    gusta
sand *n.* nisip *neut.*
sandwich *n.* sandviş *neut.*
sandy *adj.* nisipos
sapphire *n.* safir *neut.*
satisfy *v.t.* a satisface
sauce *n.* sos *neut.*
saucepan *n.* oală *f.* de gătit
saucer *n.* farfurioară *f.*
sausage *n.* cîrnat *m.*
savage *adj.* sălbatic
savory *adj.* gustos
say *v.t.*, *v.i.* a spune; *n.* cuvînt
    *neut.*
scald *v.i.* a se opări
scale *n.* cîntar *neut.* de
    persoane
scandal *n.* scandal *neut.*
scar *n.* cicatrice *f.*
scarf *n.* eşarfă *f.*
scatter *v.t.* a risipi
schedule *n.* orar *neut.*; grafic
    *neut.*
school *n.* şcoală *f.*
schoolteacher *n.* învăţător *m.*,
    învăţătoare *f.*
science *n.* ştiinţa *f.*
scientist *n.* om *m.* de ştiinţă
Scotland *n.* Scoţia *f.*
Scottish *n.*, *adj.* scoţian
scream *v.i.* a ţipa; *n.* ţipăt
    *neut.*
screwdriver *n.* şurubelniţă *f.*
scrub *v.t.*, *v.i.* a curăţa
sculptor *n.* sculptor *m.*
sculpture *n.* sculptură *f.*
sea *n.* mare *f.*
seal *n.* ştampilă *f.*
seasick, to feel a avea rău de
    mare
season *n.* sezon *neut.*
seat *n.* scaun *neut.*
second *n.* secundă *f.*
secretary *n.* secretar(ă) *m.*, *f.*
section *n.* secţiune *f.*
sedative *n.* sedativ *neut.*
seductive *adj.* seducător

see *v.t.*, *v.i.* a ( se) vedea
seed *n.* sămînţă *f.*
seek *v.t.* a căuta
seize *v.t.* a apuca
select *v.t.* a selecta; *adj.* select
sell *v.t.*, *v.i.* a vinde
selling *n.* vînzare *f.*
send *v.t.*, *v.i.* a trimite
sense *n.* simţ *neut.*
separate *adj.* separat; *v.t.* a
    separa
September *n.* septembrie *m.*
series *n.* serie *f.*
serious *adj.* serios
servant *n.* funcţionar *m.*
serve *v.i.* a servi
service *n.* serviciu *neut.*; *v.t.*,
    *v.i.* a deservi
set *v.t.* a pune; *adj.* stabilit
sew *v.t.*, *v.i.* a coase
shadow *n.* umbră *f.*; *v.i.* a
    umbri
shake *v.t.*, *v.i.* a scutura; *n.*
    zguduire *f.*
shallow *adj.* de suprafaţă
shame *n.* ruşine; *v.t.* a face de
    ruşine
shampoo *n.* şampon *neut.*
shape *n.* formă *f.*; *v.t.* a
    modela
share *n.* parte *f.*; *v.t.* a
    împărtăşi
sharp *adj.* ascuţit
shave *v.t.*, *v.i.* a (se) bărbieri
shaving cream *n.* cremă *f.* de
    ras
she *pron.* ea, dînsa
sheep *n.* oaie *f.*
sheet *n.* cearşaf *neut.*
shelf *n.* raft *neut.*
shell *n.* cochilie *f.*
shelter *n.* adăpost *neut.*; *v.t.* a
    adăposti
shepherd *n.* cioban *m.*
shine *v.i.* a (stră)luci; *n.* luciu
    *neut.*
ship *n.* navă *f.*
shipping *n.* expediţie *f.*
shirt *n.* cămaşă *f.*

shiver *v.i.* a tremura
shoe *n.* pantof *m.*
shop *n.* magazin *neut.*.; *v.i.* a
    face cumpărături
shopping, to go a merge la
    cumpărături
shore *n.* țărm *neut.*
short *adj.* scurt
shorts *n.* chiloți *m.pl.*
    bărbătești, șort *neut.*
shoulder *n.* umăr *m.*
shout *n.* strigăt *neut.*; *v.i.* a țipa
show *v.t.*, *v.i.* a arăta; *n.*
    spectacol *neut.*
shower *n.* aversă *f.*; duș *neut.*
shrewd *adj.* șiret
shrink *v.i.* a se strîmta
shut *v.t.*, *v.i.* a închide
shy *adj.* timid
sick *adj.* bolnav
side *n.* latură *f.*; parte *f.*
sidewalk *n.* trotuar *neut.*
siege *n.* asediu *neut.*
sights *n.* atracții *f.pl.* turistice
sightseeing *n.* turism *neut.*
silence *n.* liniște *f.*
silent *adj.* tăcut
silk *n.* mătase *f.*
silver *n.* argint *neut.*; *adj.*
    argintiu
similar *adj.* asemănător
simple *adj.* simplu
sin *n.* păcat *neut.*; *v.i.* a păcătui
since *adv.* de atunci; *prep.* de;
    *conj.* de cînd
sincere *adj.* sincer
sing *v.t.*, *v.i.* a cînta
singer *n.* cîntăreț *m.*
single *adj.* singur; *n.* bilet
    *neut.* simplu
sink *v.i.* a se scufunda; *n.* chi-
    uvetă *f.*
sister *n.* soră *f.*
sit *v.i.* a ședea
situation *n.* situație *f.*
size *n.* măsură *f.*
skate *n.* patină *f.*; *v.i.* a patina
skid *v.i.* a derapa
skin *n.* piele *f.*

skirt *n.* fustă *f.*
sky *n.* cer *neut.*
sleep *v.i.* a (a)dormi; *n.* somn
    *neut.*
sleeping pill *n.* somnifer *neut.*
sleeve *n.* mînecă *f.*
slice *n.* felie *f.*; *v.t.* a tăia felii
slight *adj.* ușor
slip *v.i.* a aluneca; *n.*
    combinezon *neut.*
slipper *n.* papuc *m.*
slope *n.* versant *m.*
slow *adj.* încet
small *adj.* mic
smell *v.i.* a mirosi; *n.* miros
    *neut.*
smoke *v.t.*, *v.i.* a fuma; *n.* fum
    *neut.*
snack *n.* gustare *f.*
sneakers *n.* bascheți *m.pl.*
snob *n.* snob *m.*
snow *n.* zăpadă *f.*; *v.imp.* a
    ninge
snowflake *n.* fulg *neut.* de
    zăpadă
so *adv.* așa/atît de; foarte
soap *n.* săpun *neut.*
soccer *n.* fotbal *neut.*
society *n.* societate *f.*
socket *n.* priză *f.*
sofa bed *n.* canapea-pat *f.*
soft *adj.* moale
soft drink *n.* băutură *f.*
    răcoritoare
soldier *n.* soldat *m.*
solid *adj.* solid
some *det.* ceva, niște, puțin;
    *adv.* vreo, cam
somebody *pron.* cineva
somehow *adv.* cumva
someone *pron.* cineva
something *pron.* ceva
sometimes *adv.* uneori,
    cîteodată
somewhere *adv.* undeva
son *n.* fiu *m.*
soon *adv.* curînd
sore *adj.* dureros
sort *n.* fel *neut.*; *v.t.* a sorta

soul *n.* suflet *neut.*
sound *n.* sunet *neut.*; *v.i.* a suna
soup *n.* supă *f.*
sour *adj.* acru
souvenir *n.* suvenir *neut.*
soy *n.* soia *f.*
spa *n.* stațiune *f.* termală
space *n.* spațiu *neut.*
spark *n.* scînteie *f.*; *v.i.* a
  scînteia
spark plug *n.* bujie *f.*
speak *v.i.* a vorbi
special *adj.* special
species *n.* specie *f.*
specimen *n.* specimen *neut.*
spectator *n.* spectator *m.*
speech *n.* discurs *neut.*
speed *v.i.* a accelera; *n.* viteză *f.*
spell *v.t.* a ortografia
spend *v.t.*, *v.i.* a cheltui
sphere *n.* domeniu *neut.*
spice *n.* condiment *neut.*
spicy *adj.* picant; condimentat
spinach *n.* spanac *neut.*
spine *n.* coloană *f.* vertebrală
spirit *n.* spirit *neut.*
spite, in ~ of in ciuda
splendid *adj.* superb
sponge *n.* burete *m.*
sponsor *n.* sponsor *m.*
spoon *n.* lingură *f.*
sport *n.* sport *neut.*
spray *n.* lichid *neut.*
  pulverizat; *v.i.* a stropi
spread *v.i.* a întinde
spring *n.* primăvară *f.*
sprinkle *v.i.* a pulveriza; *n.*
  stropitură *f.*
squall *n.* rafală *f.* de vînt
square *n.* pătrat *neut.*; scuar
  *neut.*
squeeze *v.t.* a apăsa
stadium *n.* stadion *neut.*
stage *n.* scenă *f.*
stain *n.* pată *f.*; *v.t.* a păta
stairs *n.* scară *f.*
stamp *n.* timbru *neut.*
stand *v.i.* a sta in picioare; *n.*
  poziție *f.*

star *n.* stea *f.*
start *v.i.* a începe; *n.* pornire *f.*
state *n.* stat *neut.*
statement *n.* afirmație *f.*
station (railway) *n.* gară *f.*
stationery *n.* papetărie *f.*
statue *n.* statuie *f.*
stay *v.i.* a sta; *n.* ședere *f.*
steak *n.* biftec *neut.*
steal *v.t.*, *v.i.* a fura
steel *n.* oțel *neut.*
stereo *adj.* stereo
still *adv.* încă; *adj.* calm
sting *v.t.*, *v.i.* a înțepa
stingy *adj.* zgîrcit
stir *v.i.* a agita; *n.* agitație *f.*
stocking *n.* ciorap *m.*
stomach *n.* stomac *neut.*
stone *n.* piatră *f.*
stop *v.i.* a opri; *n.* oprire *f.*
store *n.* magazin *neut.*
storm *n.* furtună *f.*
story *n.* relatare *f.*
straight *adj.*, *adv.* direct
strawberry *n.* căpșună *f.*
stream *n.* pîrîu *neut.*
street *n.* stradă *f.*
strength *n.* putere *f.*
strike *v.i.* a lovi; *n.* grevă *f.*
  (*labor*)
string *n.* sfoară *f.*
stroll *v.i.* a cutreiera; *n.*
  hoinăreală *f.*
strong *adj.* puternic
struggle *n.* luptă *f.*; *v.i.* a lupta
study *n.* studiu *neut.*; *v.i.* a
  studia
stunning *adj.* uluitor
stupid *adj.* stupid
stupidity *n.* prostie *f.*
style *n.* stil *neut.*
subscription *n.* abonament
  *neut.*
substitute *v.i.* a substitui; *n.*
  înlocuitor *m.*
subway *n.* metrou *neut.*
success *n.* succes *neut.*
successful *adj.* reușit
suddenly *adv.* brusc, deodată

suffer *v.i.* a suferi
suffering *n.* suferință *f.*
sufficient *adj.* suficient
sugar *n.* zahăr *neut.*
suit *n.* costum *neut.*
suitable *adj.* potrivit
suitcase *n.* valiză *f.*
sun *n.* soare *m.*
Sunday *n.* duminică *f.*
sunshine *n.* lumina *f.* soarelui
sunstroke *n.* insolație *f.*
superb *adj.* superb
supermarket *n.* magazin
    *neut.* cu autoservire
sure *adj.* sigur
surface *n.* suprafață *f.*
surgeon *n.* chirurg *m.*
surprise *n.* surpriză *f.*; *v.t.* a
    mira
surroundings *n.*
    împrejurimi *f.pl.*
survive *v.i.* a supraviețui
suspicion *n.* suspiciune *f.*
swallow *v.t.*, *v.i.* a înghiți
swear *v.i.* a jura; a înjura
sweater *n.* pulovăr *neut.*
sweep *v.i.* a mătura
sweet *adj.* dulce
swell *v.i.* a se umfla
swelling *n.* umflătură *f.*
swim *v.i.* a înota; *n.* înot *neut.*
swimmer *n.* înotător *m.*
swimsuit *n.* costum *neut.*
    de baie
switch *n.* comutator *neut.*; *v.t.*,
    *v.i.* a manevra
synthetic *adj.* sintetic


# T

table *n.* masă *f.*
tablecloth *n.* față *f.* de masă
taillight *n.* stop *neut.* (*auto*)
take *v.t.* a lua
talcum powder *n.* pudră *f.* de
    talc
tale *n.* poveste *f.*

talk *v.t.*, *v.i.* a vorbi; *n.*
    discuție *f.*
tall *adj.* înalt
tampon *n.* tampon *neut.*
tan *n.* bronzare *f.*; *v.i.* a se
    bronza
tape *n.* bandă *f.* magnetică
tape recorder *n.* casetofon
    *neut.*
taste *n.* gust *neut.*; *v.t.* a gusta
tax *n.* impozit *neut.*
taxi *n.* taxi *neut.*
tea *n.* ceai *neut.*
teacher *n.* profesor *m.*
team *n.* echipă *f.*
teamwork *n.* (muncă in)
    colaborare *f.*
tear *v.t.* a sfîșia; *n.* uzură *f.*
teaspoon *n.* linguriță *f.*
telephone *n.* telefon *neut.*
television *n.* televizor *neut.*
tell *v.t.*, *v.i.* a spune
temperature *n.* temperatură *f.*
temporary *adj.* temporar
tender *adj.* fraged
tendon *n.* tendon *neut.*
terrace *n.* terasă *f.*
terrify *v.t.* a speria
thank *v.t.* a mulțumi; *n.*
    recunoștință *f.*
thanks mulțumesc
that *pron.* acela/aceea, care
that is to say adică, cu alte
    cuvinte
theater *n.* teatru *neut.*
theft *n.* furt *neut.*
their *det.* lor
then *adv.* atunci
there *adv.* acolo
thermometer *n.*
    termometru *neut.*
these *pron.* aceștia, acestea
they *pron.* ei, ele
thick *adj.* gros
thief *n.* hoț *m.*
thigh *n.* coapsă *f.*
thin *adj.* slab
thing *n.* lucru *neut.*
think *v.i.* a gîndi; a crede

thirsty *adj.* însetat
this *pron.* acesta, aceasta
those *pron.* aceia, acelea
thought *n.* gînd *neut.*
thread *n.* fir *neut.*
threat *n.* amenințare *f.*
threaten *v.t.* a amenința
three *num.* trei
throat *n.* esofag *neut.*
through *prep.* prin; *adj., adv.*
   direct
throw away *v.t.* a arunca
throw up *v.i.* a vomita
thunder *n.* tunet *neut.*
thunderbolt *n.* trăznet *neut.*
Thursday *n.* joi *f.*
ticket *n.* bilet *neut.*
tidy *adj.* ordonat
tie *v.t.* a lega; *n.* legătură *f.*;
   cravată *f.* (*clothing*)
tight *adj.* compact
till *prep.* pînă (la)
tilt *v.t., v.i.* a răsturna
time *n.* timp *neut.*
timid *adj.* timid
tip *n.* vîrf *neut.*; bacșiș *neut.*
   (*wages*)
tire, spare *n.* roată *f.* de
   rezervă
tired *adj.* obosit
tired, to be a fi obosit
title *n.* titlu *neut.*
to *prep.* la; de; in
toast *n.* pîine *f.* prăjită
toaster *n.* prăjitor *neut.* de
   pîine
tobacco *n.* tutun *neut.*
today *adv.* astăzi
toe *n.* călcîi *neut.*
together *prep.* împreună (cu)
toilet *n.* toaletă *f.*
tolerate *v.t.* a tolera
tomato *n.* roșie *f.*
tomb *n.* mormînt *neut.*
tomorrow *adv.* mîine
tongs *n.* clește *m.*
tongue *n.* limbă *f.*
tonsils *n.* amigdale *f.pl.*
too *adv.* prea; de asemenea

tool *n.* unealtă *f.*
tooth *n.* dinte *m.*
toothache *n.* nevralgie *f.*
toothbrush *n.* periuță *f.* de
   dinți
toothpaste *n.* pastă *f.* de dinți
top *n.* vîrf *neut.*; *adj.* superior
topaz *n.* topaz *neut.*
total *adj.* total
touch *v.t., v.i.* a atinge
tough *adj.* dur; dificil
tour *n.* călătorie *f.*; tur *neut.*
tourist *n.* turist *m.*
tow *v.t.* a remorca
towards *prep.* către
towel *n.* prosop *neut.*
tower *n.* turn *neut.*
town *n.* oraș *neut.*
toy *n.* jucărie *f.*
trace *n.* urmă *f.*
track *n.* urmă *f.* (de pași)
traffic *n.* circulație *f.*
train *n.* tren *neut.*
tranquilizer *n.* tranchilizant
   *neut.*
transaction *n.* tranzacție *f.*
transformer *n.* transformator
   *neut.*
translate *v.t., v.i.* a traduce
translation *n.* traducere *f.*
transportation *n.* transport
   *neut.*
travel *v.i.* a călători; *n.*
   călătorie *f.*
travel agency *n.* agenție *f.* de
   voiaj
tree *n.* copac *m.*
tremble *v.i.* a tremura
trim *n.* tuns *neut.* potrivit
trip *n.* excursie *f.*
trolley *n.* tramvai *neut.*
trouble *n.* necaz *neut.*; *v.t.* a
   deranja
trousers *n.* pantaloni *m.pl.*
trout *n.* păstrăv *m.*
truck *n.* camion *neut.*
true *adj.* adevărat
trunk *n.* portbagaj *neut.*

trust *n.* încredere *f.*; *v.t.* a
   acorda încredere
truth *n.* adevăr *neut.*
try *v.t.*, *v.i.* a încerca; *n.* încercare *f.*
T-shirt *n.* tricou *neut.*
Tuesday *n.* marţi *f.*
tumor *n.* tumoare *f.*
tunnel *n.* tunel *neut.*
turkey *n.* curcan *m.*
turn *v.t.*, *v.i.* a întoarce
turning *n.* curbă *f.*
turnip *n.* nap *m.*
turquoise *adj.* turcoaz; *n.*
   peruzea *f.*
twilight *n.* amurg *neut.*
twin *n.* geamăn(ă), *m.*,*f.*
twist *n.* rotire *f.*; *v.t.* a răsuci

# U

ugly *adj.* urît
ulcer *n.* ulcer *neut.*
umbrella *n.* umbrelă *f.*
uncle *n.* unchi *m.*
unconscious *adj.* inconştient
uncover *v.t.* a descoperi
under *prep.* sub
understand *v.t.*, *v.i.* a înţelege
understandable *adj.* de
   înţeles
underwear *n.* lenjerie *f.*
   de corp
undress *v.t.*, *v.i.* a (se)
   dezbrăca
uneven *adj.* neregulat
unexpected *adj.* brusc
unfortunate *adj.* nefericit
unhappy *adj.* nefericit
union *n.* unire *f.*
unit *n.* unitate *f.*
United States *n.* Statele
   *neut.pl.* Unite ale Americii
   (S.U.A.)
university *n.* universitate *f.*
unleaded gas benzină fără
   plumb

unlimited mileage kilometraj
   nelimitat
unlock *v.t.* a descuia
unpleasant *adj.* neplăcut
unscrew *v.t.* a deşuruba
unsociable *adj.* nesociabil
untidiness *n.* dezordine *f.*
untidy *adj.* neîngrijit
until *prep.* pînă (la)
up *adv.* (în) sus; *prep.* de-a
   lungul
upbringing *n.* creştere *f.*
upon *prep.* pe
uproar *n.* tumult *neut.*
upstairs *adv.* la etaj
urine *n.* urină *f.*
urologist *n.* urolog *m.*
use *n.* folos *neut.*; *v.t.* a folosi
used, to get ~ (to) a se
   obişnui (cu)
useful *adj.* folositor
useless *adj.* inutil
usually *adv.* de obicei
uterus *n.* uter *neut.*

# V

vacancy *n.* post *neut.* liber
vacant *adj.* vacant
vacation *n.* vacanţă *f.*;
   concediu *neut.*
vacuum cleaner *n.* aspirator
   *neut.*
vagina *n.* vagin *neut.*
vague *adj.* vag
valid *adj.* valabil
valley *n.* vale *f.*
valuable *adj.* preţios
value *n.* valoare *f.*; *v.t.* a
   evalua
vanilla *n.* vanilie *f.*
variety *n.* specie *f.*
vase *n.* vază *f.*
veal *n.* viţel *m.*
vegetable *n.* legumă *f.*
vegetarian *n.* vegetarian *m.*
vehicle *n.* vehicul *neut.*
veil *n.* val *neut.*

vein n. venă f.
venison n. vînat neut.
verb n. verb neut.
verbal adj. verbal
verdict n. verdict neut.
verify v.t. a verifica
very adv. foarte
very much foarte mult(ă)
vest n. vestă f.
victim n. victimă f.
video n. video neut.
video cassette n. casetă f.
    video
video cassette recorder n.
    videocasetofon neut.
video player n.
    videocasetofon neut.
view n. privelişte f.
village n. sat neut.
vinegar n. oţet neut.
vineyard n. podgorie f.
violin n. vioară f.
virtue n. virtute f.
visa n. viză f.
visit n. vizită f.; v.t., v.i. a
    vizita
vitamin n. vitamină f.
voice n. voce f.
volleyball n. volei neut.
voltage n. voltaj neut.
vomit v.i. a vomita
vote v.t., v.i. a vota; n. vot
    neut.
vowel n. vocală f.
voyage n. călătorie f.; v.i. a
    călători
vulgar adj. vulgar

# W

wage n. salariu neut.
waist n. talie f.
wait v.i. a aştepta; n. aşteptare f.
waiter n. chelner m.
waitress n. chelneriţă f.
walk n. plimbare f.; v.i. a se
    plimba
wall n. zid neut.

wallet n. portofel neut.
want v.t. a vrea; n. lipsă f.
war n. razboi neut.
wardrobe n. garderobă f.,
    şifonier neut.
warehouse n. depozit neut. de
    mărfuri
warm adj. cald
wash v.t. a spăla; n. spălare f.
waste v.t. a risipi; n. irosire f.
watch n. pază f.; v.t., v.i. a păzi
water n. apă f.
watercolor n. acuarelă f.
waterfall n. cascadă f.
water heater n. boiler neut.
water-ski n. schi neut. nautic
watertight adj. etanş
wave n. val neut.
way n. drum neut.
we pron. noi
weak adj. slab
wealth n. avere f.
weapon n. armă f.
wear v.t., v.i. a purta; n.
    confecţii f.pl.
weather n. vreme f.
weather, bad vreme urîtă
weather, fine vreme
    frumoasă
weather forecast n. prognoza
    f. meteo
wedding n. cununie f., nuntă f.
week n. săptămînă f.
weekend n. weekend neut.,
    sfîrşit neut. de săptămînă
weekly adj., adv. săptămînal
weep v.i. a plînge
weigh v.i. a cîntari
weight n. greutate f.
weight, to lose a slăbi
welcome n. bun-venit neut.;
    v.t. a ura bun venit
welcome, you're ~ pentru
    puţin; nu aveţi pentru ce
well adv. bine; adj. sănătos
well done bravo; bine fript
well off adj. înstărit
west n. vest neut.; occident
    neut.

**what** *pron.* ce?, ce fel?, cum?
**wheel** *n.* roată *f.*
**when** *adv.* cînd
**where** *adv.* unde
**which** *pron.* care
**while** *conj.* în timp ce
**whim** *n.* capriciu *neut.*
**whiskers** *n.* favoriți *m.pl.*
**white** *adj.* alb
**who** *pron.* cine, pe cine, care, pe care
**whole** *adj.*, *n.* întreg *neut.*
**why** *adv.* de ce
**wide** *adj.* larg
**widow** *n.* văduvă *f.*
**wife** *n.* soție *f.*
**will** *v.aux.* voi, vei, veți, va, vom, vor; *n.* voința *f.*
**win** *v.i.* a învinge; *v.t.* a cîștiga
**wind** *n.* vînt *neut.*
**window** *n.* fereastră *f.*
**windshield** *n.* parbriz *neut.*
**wine** *n.* vin *neut.*
**wine list** *n.* listă *f.* de vinuri
**wing** *n.* aripă *f.*
**winter** *n.* iarnă *f.*
**wipe** *v.t.* a șterge
**wiper** *n.* ștergător *neut.* (de parbriz) (*windshield*)
**wise** *adj.* chibzuit
**wish** *v.t.* a dori; *n.* dorință *f.*
**with** *prep.* (împreună) cu; alături de
**withdraw** *v.t.*, *v.i.* a retrage
**within** *adv.* înăuntru
**without** *adv.* afară; *prep.* fără
**witness** *n.* martor *m.*
**witty** *adj.* spiritual
**woe** *n.* suferință *f.*
**wolf** *n.* lup *m.*
**woman** *n.* femeie *f.*
**wood** *n.* pădure *f.*
**wool** *n.* lînă *f.*

**word** *n.* cuvînt *neut.*
**work** *n.* muncă *f.*; *v.i.* a munci
**worker** *n.* muncitor *m.*
**world** *n.* lume *f.*
**worm** *n.* vierme *m.*
**worry** *v.i.* a-și face griji; *n.* îngrijorare *f.*
**wound** *n.* rană *f.*; *v.t.* a răni
**wrap** *v.t.* a înfășura
**wrist** *n.* încheietura *f.* mîinii
**write** *v.t.*, *v.i.* a scrie
**writer** *n.* scriitor *m.*
**writing** *n.* scris *neut.*
**wrong** *adj.*, *adv.* greșit; *n.* nedreptate *f.*; *v.t.* a nedreptăți

## Y

**year** *n.* an *m.*
**yellow** *adj.* galben
**yes** *adv.* da
**yesterday** *adv.* ieri
**yet** *adv.* încă; deja
**yogurt** *n.* iaurt *neut.*
**you** *pron.* tu; dumneata; dumneavoastră; voi
**young** *n.* tînăr *m.*
**your** *pron.* tău/ta; tăi/tale
**youth** *n.* tinerețe *f.*
**yummy** *adj.* delicious

## Z

**zeal** *n.* zel *neut.*
**zebra** *n.* zebră *f.*
**zero** *n.* zero *neut.*
**zest** *n.* entuziasm *neut.*
**zip code** *n.* cod *neut.* poștal
**zipper** *n.* fermoar *neut.*
**zone** *n.* zonă *f.*
**zoo** *n.* grădină *f.* zoologică

# PHRASEBOOK CONTENTS

## Everyday Expressions

Yes/No.
**Da/Nu.**

Please.
**Vă rog.**

Thank you.
**Mulţumesc.**

Thank you very much.
**Mulţumesc foarte mult.**

You're welcome.
**Cu plăcere.**

I beg your pardon?
**Poftim?**

### GREETINGS

Hello.
**Salut! Bună!**

Good morning.
**Bună dimineaţa.**

Good afternoon.
**Bună ziua.**

Good evening.
**Bună seara.**

Good night.
**Noapte bună.**

Good-bye.
**La revedere.**

See you later.
**Pe curînd.**

My name is...
**Mă numesc...**

What's your name?
**Cum vă numiți?**

This is Mr....
**Acesta este domnul...**

This is Mrs....
**Aceasta este doamna...**

Pleased to meet you.
**Mă bucur să vă cunosc.**

How are you?
**Ce mai faceți?**

Fine, thanks.
**Mulțumesc, bine.**

And you?
**Și dumneavoastră?**

I beg your pardon.
**Vă rog să mă scuzați.**

Excuse me!
**Scuzați!**

Sorry.
**Îmi pare rău.**

# Everyday Expressions

## QUESTIONS

When? How?
**Cînd? Cum?**

What? Why?
**Ce? De ce?**

Who? Which?
**Cine? Care?**

Where is/are...?
**Unde este/sînt...?**

Where can I get/find...?
**De unde pot lua...?**

Is it far?
**Este departe?**

How long?
**Cît timp durează?**

How much?
**Cît?**

How many?
**Cîți/cîte?**

A little/a lot
**Puțin/mult**

More/less
**Mai mult/mai puțin**

Enough
**Destul**

Do you speak English?
**Vorbiți englezește?**

Is there anyone here who speaks English?
**Este cineva care vorbește englezește?**

What does this mean?
**Ce înseamnă aceasta?**

I understand.
**Înțeleg.**

I don't understand.
**Nu înțeleg.**

Can you translate this for me?
**Puteți să-mi traduceți, vă rog?**

I don't speak Romanian.
**Nu vorbesc românește.**

What do you call this in Romanian?
**Cum se spune asta în românește?**

Could you speak more slowly?
**Puteți să vorbiți mai rar, vă rog?**

Could you repeat that?
**Puteți să repetați, vă rog?**

Could you spell the word?
**Puteți silabisi cuvîntul?**

Please write the word down.
**Scrieți, vă rog, cuvîntul.**

Can you help me?
**Puteți să mă ajutați?**

I can't.
**Nu pot.**

Can I have...?
**Pot avea...?**

# Everyday Expressions

May I...?
**Îmi permiteţi să...?**

Can you show me?
**Îmi puteţi arăta?**

What can I do for you?
**Cu ce vă pot fi de folos?**

How can I help you?
**Cu ce vă pot ajuta?**

Can I help you?
**Vă pot ajuta cu ceva?**

Do you need help?
**Aveţi nevoie de ajutor?**

Can you direct me to...?
**Îmi puteţi spune unde este...?**

## A FEW USEFUL WORDS

better/worse
**mai bine/mai rău**

big/small
**mare/mic**

cheap/expensive
**scump/ieftin**

early/late
**devreme/tîrziu**

good/bad
**bun/rău**

hot/cold
**cald/rece**

near/far
**aproape/departe**

right/wrong
**bine/rău**

vacant/occupied
**liber/ocupat**

## REQUESTS

What do you want?
**Ce doriţi?**

May I ask you a favor?
**Pot să vă cer un serviciu?**

I'd like…
**Aş vrea…**

We'd like…
**Am vrea…**

I want…
**vreau…**

He/she wants…
**El/ea vrea…**

We want…
**Noi vrem…**

They want…
**Ei/ele vor…**

Bring me/us…
**Aduceţi-mi/ne…**

Bring this with you.
**Luaţi aceasta cu dumneavoastră.**

# Everyday Expressions

Give me/us...
**Daţi-mi/ne...**

Show me/us...
**Arătaţi-mi/ne...**

I'm looking for...
**Caut...**

I'm lost.
**Sînt dezorientat/ă.**

I'm hungry.
**Mi-e foame.**

I'm thirsty.
**Mi-e sete.**

I'm dead tired.
**Sînt foarte obosit/ă.**

I've lost my...
**Mi-am pierdut...**

> ...handbag.
> **...poşeta.**

> ...passport.
> **...paşaportul.**

> ...wallet.
> **...portofelul.**

Where is the police station?
**Unde este circa (postul) de poliţie?**

Hurry up!
**Grăbiţi-vă!**

My car/suitcase/camera has been stolen.
**Mi s-a furat maşina/valiza/aparatul foto.**

Call this number for me please.
**Vă rog să sunaţi la numărul acesta.**

It's urgent.
**E urgent.**

It's...
**E...**

It isn't...
**Nu e...**

There it is.
**Iat-o/iată-l.**

There is/there are...
**Este/sînt ...**

There isn't/there aren't...
**Nu este/nu sînt...**

Where is the book?
**Unde este cartea?**

Here it is.
**Iat-o.**

## Descriptions and Comments

It is...
**Este...**

...above/below
**...deasupra/dedesubt**

...always/never
**...întotdeauna/niciodată**

...around/across
**...împrejur/vizavi**

...beautiful/ugly
**...frumos/urît**

...before/after
**...înainte/după**

...behind/in front
**...în spate/în faţă**

...better/worse
**...mai bun/mai rău**

...between/next to
**...între/alături de**

...big/small
**...mare/mic**

...cheap/expensive
**...ieftin/scump**

...early/late
**...devreme/tîrziu**

...easy/difficult
**...uşor/greu**

...free/occupied
**...liber/ocupat**

...from/with
**...din/cu**

...full/empty
**...plin/gol**

...good/bad
**...bun/rău**

...heavy/light
**...greu/uşor**

...hot/cold
**...cald/rece**

...last
**...ultimul**

...near/far
**...aproape/departe**

...now/then
**...acum/atunci**

...old/new
**...vechi/nou**

...old/young
**...bătrîn/tînăr**

...on/in/towards
**...pe/în/spre**

...open/closed
**...deschis/închis**

...outside/inside
**...afară/înăuntru**

...perhaps/surely
**...probabil/desigur**

...right/left
**...drept/stîng**

...since/until
**...de cînd/pînă cînd**

...something/nothing
**...ceva/nimic**

...soon/later
**...curînd/mai tîrziu**

...with/without
**...cu/fără**

It doesn't matter.
**N-are importanţă.**

I see what you mean.
**Înţeleg ce vreţi să spuneţi.**

I don't know.
**Nu ştiu.**

I don't have a clue.
**N-am idee.**

I hope so.
**Sper că da.**

I guess you're right.
**Cred că aveţi dreptate.**

I guess so.
**Cred că da.**

Maybe.
**Probabil.**

We'll try again.
**Vom încerca din nou.**

I can't wait.
**Nu pot să aştept.**

It's not worth it.
**Nu merită osteneala.**

That's fine.
**Este foarte bine.**

It's possible.
**Este posibil.**

Impossible!
**Imposibil!**

It was awesome.
**A fost minunat.**

That's good news.
**Asta-i o veste îmbucurătoare.**

That's too bad.
**Păcat.**

You never know.
**Nu se ştie niciodată.**

# Everyday Expressions

Good idea!
**Excelentă idee!**

It's very nice of you.
**Foarte drăguț din partea dumneavoastră.**

I must be off now.
**Trebuie să plec.**

## EXCLAMATIONS

Carry on.
**Continuați.**

At last!
**În sfîrșit!**

Really?
**Serios?/Adevărat?**

Good God!
**Vai, doamne!**

Heck! Damn!
**La naiba!/La dracu!**

I don't mind.
**Nu mă deranjează.**

No way!
**Nicidecum!/În nici un caz!**

Rubbish.
**Prostii.**

That's enough!
**Ajunge!**

That's true.
**Asta-i adevărat.**

Well I never!
**Nu-mi vine să cred.**

That's a piece of cake.
**Asta-i floare la ureche.**

## To Be and to Have

I am/I am not...
**Eu sînt/nu sînt...**

You are/you are not...
**Tu eşti/nu eşti...**

He/she is...
**El/ea este...**

He/she is not...
**El/ea nu este...**

We are/we are not...
**Noi sîntem/nu sîntem...**

You are/you are not... (*pl.*)
**Voi sînteţi/nu sînteţi...**

They are...
**Ei/ele sînt...**

They are not...
**Ei/ele nu sînt...**

I have/I have not...
**Eu am/nu am...**

You have/you have not...
**Tu ai/nu ai**...

He/she has...
**El/ea are**...

He/she has not...
**El/ea nu are**...

We have/we have not...
**Noi avem/nu avem**...

You have/you have not... (*pl.*)
**Voi aveţi/nu aveţi**...

They have...
**Ei/ele au**...

They have not...
**Ei/ele nu au**...

## TIME AND DATES

Times of the day
**Orele zilei**

Noon
**Miezul zilei**

Midnight
**Miezul nopţii**

What time is it?
**Cît e ora/ceasul?**

It is...o'clock.
**Este ora...**

Ten o'clock
**Ora zece**

Quarter past ten
**Zece şi un sfert**

Half past ten
**Zece jumătate**

Quarter to seven
**Şapte fără un sfert**

Five to eleven
**Unsprezece fără cinci**

Excuse me. Can you tell me the time?
**Scuzaţi. Îmi puteţi spune cît e ora?**

It's eight o'clock.
**Este ora opt.**

It's a quarter past nine.
**Este nouă şi un sfert.**

In the morning
**Dimineaţa**

At noon
**La prînz**

In the afternoon
**După amiază**

In the evening
**Seara**

At midnight
**La miezul nopţii**

# Everyday Expressions

Yesterday
**Ieri**

The day before yesterday
**Alaltăieri**

Today
**Astăzi**

Tomorrow
**Mîine**

The day after tomorrow
**Poimîine**

Two days ago
**Acum două zile**

In three days
**În trei zile**

This week
**Săptămîna aceasta**

Next week
**Săptămîna viitoare**

Last week
**Săptămîna trecută**

In two weeks
**În două săptămîni**

Ten at night
**Zece seara**

My watch is fast.
**Ceasul meu este înainte.**

My watch is slow.
**Ceasul meu este înapoi.**

Year
**An**

Day
**Zi**

Hour
**Oră**

Minute
**Minut**

Second
**Secundă**

When?
**Cînd?**

Now
**Acum**

This morning
**Azi dimineaţă**

Tonight
**Deseară**

Last night
**Aseară**

Yesterday morning
**Ieri dimineaţă**

Tomorrow afternoon
**Mîine după amiază**

Tomorrow night
**Mîine seară**

In the morning
**Dimineața**

In the afternoon
**După amiază**

In the evening
**Seara**

Three days from now
**Peste trei zile**

Last year
**Anul trecut**

The year before last
**Acum doi ani**

The year after next
**Peste doi ani**

What date is it today?
**Ce dată este astăzi?**

# Arrival

## CUSTOMS

Customs
**Vama**

Passport control
**Controlul paşaportului**

Here is my passport.
**Iată paşaportul meu.**

I'll be staying...
**Voi sta...**

> ...a few days.
> **...cîteva zile.**

> ...a week.
> **...o săptămînă.**

> ...six months.
> **...şase luni.**

I don't know yet.
**Nu ştiu încă.**

I'm visiting relatives.
**Sînt în vizită la rude.**

I'm here on vacation.
**Sînt aici in vacanţă.**

I'm here on business.
**Sînt aici în interes de afaceri.**

I'm taking courses at the university.
**Urmez (nişte) cursuri la universitate.**

I'm sorry, I don't understand.
**Îmi pare rău, nu înțeleg.**

This is my luggage.
**Acesta este bagajul meu.**

I have nothing to declare.
**Nu am nimic de declarat.**

I have a bottle of whiskey.
**Am o sticlă de whiskey.**

Do I have to pay duty on these items?
**Trebuie să plătesc vamă pentru aceste articole?**

It's for my personal use.
**Este pentru uzul personal.**

There's one suitcase missing.
**Îmi lipsește o valiză.**

## FILLING IN FORMS

Name
**Numele**

Address
**Adresa**

Date of birth
**Data nașterii**

Place of birth
**Locul nașterii**

Nationality
**Naționalitatea**

Age
**Vîrsta**

Sex
**Sexul**

Male
**Bărbat**

Female
**Femeie**

Reason for travel
**Motivul călătoriei**

Business
**Afaceri**

Tourism
**Turism**

Work
**Muncă**

Personal
**Personal**

Profession
**Profesiunea**

Date
**Data**

Date of arrival
**Data sosirii**

Date of departure
**Data plecării**

# Arrival

Passport number
**Seria paşaportului**

Visa
**Viza**

Signature
**Semnătura**

Currency
**Valuta**

## CHANGING MONEY

Can you change dollars?
**Puteţi schimba dolari?**

What's your exchange rate for dollars?
**Care este cursul de schimb pentru dolari?**

What is the commission?
**Cît este comisionul?**

Any extra fee?
**Mai e vreo taxă suplimentară?**

I would like...
**Aş vrea...**

> ...small bills.
> **...bancnote mici.**

> ...large bills.
> **...bancnote mari.**

> ...coins.
> **...monede.**

> ...small change.
> **...mărunţiş.**

Where is a cash machine?
**Unde găsesc un bancomat?**

Where is the bank?
**Unde este banca?**

Is there an exchange office around?
**Este vreun birou de schimb prin apropiere?**

Do you accept credit cards?
**Acceptaţi plata cu carte de credit?**

## Accommodations

### RESERVATIONS

Can you recommend a hotel in…?
**Imi puteţi recomanda un hotel în…?**

Is it downtown?
**Este în centru?**

How much is it per night?
**Cît costă pe noapte?**

Is there anything cheaper?
**Este altceva mai ieftin?**

Could you reserve me a room (there), please?
**Îmi puteţi rezerva o cameră acolo, vă rog?**

How do I get there?
**Cum ajung acolo?**

### AT THE HOTEL

Do you have any vacancies?
**Aveţi camere libere?**

I'm sorry, we're full.
**Îmi pare rău, totul este ocupat.**

Is there another hotel nearby?
**Mai este un alt hotel prin apropiere?**

I'd like a single/double room.
**Aş vrea o cameră pentru o persoană/două persoane.**

A room with...
**O cameră cu...**

    ...twin beds.
    **...două paturi.**

    ...a double bed.
    **...un pat dublu.**

    ...a bath/shower.
    **...baie/duş.**

    ...a balcony.
    **...balcon.**

How long will you be staying?
**Cît timp veţi sta?**

How many nights?
**Cîte nopţi?**

I'm going to stay for...
**Voi sta...**

    ...one day.
    **...o zi.**

    ...two days.
    **...două zile.**

    ...one week.
    **...o săptămînă.**

How much is it per night?
**Cît costă pentru o noapte?**

How much is it per person?
**Cît costă de persoană?**

# Accommodations

How much is it per week?
**Cît costă pe săptămînă?**

It's... per day.
**Costă... pe zi.**

It's... per person.
**Costă... de persoană.**

Can I see the room?
**Pot să văd camera?**

Are there any others?
**Mai sînt şi altele?**

It's fine, I'll take it.
**E bună, o iau.**

Do you have anything...
**Aveţi altă cameră...**

...bigger/cheaper?
**...mai mare/mai ieftină?**

...quieter/warmer?
**...mai liniştită/mai călduroasă?**

Does the price include...
**Preţul include...**

...breakfast?
**...micul dejun?**

...service?
**...serviciul?**

Do I have to pay a deposit?
**Trebuie să achit un avans?**

Is there a discount for children?
**Este vreo reducere pentru copii?**

That's too expensive.
**Este prea scump.**

Could you put an extra bed in the room?
**Aţi putea pune un pat suplimentar în cameră?**

## NEEDS

The key to room…, please.
**Cheia de la camera…, vă rog.**

I've locked myself out of my room.
**M-am închis pe dinafară.**

Could you wake me at…?
**M-aţi putea trezi la…?**

I'd like breakfast in my room.
**Aş vrea micul dejun în cameră.**

Can I leave this in the safe?
**Pot lăsa aceasta în seif?**

Could I have my things from the safe?
**Puteţi să-mi daţi lucrurile din seif?**

Where can I park my car?
**Unde pot parca maşina?**

Where's the elevator?
**Unde este liftul?**

Where's the restroom?
**Unde este toaleta?**

# Accommodations

I'd like another…
**Aş mai vrea…**

> …blanket.
> **…o pătură.**

> …glass.
> **…un pahar.**

> …pillow.
> **…o pernă.**

> …sheet.
> **…un cearşaf.**

> …towel.
> **…un prosop.**

Where can I wash/hang my laundry?
**Unde pot spăla/atîrna rufele?**

What time is breakfast?
**La ce oră se serveşte micul dejun?**

Could you clean/iron these clothes?
**Puteţi curăţa/călca hainele acestea?**

When will they be ready?
**Cînd vor fi gata?**

I need them as soon as possible.
**Îmi trebuie cît de repede posibil.**

Can you mend this?
**Puteţi repara asta?**

Can you sew on this button?
**Puteţi coase acest nasture?**

Can you get this stain out?
**Puteți scoate această pată?**

Is my laundry ready?
**Sînt gata rufele mele?**

Come with me.
**Veniți cu mine.**

I have a problem in my room.
**Am o problemă cu camera.**

The bed is too soft/hard.
**Patul este prea moale/tare.**

The heating/air-conditioner doesn't work.
**Încălzirea/aerul condiționat nu funcționează.**

There is no hot water.
**Nu este apă caldă.**

My room has not been made up.
**Camera mea nu a fost făcută.**

There's too much noise next door.
**Este prea mult zgomot în camera de alături.**

Could you have that taken care of?
**Ați putea să vă ocupați de asta?**

I'd like to move to another room.
**Aș vrea să mă mut în altă cameră.**

I'd like to speak to the manager.
**Aș vrea să vorbesc cu directorul.**

## Accommodations

Where's the...
**Unde este...**

> ...bar?
> **...barul?**

> ...parking lot?
> **...parcajul?**

> ...swimming pool?
> **...piscina?**

> ...TV room?
> **...sala tv?**

I'd like to stay another night.
**Aş vrea să mai stau o noapte.**

### RENTING

We've reserved an apartment in the name of...
**Am rezervat un apartament pe numele...**

Where do we pick up the keys?
**De unde luăm cheile?**

Where is the...
**Unde este...**

> ...electricity meter?
> **...contorul electric?**

> ...fuse box?
> **...tabloul de siguranţă?**

> ...water heater?
> **...boilerul?**

Are there any spare sheets?
**Aveţi cearşafuri suplimentare?**

Which day does the cleaner come?
**În ce zi vine îngrijitoarea?**

When do I put out the trash?
**Cînd scot afară gunoiul?**

Is the cost of electricity included?
**Costul electricităţii este inclus?**

Where can I contact you?
**Unde vă pot găsi?**

We have accidentally broken...
**Am stricat din greşeală...**

That was already damaged when we arrived.
**Era deja stricat cînd am venit noi.**

We need...
**Ne trebuie...**

> ...cutlery.
> **...tacîmuri.**

> ...dishes.
> **...veselă.**

> ...a frying pan.
> **...o tigaie.**

> ...a kettle.
> **...un ceainic.**

> ...a saucepan.
> **...o oală de gătit.**

> ...a toaster.
> **...un prăjitor de pîine.**

...a refrigerator.
**...un frigider.**

...a washing machine.
**...o maşină de spălat rufe.**

...a dishwasher.
**...o maşină de spălat vase.**

...dishwashing liquid.
**...detergent de vase.**

## CHECKING OUT

I leave/We leave...
**Plec/Plecăm...**

...today/tomorrow.
**...astăzi/mîine.**

...very early.
**...foarte devreme.**

Please have my bill ready.
**Vă rog să pregătiţi nota de plată.**

When is check-out time?
**La ce oră trebuie eliberate camerele?**

Can I pay now?
**Pot plăti acum?**

May I please have my bill?
**Îmi puteţi face nota de plată, vă rog?**

I'd like to pay by credit card.
**Aş vrea să plătesc cu cartea de credit.**

The bill, please.
**Nota de plată, va rog.**

I think there's a mistake in this bill.
**Cred că este o eroare în nota de plată.**

Can I leave my luggage here until...?
**Pot lăsa aici bagajul pînă la...?**

Can you get me a taxi, please?
**Puteți, vă rog, chema un taxi?**

Please forward my mail to this address.
**Vă rog să-mi trimiteți corespondența la această adresă.**

# Meeting People

## Meeting People

### INTRODUCTIONS

Good morning.
**Bună dimineața.**

Good evening.
**Bună seara.**

Good night.
**Noapte bună.**

Good-bye.
**La revedere.**

See you tomorrow.
**Pe mîine.**

Welcome.
**Bine ați venit.**

Bon voyage.
**Călătorie plăcută.**

What is your name?
**Cum vă numiți?**

My name is…
**Mă numesc…**

How are you?
**Ce mai faceți?**

Fine, thanks.
**Mulțumesc, bine.**

And you?
**Şi dumneavoastră?**

Where are you from?
**De unde sînteţi?**

I am from...
**Sînt din...**

...Australia.
**...Australia.**

...Canada.
**...Canada.**

...England.
**...Anglia.**

...Europe.
**...Europa.**

...France.
**...Franţa.**

...Germany.
**...Germania.**

...Great Britain.
**...Marea Britanie.**

...India.
**...India.**

...Ireland.
**...Irlanda.**

...Italy.
**...Italia.**

...Japan.
**...Japonia.**

...Korea.
**...Coreea.**

...New Zealand.
**...Noua Zeelandă.**

...Northern Ireland.
**...Irlanda de Nord.**

...Scotland.
**...Scoţia.**

...Sweden.
**...Suedia.**

...the United States.
**...Statele Unite ale Americii.**

...Wales.
**...Ţara Galilor.**

I am...
**Sînt...**

...American.
**...american.**

...Australian.
**...australian.**

...British/English.
**...britanic/englez.**

...Canadian.
**...canadian.**

...French.
**...francez.**

...German.
**...german.**

...Indian.
**...indian.**

...Irish.
**...irlandez.**

...Italian.
**...italian.**

...Japanese.
**...japonez.**

...Korean.
**...coreean.**

...Scottish.
**...scoțian.**

...Swedish.
**...suedez.**

...Welsh.
**...galez.**

I am with my...
**Sînt cu...**

...wife.
**...soția.**

...husband.
**...soțul.**

# Meeting People

...family.
**...familia.**

...boyfriend.
**...prietenul meu.**

...girlfriend.
**...prietena mea.**

I am on my own.
**Sînt singur.**

I am here on vacation.
**Sînt aici în vacanță.**

I am here on business.
**Sînt aici în interes de afaceri.**

## OCCUPATIONS

What do you do?
**Cu ce vă ocupați?**

I am a/an...
**Sînt...**

...accountant.
**...contabil.**

...administrator.
**...administrator.**

...agronomist.
**...agronom.**

...architect.
**...arhitect.**

...artist.
**...artist.**

...business person.
**...om de afaceri.**

...carpenter.
**...tîmplar.**

...consultant.
**...consultant.**

...dentist.
**...dentist.**

...diplomat.
**...diplomat.**

...doctor .
**...doctor.**

...economist.
**...economist.**

...engineer.
**...inginer.**

...farmer.
**...fermier.**

...filmmaker.
**...cineast.**

...journalist.
**...ziarist/jurnalist.**

...lawyer.
**...avocat.**

...manual worker.
**...muncitor manual.**

...mechanic.
**...mecanic.**

...nurse.
**...infirmieră.**

...observer.
**...observator.**

...office worker.
**...funcţionar.**

...pilot.
**...pilot.**

...political scientist.
**...specialist în ştiinţe politice.**

...scientist.
**...om de ştiinţă.**

...secretary.
**...secretar/ă.**

...soldier.
**...soldat.**

...student.
**...student.**

...surgeon.
**...chirurg.**

...teacher.
**...învăţător.**

...telecommunications specialist.
**...specialist în telecomunicaţii.**

...tourist.
**...turist.**

...writer.
**...scriitor.**

## FAMILY

Are you married?
**Sînteți căsătorit/ă?**

I am single.
**Sînt necăsătorit/ă.**

How many children do you have?
**Cîți copii aveți?**

I don't have any children.
**Nu am copii.**

I have a son.
**Am un băiat.**

I have a daughter.
**Am o fată.**

What is his/her name?
**Cum se numește?**

How many sisters do you have?
**Cîte surori aveți?**

How many brothers do you have?
**Cîți frați aveți?**

My father/mother is fifty years old.
**Tata/mama are cincizeci de ani.**

# Meeting People

I am here with my husband/wife.
**Sînt aici cu soțul/soția.**

I have a large family.
**Am o familie numeroasă.**

Our grandmother/grandfather visits us fairly often.
**Bunica/bunicul ne vizitează destul de des.**

## INVITATIONS

May I invite you for coffee?
**Vă pot invita la o cafea?**

We're having a party.
**Avem o petrecere.**

Would you like to join us?
**Ați vrea să veniți și dumneavoastră?**

That's very kind of you.
**Este foarte amabil din partea dumneavoastră.**

I'd love to come.
**Mi-ar plăcea să vin.**

What time shall I come?
**La ce oră să vin?**

What can I bring?
**Ce pot să aduc?**

May I bring a friend?
**Pot să aduc și un prieten?**

Do you mind my smoking?
**Va deranjează dacă fumez?**

Would you like a cigarette?
**Aţi vrea o ţigară?**

Would you care for a drink?
**Aţi vrea ceva de băut?**

Are you free this evening?
**Sînteţi liber/ă astă seară?**

Would you like to go out with me?
**Aţi vrea să ieşiţi împreună cu mine?**

I'd love to, thank you.
**Aş fi încîntat/ă, vă mulţumesc.**

Thank you, but I am busy.
**Mulţumesc, dar sînt ocupat/ă.**

Why are you laughing?
**De ce rîdeţi?**

Is my Romanian so bad?
**Vorbesc aşa de prost româneşte?**

Where shall we meet?
**Unde ne întîlnim?**

Here's my phone number.
**Iată numărul meu de telefon.**

May I have your number?
**Îmi puteţi da numărul dumneavoastră?**

I'll call in case something comes up.
**Vă voi suna în caz că survine ceva.**

Can I see you again tomorrow?
**Vă pot vedea din nou mîine?**

## Meeting People

### THE WEATHER

What's the weather like?
**Cum e vremea?**

What a gorgeous day!
**Ce zi frumoasă!**

What horrible weather!
**Ce vreme îngrozitoare!**

What's the temperature?
**Ce temperatură e?**

The weather is getting bad/is improving.
**Vremea se înrăutăţeşte/se face frumoasă.**

Is it going to be nice tomorrow?
**Vremea va fi frumoasă mîine?**

Is it going to rain?
**O să plouă?**

What's the weather forecast?
**Care este prognoza meteo?**

The weather is bad/good/fine.
**Vremea este urîtă/bună/frumoasă.**

It's...
**Este...**

> ...cold/hot.
> **...rece/cald.**

> ...very cloudy.
> **...foarte înnorat.**

There's going to be a thunderstorm.
**Va fi o furtună.**

# Eating Out

### FINDING A PLACE TO EAT

Can you recommend a good restaurant?
**Îmi puteţi recomanda un restaurant bun?**

I'd like to go to a...
**Aş vrea să merg la un...**

>...traditional local restaurant.
>**...restaurant local tradiţional.**

>...inexpensive restaurant.
>**...restaurant ieftin.**

>...vegetarian restaurant.
>**...restaurant vegetarian.**

>...restaurant with a terrace.
>**...restaurant cu terasă.**

Where can I find a...
**Unde este o...**

>...café?
>**...cafenea?**

>...pizzeria?
>**...pizzeria?**

I'd like to reserve a table for two today at...
**Aş vrea să rezerv o masă pentru două persoane pentru astăzi la ora...**

We'll come at 8:00.
**Vom veni la ora opt.**

A table for two, please.
**O masă pentru două persoane, vă rog.**

## Eating Out

We have a reservation.
**Avem o masă rezervată.**

Could we sit…
**Am putea sta…**

…over there/outside?
**…acolo/afară?**

…by the window?
**…lîngă fereastră?**

### BREAKFAST

I'd like breakfast, please.
**Aş vrea micul dejun, vă rog.**

What's for breakfast?
**Ce avem la micul dejun?**

| | |
|---|---|
| sausage and eggs | **ouă cu cîrnăciori** |
| bacon and eggs | **ouă cu şuncă** |
| two eggs sunny side up | **două ouă ochiuri** |
| a boiled egg | **un ou fiert** |
| omelet with onion/ | **omletă cu ceapă/** |
| vegetables/grated cheese | **legume/brînză rasă** |
| bread | **pîine** |
| toast | **pîine prăjită** |
| jelly | **gem** |
| yogurt | **iaurt** |
| butter | **unt** |
| milk | **lapte** |
| cereal | **fulgi de porumb** |
| fruit juice | **suc de fructe** |
| orange juice | **suc de portocale** |
| coffee | **cafea** |
| tea with lemon | **ceai cu lămîie** |
| tea with milk | **ceai cu lapte** |

## ORDERING

Waiter!
**Ospătar (Chelner)!**

May I see the wine list, please?
**Îmi puteţi arăta lista de vinuri, vă rog?**

Do you have a set menu?
**Aveţi un meniu fix?**

Can you recommend some typical local dishes?
**Îmi puteţi recomanda nişte mîncăruri locale
    tradiţionale?**

Could you tell me what… is?
**Îmi puteţi spune ce este…?**

What is in it?
**Ce conţine?**

What kind of… do you have?
**Ce fel de… aveţi?**

What's your favorite?
**Care este mîncarea dumneavoastră preferată?**

Is it…
**Este…**

      …good?
      **…bună?**

      …expensive?
      **…scumpă?**

      …light?
      **…uşoară?**

# Eating Out

What is fast?
**Ce aveţi deja pregătit?**

What is local?
**Ce mîncăruri tradiţionale (româneşti) aveţi?**

Do you have an English menu?
**Aveţi un meniu în limba engleză?**

Would you bring us…, please?
**Vreţi să ne aduceţi vă rog…?**

…an ashtray
**…o scrumieră**

…an extra chair
**…încă un scaun**

…an extra dish
**…încă o farfurie**

…a fork
**…o furculiţă**

…a glass
**…un pahar**

…a knife
**…un cuţit**

…a napkin
**…un şerveţel**

…a plate
**…o farfurie**

…a saucer
**…o farfurioară**

…a spoon
**…o lingură**

There's a plate missing.
**Lipseşte o farfurie.**

May I have some...
**Îmi puteţi da nişte...**

    ...bread?
    **...pîine?**

    ...margarine?
    **...margarină?**

    ...oil?
    **...ulei?**

    ...pepper?
    **...piper?**

    ...salt?
    **...sare?**

    ...sugar?
    **...zahăr?**

    ...vinegar?
    **...oţet?**

I'm on a diet.
**Mănînc regim.**

I'm allergic to...
**Sînt alergic la...**

I cannot eat...
**Nu mănînc...**

    ...beef/pork.
    **...carne de vită/de porc.**

    ...dairy products.
    **...(produse) lactate.**

I'm a diabetic.
**Sînt diabetic.**

No fat.
**Fără grăsime.**

Low-fat meal.
**Mîncare de regim.**

Do you have vegetarian dishes?
**Aveți mîncăruri pentru vegetarieni?**

May I have a glass of water, please?
**Îmi puteți da, vă rog, un pahar cu apă?**

I'd like some more.
**Mai vreau încă puțin.**

Just a small portion.
**Doar o porție mică.**

Enjoy your meal!
**Poftă bună!**

I'd like a bottle/glass/half a bottle of white/red wine.
**Aş vrea o sticlă/un pahar/o jumătate de sticlă de vin alb/roşu.**

Can I have a glass of beer?
**Îmi puteți da un pahar de bere?**

Nothing more, thanks.
**Nimic altceva, mulțumesc.**

Check, please. (The bill, please).
**Nota, vă rog.**

We'd like to pay separately.
**Am vrea să plătim separat.**

## MENU

The chef recommends...
**Bucătarul şef recomandă...**

Service included
**Serviciul inclus**

Service not included
**Serviciul nu e inclus**

| | |
|---|---|
| aperitif | **aperitiv** |
| appetizers | **gustări** |
| main meal | **felul al doilea** |
| first course | **felul întîi** |
| second course | **felul al doilea** |
| daily special | **specialitatea zilei** |
| specialties | **specialităţi** |
| cold dish | **hrană rece** |
| soups | **supe** |
| pasta | **paste** |
| noodles | **tăiţei** |
| pizza | **pizza** |
| sauces | **sosuri** |
| rice | **orez** |
| fish | **peşte** |
| meat | **carne** |
| venison | **vînat** |
| poultry | **carne de pasăre** |
| vegetables | **legume** |
| vegetables in season | **legume de sezon** |
| salads | **salate** |
| spices | **condimente** |
| cheese | **brînză** |
| fruit | **fructe** |
| dessert | **desert** |

## Soups

| | |
|---|---|
| soup | **supă** |
| chicken soup with rice | **supă de pasăre cu orez** |
| fish soup | **ciorbă de peşte** |
| noodle soup | **supă cu tăiţei** |
| meat broth with vegetables | **supă de carne cu legume** |
| onion soup | **supă de ceapă** |
| vegetable soup | **supă de legume** |

## Meat

| | |
|---|---|
| beef | **carne de vacă** |
| brains | **creer** |
| chicken | **carne de pasăre** |
| chop/cutlet | **cotlet de porc** |
| lamb | **carne de miel** |
| liver | **ficat** |
| pork | **carne de porc** |
| roastbeef | **friptură de vită** |
| salami | **salam** |
| steak | **biftec** |
| tongue | **limbă** |
| turkey | **curcan** |
| veal | **viţel** |

## Vegetables and Salads

| | |
|---|---|
| asparagus | **sparanghel** |
| beans | **fasole** |
| beets | **sfeclă** |
| cabbage | **varză** |
| carrots | **morcovi** |
| cauliflower | **conopidă** |
| corn | **porumb** |
| cucumbers | **castraveţi** |
| eggplants | **vinete** |
| garlic | **usturoi** |
| green salad | **salată verde** |
| leeks | **praz** |

| | |
|---|---|
| mushrooms | **ciuperci** |
| olives | **măsline** |
| onions | **ceapă** |
| peas | **mazăre** |
| peppers | **ardei** |
| potatoes | **cartofi** |
| diced boiled potatoes and carrots with mayonnaise | **salată à la russe** |
| salad | **salată** |
| spinach | **spanac** |
| tomatoes | **roşii** |
| tomato and lettuce salad | **salată asortată** |

## FRUIT AND DESSERT

| | |
|---|---|
| apples | **mere** |
| cherries | **cireşe** |
| oranges | **portocale** |
| peaches | **caise** |
| pears | **pere** |
| plums | **prune** |
| strawberries | **căpşuni** |
| cake | **prăjitură** |
| fruit cake | **prăjitură cu fructe** |
| ice cream | **îngheţată** |

## DRINKS

| | |
|---|---|
| beverages | **băuturi** |
| beer | **bere** |
| brandy | **coniac** |
| plum brandy | **ţuică** |
| champagne | **şampanie** |
| coffee | **cafea** |
| mineral water | **apă minerală** |
| wine | **vin** |
| dry/sweet white wine | **vin alb sec/dulce** |
| red/white/rose wine | **vin roşu/alb/roze** |
| sparkling wine | **vin spumant** |
| table wine | **vin de masă** |

## COMPLAINTS

I have no knife/fork/spoon.
**Nu am cuțit/furculiță/lingură.**

There must be some mistake.
**Trebuie să fie o greșeală.**

That's not what I ordered.
**Nu am comandat asta.**

I asked for…
**Am cerut…**

I can't eat this.
**Nu pot mînca asta.**

The meat is…
**Carnea este…**

> …overdone.
> **…prea prăjită.**

> …rare.
> **…în sînge.**

> …too tough.
> **…prea tare.**

This is too bitter/sour.
**Aceasta este prea amară/acră.**

The food is cold.
**Mîncarea este rece.**

This isn't fresh.
**Aceasta nu este proaspătă.**

We can't wait any longer.
**Nu mai putem aştepta.**

We're leaving.
**Plecăm.**

PAYING

The bill, please.
**Nota de plată, vă rog.**

We'd like to pay separately.
**Am vrea să plătim separat.**

Separate checks
**Note separate**

Together
**Împreună**

I think there's a mistake in this check.
**Cred că e o greşeală în nota de plată.**

What is this amount for?
**Pentru ce este suma aceasta?**

I didn't have that. I had...
**N-am servit asta. Am servit...**

Is service included?
**Serviciul este inclus?**

I've forgotten my wallet.
**Mi-am uitat portmoneul.**

Can I pay with this credit card?
**Pot plăti cu cartea de credit?**

# Eating Out

That was a very good meal.
**A fost o masă foarte bună.**

Keep the change.
**Păstraţi restul.**

This is for you.
**Asta este pentru dumneavoastră.**

# Travel

### DRIVING

Is this the right road for...?
**Acesta este drumul spre...?**

How far is it to... from here?
**Ce distanță este pînă la... de aici?**

How do I get onto the freeway?
**Cum ajung la autostradă?**

What's the next town called?
**Cum se numește următorul oraș?**

How long does it take by car?
**Cît durează cu mașina?**

Where is the nearest gas station?
**Unde este cea mai apropiată stație de benzină?**

Is it self-service?
**Este cu autoservire?**

Fill the tank.
**Umpleți rezervorul.**

Fill'er up, please.
**Faceți plinul, vă rog.**

I need regular/super/diesel gas.
**Îmi trebuie benzină regular/super/diesel.**

Do you have unleaded gas?
**Aveți benzină fără plumb?**

Please check the...
**Verificați, vă rog...**

...air in the tires.
**...presiunea pneurilor.**

...battery.
**...bateria.**

...brakes.
**...frînele.**

...car mirror.
**...oglinda retrovizoare.**

...directional signal.
**...semnalul de direcție.**

...fuses.
**...siguranțele.**

...headlights.
**...farurile.**

...oil.
**...uleiul.**

...radiator.
**...radiatorul.**

...spark plugs.
**...bujiile.**

...tail lights.
**...stopurile (lumina din spate).**

Please change the...
**Vă rog schimbați...**

      ...brake fluid.
      **...lichidul de frînă.**

      ...bulb.
      **...becul.**

      ...fanbelt.
      **...cureaua ventilatorului.**

      ...filter.
      **...filtrul (de aer).**

      ...wipers.
      **...ștergătoarele.**

Where can I park?
**Unde pot parca?**

May I park here?
**Pot parca aici?**

Where's the nearest garage?
**Unde este garajul cel mai apropiat?**

How long can I park here?
**Cît timp pot parca aici?**

Must I pay to park here?
**Trebuie să plătesc pentru a parca aici?**

## BREAKDOWN

Excuse me. My car broke down.
**Scuzați. Mașina mea a căzut în pană.**

May I use your phone?
**Pot folosi telefonul dumneavoastră?**

Can you send a mechanic?
**Puteţi trimite un mecanic?**

I need a tow-truck.
**Îmi trebuie o autoremorcă.**

Can you send one?
**Îmi puteţi trimite una?**

My car won't start.
**Motorul nu porneşte.**

I've run out of gas.
**Am rămas fără benzină.**

The battery is dead.
**Bateria e descarcată.**

The engine is overheating.
**Motorul se încălzeşte prea tare.**

There's something wrong with the…
**Ceva nu este în ordine cu…**

> …air conditioner.
> **…instalaţia de aer condiţionat.**

> …front/back wheels.
> **…roţile din faţă/din spate.**

> …ignition/brakes.
> **…aprinderea/frînele.**

> …radiator/exhaust pipe.
> **…radiatorul/ţeava de eşapament.**

Do you do repairs?
**Va ocupaţi de reparaţii?**

Can you repair it?
**O puteţi repara?**

Can you repair it today?
**O puteţi repara astăzi?**

Can I wait for it?
**Pot să aştept pînă o reparaţi?**

When will it be ready?
**Cînd va fi gata?**

How much will it cost?
**Cît va costa?**

Can I have a receipt for the insurance?
**Îmi puteţi da o chitanţă pentru asigurare?**

## AUTO ACCIDENT

There has been an accident.
**A avut loc un accident.**

There are people injured.
**Există persoane rănite.**

Where's the nearest phone?
**Unde este telefonul cel mai apropiat?**

Call...
**Chemaţi...**

...an ambulance.
**...salvarea.**

...a doctor.
**...un doctor.**

...the fire station.
**...pompierii.**

...the police.
**...poliţia.**

No one is hurt.
**Nu e nimeni rănit**.

He can't breathe/move.
**El nu poate respira/nu se poate mişca.**

Don't move him.
**Nu-l mişcaţi din loc.**

He is seriously bleeding.
**El are o hemoragie puternică.**

She's unconscious.
**Ea şi-a pierdut cunoştinţa.**

## LEGAL MATTERS

What's your name and address?
**Care este numele şi adresa dumneavoastră?**

What's your insurance company?
**La ce companie sînteţi asigurat?**

He was driving too fast/too close.
**Conducea prea repede/prea aproape.**

He ran into me.
**El a intrat în maşina mea.**

He did not give way.
**El nu a cedat trecerea (prioritate).**

I had right of way.
**Eu aveam prioritate.**

I was only driving at… kilometers/per hour.
**Conduceam numai cu… kilometri pe oră.**

I'd like an interpreter.
**Aş dori un interpret.**

I didn't see the sign.
**Nu am văzut semnul.**

He/she saw it happen.
**El/ea a văzut cînd s-a întîmplat.**

Are there any witnesses?
**Este vreun martor?**

You were speeding.
**Mergeaţi cu viteză excesivă.**

## By Bus and by Streetcar

Excuse me. Where can I get a bus to...?
**Scuzaţi. De unde pot lua un autobuz spre...?**

Is there a bus to...?
**Este un autobuz spre...?**

Where's the bus stop?
**Unde este staţia de autobuz?**

How much is the fare to...?
**Cît costă biletul pînă la...?**

Do I have to change buses?
**Trebuie să schimb autobuzul?**

I want to get off at...
**Vreau să cobor la...**

Could you tell me when to get off?
**Îmi puteţi spune cînd trebuie să cobor?**

It's the next stop.
**Este stația urmatoare.**

Next stop, please!
**Stația următoare, vă rog!**

## BY SUBWAY

Where's the nearest subway station?
**Unde este cea mai apropiată stație de metrou?**

Where do I buy tickets?
**Unde cumpăr bilete?**

Could I have a map of the subway?
**Îmi puteți da o hartă a metroului?**

Which line should I take for...?
**Ce linie trebuie să iau spre...?**

Is this the train for...?
**Acesta este trenul spre...?**

Which stop is it for...?
**La ce stație trebuie să cobor pentru...?**

How many stops is it to...?
**Cîte stații sînt pînă la...?**

Is the next stop...?
**Stația următoare este...?**

Where are we?
**Unde sîntem?**

Where do I change for...?
**Unde trebuie să schimb pentru...?**

What time is the last train to...?
**La ce oră este ultimul tren spre...?**

## BY TRAIN

I'd like a one-way/round trip ticket.
**Vreau un bilet dus/dus-întors.**

Can I buy a ticket on board?
**Pot cumpăra bilet în tren?**

Is there a sleeping car?
**Are vagon de dormit?**

I want a first/second class ticket.
**Vreau un bilet clasa întîi/a doua.**

I'd like a window seat.
**Aş vrea un loc la fereastră.**

Is there a discount for children/families?
**Este reducere pentru copii/familie?**

Do I have to change trains?
**Trebuie să schimb trenul?**

It's a direct train
**E un tren direct.**

You have to change at...
**Trebuie să schimbaţi la...**

How long is this ticket valid for?
**Cît timp este valabil acest bilet?**

Which car/coach is my seat in?
**În care vagon este locul meu?**

Is there a dining car on the train?
**Trenul are vagon restaurant?**

What time does the train arrive in...?
**La ce oră soseşte trenul la...?**

How long is the trip?
**Cît durează călătoria?**

Where is platform...?
**Unde este peronul...?**

Where do I change for...?
**Unde trebuie să schimb pentru...?**

How long will I have to wait for a connection?
**Cît trebuie să aştept legătura?**

How long are we stopping here for?
**Cît timp opreşte aici?**

When do we get to...?
**Cînd sosim la...?**

Is this seat taken?
**Locul acesta este ocupat?**

I think this is my seat.
**Cred că acesta este locul meu.**

### BY PLANE

When is the first/next/last flight to...?
**La ce oră este prima/următoarea/ultima cursă spre...?**

I'd like two first/economy class tickets to...
**Aş vrea două bilete clasa întîi/clasa turist pentru...**

I'd like to cancel/change/confirm my reservation for
flight number...
**Aş vrea să anulez/schimb/confirm rezervarea pentru
cursa numărul...**

How long is the flight?
**Cît durează zborul?**

What time does the plane leave?
**La ce oră pleacă avionul?**

What time will we arrive?
**La ce oră vom sosi?**

What time do I have to check in?
**La ce oră trebuie să mă prezint la aeroport?**

Where is the check-in desk for flight...?
**Unde este ghişeul de înregistrare pentru cursa...?**

Would you like a window or an aisle seat?
**Preferaţi un loc la fereastră sau la mijloc?**

Smoking or non-smoking?
**Fumător sau nefumător?**

I have three suitcases and two pieces of hand luggage.
**Am trei valize şi două bagaje de mînă.**

I feel airsick.
**Am rău de înălţime.**

Is there any delay on flight...?
**Cursa... are vreo întirziere?**

Has the flight from... landed?
**A aterizat cursa de la...?**

My luggage has been lost/stolen.
**Bagajul meu s-a pierdut/a fost furat.**

My suitcase was damaged.
**Valiza mea a fost deteriorată.**

Our luggage has not arrived.
**Bagajul nostru nu a sosit.**

## ASKING DIRECTIONS

I am going to…
**Merg la…**

How do I get to…?
**Cum ajung la…?**

How far is it from here to…?
**Ce distanţă este de aici pînă la…?**

Where can I find this address?
**Unde pot găsi această adresă?**

Can you show me where I am on the map?
**Îmi puteţi arăta pe hartă unde mă aflu?**

I've lost my way.
**M-am rătăcit.**

Can you repeat that, please?
**Puteţi repeta, vă rog?**

More slowly, please.
**Mai rar, vă rog.**

Thanks for your help.
**Vă mulţumesc pentru ajutor.**

What's the best/fastest/most interesting route to...?
**Care este ruta cea mai bună/cea mai rapidă/cea mai interesantă spre...?**

Where am I?
**Unde mă aflu?**

How many kilometers to...?
**Cîţi kilometri sînt pînă la...?**

How many hours by car/by bicycle?
**Cîte ore cu maşina/cu bicicleta?**

It's...
**Este...**

...straight ahead.
**...drept înainte.**

...on the left.
**...la stînga.**

...on the right.
**...la dreapta.**

...on the other side of the street.
**...pe cealaltă parte a străzii.**

...on the corner.
**...la colţ.**

...around the corner.
**...după colţ.**

...in the direction of...
**...în direcţia...**

...opposite/behind...
**...vizavi/în spate...**

Go down the side street/main street.
**Mergeţi pe strada laterală/strada principală.**

Cross the square/bridge.
**Traversaţi scuarul/podul.**

Turn left...
**Luaţi-o la stînga...**

>...after the first traffic lights.
>**...după primul stop.**

>...at the second intersection.
>**...la cea de-a doua intersecţie.**

# Leisure

### TOURIST INFORMATION

Where's the tourist office?
**Unde este agenţia de turism?**

What are the main points of interest?
**Care sînt principalele puncte de atracţie?**

We're here for...
**Sîntem aici pentru...**

> ...only a few hours.
> **...numai cîteva ore.**

> ...a day.
> **...o zi.**

> ...a week.
> **...o săptămînă.**

Can you recommend...
**Puteţi recomanda...**

> ...an excursion?
> **...o excursie?**

> ...a boat trip?
> **...o călătorie cu vaporul?**

> ...a sightseeing tour?
> **...un tur de vizitare a oraşului?**

Do you have information on...?
**Aveţi materiale informative despre...?**

Are there any trips to...?
**Se organizează excursii la...?**

# Leisure

## SIGHTSEEING

Where is the...
**Unde este...**

...art gallery?
**...galeria de artă?**

...best view?
**...vederea cea mai frumoasă?**

...botanical garden?
**...grădina botanică?**

...castle?
**...castelul?**

...cathedral?
**...catedrala?**

...concert hall?
**...sala de concerte?**

...main square?
**...piața principală?**

...market?
**...piața?**

...museum?
**...muzeul?**

...old town center?
**...centrul vechi al orașului?**

...opera house?
**...opera?**

...palace?
**...palatul?**

...park?
**...parcul?**

...parliament building?
**...clădirea parlamentului?**

...shopping area?
**...centrul comercial?**

...stadium?
**...stadionul?**

...theater?
**...teatrul?**

...university?
**...universitatea?**

...zoo?
**...grădina zoologică?**

Can we stop here...
**Putem opri aici...**

...to buy postcards?
**...să cumpărăm ilustrate?**

...for the restrooms?
**...pentru toaletă?**

...to take photographs?
**...să facem poze?**

What is this monument?
**Ce reprezintă acest monument?**

# Leisure

Who is that statue of?
**A cui este statuia aceea?**

Is it free?
**Este gratuit?**

Is there an entrance fee?
**Este taxă de intrare?**

## ADMISSION

How much is the entrance fee?
**Cît este taxa de intrare?**

Are there discounts for...
**Sînt reduceri pentru...**

> ...children?
> **...copii?**

> ...disabled?
> **...handicapaţi?**

> ...retirees?
> **...pensionari?**

> ...students/groups?
> **...studenţi/grupuri?**

Is the... open to the public?
**Este... deschis pentru public?**

What are the opening hours?
**Care sînt orele de funcţionare?**

When does it close?
**Cînd se închide?**

Is the ticket valid all day?
**Biletul este valabil toată ziua?**

What time is the last entry?
**Pînă la ce oră se poate intra?**

Please let me in.
**Permiteți-mi să intru, vă rog.**

## NIGHTLIFE

What is there to do in the evening?
**Ce se poate face seara?**

Can you recommend a...
**Îmi puteți recomanda...**

>>...bar?
>>**...un bar?**

>>...casino?
>>**...un cazinou?**

>>...discoteque?
>>**...o discotecă?**

>>...nightclub?
>>**...un club de noapte?**

Is there a floorshow/cabaret?
**Este un spectacol de revistă/varietăți?**

What type of music do they play?
**Ce fel de muzică se cîntă?**

How do I get there?
**Cum ajung acolo?**

What time does the show start?
**La ce oră începe spectacolul?**

Is evening dress required?
**Ținuta de seară este obligatorie?**

Is there a cover charge?
**Se plătește taxă de intrare?**

Is a reservation necessary?
**Este necesar să facem rezervare?**

I'd like a good table.
**Aș vrea o masă bună.**

## IMPRESSIONS

It's so...
**Este atît de...**

> ...beautiful.
> **...frumos.**

> ...boring.
> **...plictisitor.**

> ...interesting.
> **...interesant.**

> ...ugly.
> **...urît.**

> ...weird.
> **...ciudat.**

Wow!
**Extraordinar!**

I like it.
**Îmi place.**

I don't like it.
**Nu-mi place.**

It's good value.
**Merită banii.**

It's...
**Este...**

...amazing.
**...uimitor.**

...bizarre.
**...bizar.**

...brilliant.
**...strălucit.**

...great fun.
**...foarte amuzant.**

...magnificent.
**...minunat.**

...pretty.
**...drăguț.**

...romantic.
**...romantic.**

...stunning.
**...uluitor.**

...superb.
**...superb.**

We're interested in...
**Ne interesează...**

...antiques.
**...antichităţile.**

...archaeology.
**...arheologia.**

...art.
**...arta.**

...ceramics.
**...ceramica.**

...coins.
**...numismatica.**

...fauna.
**...fauna.**

...flora.
**...flora.**

...furniture.
**...mobila.**

...handicrafts.
**...artizanatul.**

...history.
**...istoria.**

...music.
**...muzica.**

...ornithology.
**...ornitologia.**

…painting.
**…pictura.**

…pottery.
**…olăritul.**

…religion.
**…religia.**

…sculpture.
**…sculptura.**

### SPORTS

Is there a soccer game this Saturday?
**Este vreun meci de fotbal sîmbăta aceasta?**

Which teams are playing?
**Ce echipe joacă?**

Can you get me a ticket?
**Îmi puteţi procura un bilet?**

Where's the golf course?
**Unde este terenul de golf?**

Where are the tennis courts?
**Unde sînt terenurile de tenis?**

Is it possible to go fishing around here?
**Se poate pescui în împrejurimi?**

Do I need a permit?
**Am nevoie de permis?**

What's the charge per day/hour?
**Cît se plăteşte pe zi/oră?**

# Leisure

Where can I rent...
**Unde pot închiria...**

...boots?
**...ghete?**

...equipment?
**...echipament?**

...a pair of skis?
**...o pereche de schiuri?**

...a racket?
**...o rachetă?**

...skates?
**...patine?**

Is there an aerobics class?
**Este un curs de gimnastică aerobică?**

Do you have a fitness room?
**Aveţi o sală de gimnastică?**

Can I join in?
**Pot să vin şi eu?**

Is there a swimming pool here?
**Este o piscină aici?**

I'd like to learn skiing.
**Aş vrea să învăţ să schiez.**

Are there courses for beginners?
**Exista cursuri pentru începători?**

Where can I buy a ticket?
**Unde pot cumpăra un bilet?**

When does it start?
**Cînd începe?**

When does it end?
**Cînd se termină?**

### ENTERTAINMENT

What is the best place to dance nearby?
**Care este cel mai bun loc de dans din apropiere?**

Do you want to dance?
**Doriți să dansați?**

Let's celebrate.
**Haideți să sărbătorim.**

Let's have fun.
**Haideți să ne distrăm.**

What's playing at the movies?
**Ce filme rulează la cinema?**

Is the movie dubbed/subtitled?
**Filmul este dublat sau are subtitluri?**

Is the movie in the original English?
**Filmul este în limba engleză originală?**

Who's the main actor/actress?
**Cine este actorul/actrița principal/ă?**

What's playing at the... Theater?
**Ce se joacă la Teatrul...?**

Who's the playwright?
**Cine este autorul piesei?**

Do you think I'd enjoy it?
**Credeți că mi-ar plăcea?**

Where's the opera house?
**Unde este opera?**

Who's the composer/soloist?
**Cine este compozitorul/solistul?**

Is formal dress expected?
**Trebuie să mergi în ținută de rigoare?**

Who's dancing?
**Cine dansează?**

I'm interested in contemporary dance.
**Mă interesează dansul contemporan.**

Where's the concert hall?
**Unde este sala de concerte?**

Which orchestra/band is playing?
**Ce orchestră/formație cîntă?**

What are they playing?
**Ce cîntă?**

Who's the conductor?
**Cine este dirijorul?**

I really like...
**Îmi place mult...**

...country music.
**...muzica country.**

...folk music.
**...muzica populară.**

...jazz.
**...jazul.**

...music of the '60s.
**...muzica anilor şaizeci.**

...pop/rock music.
**...muzica pop/rock.**

...rap music.
**...muzica rap.**

...soul music.
**...muzica soul.**

## IN THE COUNTRYSIDE

I'd like a map of...
**Aş vrea o hartă...**

...this region.
**...a acestei regiuni.**

...walking routes.
**...a itinerariului.**

...bicycle routes.
**...a itinerariului de biciclete.**

How far is it to...?
**Ce distanţă este pînă la...?**

Is there a trail/scenic route to...?
**Există o cărare marcată/un drum pitoresc spre...?**

Can you show me on the map?
**Îmi puteţi arăta pe hartă?**

When does the guided tour start?
**La ce oră începe turul organizat?**

When will we return?
**Cînd ne întoarcem?**

What is the hike like?
**Cum este urcuşul?**

It's...
**Este...**

       ...gentle/medium.
       **...uşor/mediu.**

       ...tough.
       **...greu.**

I'm exhausted.
**Sînt epuizat/ă.**

What kind of animal/bird is that?
**Ce fel de animal/pasăre este acela/aceea?**

What kind of flower/tree is this?
**Ce fel de floare/copac este aceasta/acesta?**

## AT THE BEACH

Is it safe to swim here?
**Se poate înota în siguranţă aici?**

Is it safe for children?
**Copiii sînt în siguranţă aici?**

Is there a lifeguard?
**Există un serviciu salvamar?**

I want to rent a...
**Vreau să închiriez...**

> ...deck chair.
> **...un şezlong.**

> ...motorboat.
> **...o barcă cu motor.**

> ...rowing boat.
> **...o barcă.**

> ...waterskis.
> **...schiuri acvatice.**

## GEOGRAPHIC FEATURES

I'd like to see a...
**Aş vrea să văd...**

> ...bridge.
> **...un pod.**

> ...cave.
> **...o peşteră.**

> ...cliff.
> **...o faleză.**

> ...farm.
> **...o fermă.**

> ...field.
> **...un cîmp.**

> ...footpath.
> **...o cărare.**

...forest.
**...o pădure.**

...hill.
**...un deal.**

...lake.
**...un lac.**

...mountain.
**...un munte.**

...mountain pass.
**...o trecătoare.**

...mountain range.
**...un lanţ muntos.**

...nature reserve.
**...o rezervaţie naturală.**

...park.
**...un parc.**

...peak.
**...un vîrf de munte.**

...picnic area.
**...un spaţiu pentru picnic.**

...pond.
**...un iaz.**

...river.
**...un rîu/fluviu.**

...sea.
**...o mare.**

...stream.
**...un pîrîu.**

...valley.
**...o vale.**

...village.
**...un sat.**

...vineyard.
**...o podgorie.**

...waterfall.
**...o cascadă.**

## Shops, Stores, and Services

### OPENING HOURS

When does… open/close?
**Cînd se deschide/închide…?**

Are you open in the evening?
**Este deschis seara?**

Do you close for lunch?
**Închideţi la ora prînzului?**

Where is…?
**Unde este…?**

It's on the first/second floor.
**Este la etajul unu/doi.**

### GENERAL EXPRESSIONS

Where is…
**Unde este…**

>    …an antique shop?
>    **…un magazin de antichităţi?**
>
>    …an art gallery?
>    **…o galerie de artă?**
>
>    …a bakery?
>    **…o brutărie?**
>
>    …a bank?
>    **…o bancă?**
>
>    …a barber shop?
>    **…o frizerie?**

...a beauty salon?
**...un salon de coafură?**

...a bookstore?
**...o librărie?**

...a camera shop?
**...un magazin foto?**

...a department store?
**...un magazin universal?**

...a dry cleaner?
**...o curățătorie chimică?**

...a grocery store?
**...o băcănie?**

...a jewelry shop?
**...un magazin de bijuterii?**

...a laundromat?
**...o spălătorie?**

...a library?
**...o bibliotecă?**

...a market?
**...o piață?**

...a newsstand?
**...un chioșc de ziare?**

...an optician?
**...un optician?**

...a pharmacy?
**...o farmacie?**

# Shops, Stores, and Services

...a post office?
**...un oficiu poştal?**

...a shopping mall?
**...un centru comercial?**

...a supermarket?
**...un magazin cu autoservire?**

...a toy store?
**...un magazin de jucării?**

...a travel agency?
**...o agenţie de voiaj?**

...a wine shop?
**...un magazin de vinuri?**

How do I get to...?
**Cum ajung la...?**

Can you help me?
**Mă puteţi ajuta?**

We're just looking.
**Vrem doar să ne uitam.**

I want...
**Vreau...**

Do you have...?
**Aveţi...?**

Can you show me...
**Îmi puteţi arăta...**

...this?
**...pe acesta?**

...that one?
**...pe acela?**

...that one over there?
**...pe acela/aceea de acolo?**

...the one in the window?
**...pe cel/cea din vitrină?**

I don't want anything too expensive.
**Nu vreau ceva prea scump.**

Can you show me something...
**Îmi puteţi arăta ceva...**

    ...better?
    **...mai bun?**

    ...cheaper?
    **...mai ieftin?**

    ...larger?
    **...mai mare?**

    ...smaller?
    **...mai mic?**

How much is this?
**Cît costă ace(a)sta?**

How much are they?
**Cît costă aceştia/acestea?**

I'll take it.
**Îl/o iau.**

No, I don't like it.
**Nu, nu-mi place.**

Can you order it for me?
**Mi-l/mi-o puteţi comanda?**

How long will it take?
**Cît timp va dura?**

Please send it to this address.
**Vă rog să-l/s-o trimiteți la această adresă.**

Can I pay by credit card?
**Pot plăti cu cartea de credit?**

Do you accept American dollars?
**Acceptați dolari americani?**

Can you please exchange this?
**Puteți vă rog schimba acest articol?**

I'd like to return this.
**Vreau să dau înapoi acest articol.**

Here's the receipt.
**Poftiți bonul.**

Can I see more?
**Pot să mai văd și altele?**

This one.
**Ace(a)sta.**

Can I try it on?
**Îl/o pot încerca?**

A mirror?
**O oglindă?**

Machine washable?
**Se spală la mașină?**

Will it shrink?
**Intră la apă?**

Can you ship this?
**Îl/o puteți expedia?**

Tax-free?
**Scutit de taxă?**

Is that your lowest price?
**Acesta este ultimul dumneavoastră preţ?**

My last offer.
**Ultima mea ofertă.**

## Repairs and Cleaning

This is broken.
**Ace(a)sta este stricat/ă.**

Can you fix it?
**Îl/o puteţi repara?**

How much will it cost?
**Cît o să coste?**

When will it be ready?
**Cînd va fi gata?**

I need it by...
**Îmi trebuie pînă la...**

I'd like this cleaned/pressed.
**Aş vrea să-mi curăţaţi/călcaţi acest articol.**

This doesn't work.
**Ace(a)sta nu merge (funcţionează).**

Can you exchange this, please?
**Puteţi schimba ace(a)sta, vă rog?**

I'd like a refund.
**Vreau să-mi restituiţi banii.**

## Shops, Stores, and Services

### NEWSSTAND, BOOKSTORE, AND STATIONERY

Do you sell English language books/newspapers?
**Vindeţi cărţi/ziare in limba engleză?**

I'd like a...
**Aş vrea...**

> ...box of matches.
> **...o cutie de chibrituri.**

> ...lighter.
> **...o brichetă.**

> ...magazine.
> **...o revistă.**

> ...map of the town.
> **...o hartă a oraşului.**

> ...postcard.
> **...o carte poştală.**

I'm interested in...
**Mă interesează...**

> ...art books.
> **...cărţi de artă.**

> ...geography.
> **...geografia.**

> ...phrasebooks.
> **...ghiduri de conversaţie.**

> ...tourist guides.
> **...ghiduri turistice.**

> ...travel books.
> **...cărţi de călătorie.**

Where's the nearest stationery store?
**Unde este papetăria cea mai apropiată?**

I need...
**Îmi trebuie...**

...a calculator.
**...un calculator.**

...a notebook.
**...un caiet.**

...a pen.
**...un stilou.**

...a pencil.
**...un creion.**

...writing paper.
**...hîrtie de scris.**

## SOUVENIRS AND ARTS AND CRAFTS

Where can I buy...
**Unde pot cumpăra...**

...antiques?
**...antichităţi?**

...ceramics?
**...(obiecte de) ceramică?**

...a CD of Romanian music?
**...un disc compact cu muzică românească?**

...glassware?
**...sticlărie?**

...knitwear?
**...articole tricotate de mînă?**

...leatherwork?
**...obiecte de piele?**

...needlework?
**...lucru de mînă?**

...paintings?
**...tablouri?**

...porcelain?
**...porţelanuri?**

...silk?
**...articole de mătase?**

...toys?
**...jucării?**

...a vase?
**...o vază?**

...a video about Romanian church architecture?
**...o casetă video despre arhitectura bis-
ericească din România?**

...watercolors?
**...acuarele?**

...woodwork?
**...sculptură în lemn?**

How old is this?
**Ce vechime are acest obiect?**

Can you ship it to me?
**Mi-l/mi-o puteți expedia?**

Will I have problems with customs?
**Voi avea dificultăți la vamă?**

Is there a certificate of authenticity?
**Îmi puteți da un certificat de autenticitate?**

## PHOTOGRAPHY

How much does it cost to process this film?
**Cît costă developatul acestui film?**

When will it be ready?
**Cînd va fi gata?**

I'd like film for this camera.
**Aș vrea un film pentru acest aparat.**

Would you enlarge this, please?
**Vreți să măriți poza aceasta, vă rog?**

I want a...
**Vreau...**

> ...battery.
> **...o baterie.**

> ...color film.
> **...un film color.**

> ...filter.
> **...un filtru.**

> ...lens.
> **...o lentilă.**

# Shops, Stores, and Services

## PHARMACY

Where's the nearest pharmacy?
**Unde este farmacia cea mai apropiată?**

Would it be open now?
**Este deschisă acum?**

What would you recommend for...?
**Ce ați recomanda pentru...?**

I need something for...
**Îmi trebuie ceva pentru...**

> ...a cold.
> **...răceală.**

> ...a cough.
> **...tuse.**

> ...fever.
> **...febră.**

> ...headache.
> **...migrenă.**

> ...an insect bite.
> **...o înțepătură de insecte.**

> ...sunburn.
> **...arsuri de soare.**

> ...toothache.
> **...nevralgie.**

> ...an upset stomach.
> **...deranjament la stomac.**

Can you make up this prescription for me?
**Îmi puteți prepara această rețetă?**

I need...
**Am nevoie de...**

> ...an aspirin.
> **...o aspirină.**

> ...contraceptives.
> **...anticoncepționale.**

> ...cough drops.
> **...picături pentru tuse.**

> ...some disinfectant.
> **...un dezinfectant.**

> ...ear drops.
> **...picături pentru urechi.**

> ...eye drops.
> **...picături pentru ochi.**

> ...insect repellent.
> **...sprei contra insectelor.**

> ...iodine.
> **...iod.**

> ...laxative.
> **...laxativ.**

> ...nose drops.
> **...picături pentru nas.**

> ...sanitary napkins.
> **...tampoane igienice.**

...sleeping pills.
**...somnifere.**

...a thermometer.
**...un termometru.**

...tranquilizers.
**...tranchilizante.**

...vitamins.
**...vitamine.**

## TOILETRIES

I'd like...
**Aş vrea...**

...after-shave lotion.
**...loţiune după ras.**

...bath tissue.
**...hîrtie igienică.**

...condoms.
**...prezervative.**

...a deodorant.
**...un deodorant.**

...face powder.
**...pudră de faţă.**

...hair spray.
**...sprei pentru păr.**

...hand cream.
**...cremă pentru mîini.**

...lipstick.
**...ruj de buze.**

...a nail file.
**...o pilă de unghii.**

...perfume.
**...parfum.**

...an electric razor.
**...un aparat de ras electric.**

...razor blades.
**...lame de ras.**

...shampoo.
**...şampon.**

...shaving cream.
**...cremă de ras.**

...soap.
**...săpun.**

...suntan cream/lotion.
**...cremă de bronzat.**

...a toothbrush.
**...o periuţă de dinţi.**

...toothpaste.
**...pastă de dinţi.**

## CLOTHES AND ACCESSORIES

I'd like...
**Aş vrea...**

...a bathing suit.
**...un costum de baie.**

...a bathrobe.
**...un halat de baie.**

...a belt.
**...un cordon/o curea.**

...a blouse.
**...o bluză.**

...a bra.
**...un sutien.**

...a button.
**...un nasture.**

...a coat.
**...o jachetă.**

...a dress.
**...o rochie.**

...gloves.
**...mănuşi.**

...a handbag.
**...o poşetă.**

...a handkerchief.
**...o batistă.**

...a hat.
**...o pălărie.**

...a jacket.
**...o jachetă.**

...jeans.
**...blugi.**

...pajamas.
**...o pijama.**

…panties.
**…chiloți de damă.**

…pants.
**…pantaloni.**

…a raincoat.
**…o manta de ploaie.**

…a scarf.
**…un fular.**

…a shirt.
**…o cămașă.**

…shorts.
**…un șort.**

…a skirt.
**…o fustă.**

…a slip.
**…un combinezon.**

…stockings.
**…ciorapi.**

…a suit.
**…un costum.**

…a sweater.
**…un pulovăr.**

…a swimsuit.
**…un costum de baie.**

…a tie.
**…o cravată.**

...a T-shirt.
**...un tricou.**

...an umbrella.
**...o umbrelă.**

...underwear.
**...lenjerie de corp (intimă).**

...a zipper.
**...un fermoar.**

What color did you want?
**Ce culoare doriți?**

I prefer something in...
**Prefer ceva de culoare...**

...beige.
**...bej.**

...black.
**...neagră.**

...blue.
**...albastră.**

...brown.
**...maro.**

...gray.
**...gri.**

...green.
**...verde.**

...orange.
**...portocalie.**

...pink.
**...roz.**

...purple.
**...mov.**

...red.
**...roşie.**

...silver.
**...argintie.**

...turquoise.
**...turcoaz.**

...white.
**...albă.**

...yellow.
**...galbenă.**

I want a lighter/darker shade.
**Vreau o nuanţă mai deschisă/închisă.**

Do you have the same in gray?
**Îl/o aveţi şi pe gri?**

I want something to match this.
**Vreau ceva care să se asorteze cu ace(a)sta.**

I don't like the color.
**Nu-mi place culoarea.**

Do you have any better quality?
**Aveţi ceva de calitate mai bună?**

I want something for a 7-year old boy/girl.
**Vreau ceva pentru un băieţel/o fetiţă de şapte ani.**

# Shops, Stores, and Services

Is it...
**Este...**

...machine washable?
**...lavabil la maşină?**

...pure (virgin) wool?
**...lînă pură?**

...synthetic?
**...sintetic?**

...wrinkle resistant?
**...neşifonabil?**

I take American size 12.
**Port măsura doisprezece americană.**

I don't know Romanian sizes.
**Nu cunosc măsurile româneşti.**

Could you measure me?
**Mă puteţi măsura?**

Can I try it on?
**Îl/o pot încerca?**

It fits very well.
**Se potriveşte foarte bine.**

It doesn't fit.
**Nu se potriveşte.**

It's too...
**Este prea...**

...tight.
**...strîmt/ă.**

...loose.
**...larg/ă.**

...short.
**...scurt/ă.**

...long.
**...lung/ă.**

Can you have it altered?
**Îl/o puteţi modifica?**

How long will it take?
**Cît timp durează?**

What size is this?
**Ce măsură este ace(a)sta?**

Do you have this in size...?
**Aveţi asta în măsura...?**

## SHOES

I need a pair of...
**Îmi trebuie o pereche de...**

...sandals.
**...sandale.**

...shoes.
**...pantofi.**

...slippers.
**...papuci.**

These are too...
**Aceştia sînt prea...**

...small/large.
**...mici/mari.**

...wide/narrow.
**...largi/strîmţi.**

Do you have the same in brown?
**Aveţi şi de culoare maro?**

Is this genuine leather?
**Este piele veritabilă?**

Can you repair these shoes?
**Puteţi repara aceşti pantofi?**

I need them as soon as possible.
**Îmi trebuie cît se poate de repede.**

## GROCERY

I'd like a loaf of bread.
**Aş vrea o pîine.**

I'd like also some of this cheese.
**Aş vrea puţin şi din brînza aceasta.**

I also need...
**Îmi mai trebuie...**

> ...a kilo (two pounds) of apples.
> **...un kilogram de mere.**

> ...a half a kilo (one pound) of tomatoes.
> **...o jumătate de kilogram de roşii.**

> ...a liter (quart) of milk.
> **...un litru de lapte.**

> ...a dozen eggs.
> **...o duzină de ouă.**

> ...a kilo (two pounds) of flour.
> **...un kilogram de făină.**

> ...tea/coffee/sugar.
> **...ceai/cafea/zahăr.**

...100 grams (3.5 ounces, one third of a pound)
of butter.
**...o sută de grame de unt.**

...a kilo (two pounds) of onions.
**...un kilogram de ceapă.**

...some carrots.
**...nişte morcovi.**

...some heads of garlic.
**...nişte căpăţîni de usturoi.**

...a can of cola.
**...o cutie de coca cola.**

...a bottle of olive oil.
**...o sticlă de ulei de măsline.**

...a jar of jam.
**...un borcan de gem.**

...a can of tomato sauce/paste.
**...o cutie de sos/pastă de roşii.**

...a tube of mustard.
**...un tub de muştar.**

...a box of chocolate.
**...o cutie de ciocolată.**

...a bottle of wine.
**...o sticlă de vin.**

Anything else?
**Mai doriţi ceva?**

That's all, thanks.
**Asta-i tot, mulţumesc.**

### ELECTRICAL APPLIANCES

I'd like…
**Aş vrea…**

> …an adaptor.
> **…un adaptor.**

> …a bulb.
> **…un bec.**

> …a CD (compact disc).
> **…un disc compact.**

> …a clock radio.
> **…un radio cu ceas.**

> …an extension cord
> **…un (cablu) prelungitor.**

> …a fan.
> **…un ventilator.**

> …a hair dryer.
> **…un uscător de păr.**

> …an iron.
> **…un fier de călcat.**

> …a tape recorder.
> **…un casetofon.**

> …a portable TV.
> **…un televizor portabil.**

> …a video player.
> **…un videocasetofon.**

...a videotape.
**...o casetă video.**

...a transformer.
**...un transformator de curent.**

## JEWELRY

I need...
**Am nevoie de...**

...an alarm clock.
**...un ceas deşteptător.**

...a bracelet.
**...o brăţară.**

...a brooch in silver.
**...o broşă de argint.**

...a chain in gold.
**...un lanţ de aur.**

...a cross in silver.
**...o cruce de argint.**

...a digital watch.
**...un ceas digital.**

...earrings.
**...cercei.**

...an engagement ring.
**...un inel de logodnă.**

...a jewel box.
**...o cutie de bijuterii.**

...a necklace.
**...un colier.**

...a pearl.
**...o perlă.**

...a ring.
**...un inel.**

...a tie clip.
**...un ac de cravată.**

...a wedding ring.
**...o verighetă.**

This is...
**Acesta este...**

...alabaster/amethyst.
**...alabastru/ametist.**

...copper/coral.
**...cupru/coral.**

...crystal/diamond.
**...cristal/diamant.**

...emerald/enamel.
**...smarald/email.**

...gold/ivory.
**...aur/fildeş.**

...platinum/ruby.
**...platină/rubin.**

...sapphire/silver.
**...safir/argint.**

…stainless steel.
**…oțel inoxidabil.**

…topaz/turquoise.
**…topaz/peruzea.**

Could I see that?
**Pot să-l/s-o vad?**

It's in the window.
**Este în vitrină.**

## OPTICIAN

I've broken my glasses.
**Mi-am spart ochelarii.**

Can you repair these glasses?
**Puteți repara acești ochelari?**

Can you repair this frame?
**Puteți repara această ramă?**

Can you change the lenses?
**Puteți înlocui lentilele?**

I need new lenses.
**Îmi trebuie lentile noi.**

When will they be ready?
**Cînd vor fi gata?**

I've lost one of my contact lenses.
**Mi-am pierdut o lentilă de contact.**

Could you give me a replacement?
**Mi-ați putea-o înlocui?**

I'd like to buy a pair of binoculars.
**Aș vrea să cumpăr un binoclu.**

### HAIRDRESSER

I'd like a...
**Vreau un...**

> ...cut.
> **...tuns.**

> ...cut and blow-dry.
> **...tuns şi uscat cu fenul.**

> ...shampoo and set.
> **...spălat şi permanent.**

> ...trim.
> **...tuns potrivit.**

I'd like my hair permed.
**Vreau să-mi faceţi permanent.**

Don't cut it too short.
**Nu-l scurtaţi prea mult.**

A little more off the...
**Mai luaţi puţin din...**

> ...back/front.
> **...spate/faţă.**

> ...sides.
> **...părţi.**

> ...top.
> **...vîrf.**

### IN CASE OF EMERGENCY

Where is the nearest police station?
**Unde este circa de poliţie cea mai apropiată?**

Does anyone here speak English?
**Vorbeşte cineva de aici englezeşte?**

---

I want to report...
**Vreau să anunţ...**

    ...an accident/attack.
    **...un accident/atac.**

    ...a mugging/rape.
    **...o agresiune/un viol.**

My son/daughter is missing.
**Fiul/fiica mea a dispărut.**

Here's a photo of him/her.
**Iată o fotografie a lui/a ei.**

I need an English-speaking lawyer.
**Am nevoie de un avocat care vorbeşte englezeşte.**

I need to make a phone call.
**Trebuie să dau un telefon.**

I want to report a theft/break-in.
**Vreau să declar un furt/o spargere.**

My car's been broken into.
**Maşina mea a fost prădată.**

My camera/credit card/passport/watch/wallet has been
    stolen
**Mi s-a furat aparatul foto/cartea de credit/paşaportul/
    ceasul/portmoneul.**

I've been ripped off.
**Am fost jefuit.**

Help me!
**Ajutaţi-mă!**

Help!
**Ajutor!**

Emergency.
**Urgenţă.**

There's been an accident.
**A avut loc un accident.**

Call the doctor.
**Chemaţi un doctor.**

Call the ambulance.
**Chemaţi salvarea.**

Is anyone hurt?
**Este cineva rănit?**

Don't move!
**Nu vă mişcaţi!**

Get help quickly!
**Chemaţi repede în ajutor!**

Call the police.
**Chemaţi poliţia.**

My possessions are insured.
**Am bunurile asigurate.**

I didn't do it.
**Nu am făcut-o eu.**

I'm sorry.
**Îmi pare rău.**

I apologize.
**Vă rog să mă iertaţi.**

I didn't realize anything was wrong.
**Nu mi-am dat seama că fac ceva greşit.**

I want to contact my embassy/consulate.
**Vreau să iau legătura cu ambasada/consulatul.**

## Finance and Money

### AT THE BANK

Where's the nearest bank?
**Unde este banca cea mai apropiată?**

Where can I change some money?
**Unde pot schimba niște bani?**

I want to change some dollars.
**Vreau să schimb (niște) dolari.**

What's the exchange rate?
**Care este cursul de schimb?**

What is the commission?
**Cît este comisionul?**

I want to cash a travelers check.
**Vreau să încasez un cec de călătorie.**

Can I get a cash advance on my credit card?
**Pot obține numerar cu cartea de credit?**

I'd like to open a temporary account.
**Aș vrea să deschid un cont temporar.**

I'd like to transfer a sum of money from my bank account
in New York.
**Aș vrea să transfer o sumă din contul meu din New York.**

I'd like to withdraw $100 in Romanian lei from my
account.
**Aș vrea să retrag o sută de dolari în lei din contul meu.**

Do you have a calculator?
**Aveți un calculator?**

Could you please check that again?
**Ați putea verifica din nou, vă rog?**

## Communications

### AT THE POST OFFICE

Where is the post office?
**Unde este oficiul poştal?**

What time does the post office open/close?
**La ce oră se deschide/închide oficiul poştal?**

Where is the mailbox?
**Unde este cutia de scrisori?**

What's the postage for a letter to the United States?
**Cît costă timbrul pentru o scrisoare în Statele Unite?**

A stamp for this letter/postcard, please.
**Un timbru pentru această scrisoare/carte poştală, vă rog.**

I'd like to send this parcel by...
**Vreau să trimit coletul acesta...**

> ...airmail.
> **...par avion.**

> ...express mail.
> **...expres.**

> ...insured mail.
> **...cu asigurare.**

> ...registered mail.
> **...recomandat.**

How long would it take for this to get there?
**În cît timp va ajunge ace(a)sta la destinaţie?**

I would like some stamps.
**Aş vrea nişte timbre.**

I'd like to rent a post office box.
**Aş vrea să închiriez o căsuţă poştala.**

I'd like a money order for 100,000 lei.
**Aş vrea un mandat poştal pentru o sută de mii lei.**

## TELEPHONING

Where is the telephone?
**Unde este telefonul?**

Where can I rent a cell phone?
**Unde pot închiria un telefon celular?**

Can I telephone from here?
**Pot telefona de aici?**

May I use your phone?
**Pot folosi telefonul dumneavoastră?**

Can you help me get this number?
**Mă puteţi ajuta să obţin acest număr?**

I'd like to place a person-to-person call.
**Aş vrea să fac o convorbire particulară.**

I would like to make a phone call.
**Aş vrea să fac o convorbire telefonică.**

Hello! This is....
**Alo! Aici e...**

I want to speak to...
**Vreau să vorbesc cu...**

# Communications

Would you please take a message?
**Pot să vă las un mesaj, vă rog?**

The line is busy.
**Linia este ocupată.**

There's no answer.
**Nu răspunde (nimeni).**

I've been cut off.
**Am fost întrerupt/ă.**

Wait a moment.
**Așteptați o clipă.**

Don't hang up.
**Nu închideți.**

Can I dial direct?
**Pot să chem direct?**

My number is...
**Numărul meu este...**

What is the code for...?
**Care este prefixul pentru...?**

What is the international code?
**Care este prefixul internațional?**

The number is...
**Numărul este...**

The extension is...
**Interiorul este...**

Just a moment, please.
**O clipă, vă rog.**

Hold on, please.
**Staţi pe fir, vă rog.**

Do you have a telephone book?
**Aveţi o carte de telefon?**

Where is the nearest pay-phone?
**Unde este cel mai apropiat telefon public?**

The telephone is out of service.
**Telefonul este defect.**

I'd like to send a fax.
**Aş vrea să trimit un fax.**

I want to pay for the call.
**Vreau să plătesc pentru convorbire.**

## INTERNET

I'd like to send a message by E-mail.
**Aş vrea să trimit un mesaj prin poşta electronică.**

What's your E-mail address?
**Care este adresa dumneavoastră de poştă electronică?**

Can I access the Internet here?
**Pot accesa reţeaua Internet aici?**

What are the charges per hour?
**Cît se plăteşte pe oră?**

How do I log on?
**Cum intru pe Internet?**

Can you recommend a local Internet company?
**Îmi puteţi recomanda o companie locală de Internet?**

## Communications

I'd like to open a temporary E-mail account.
**Aş vrea să deschid un cont E-mail temporar.**

Do I have unlimited access?
**Am acces nelimitat?**

I'd like to have this picture scanned and attached to my
  E-mail message.
**Aş vrea să scanez această poză şi s-o trimit ca anexă la
  mesajul electronic.**

I'd like to send/print/delete this message.
**Aş vrea să trimit/tipăresc/şterg acest mesaj.**

## THE CONFERENCE

Can we go to the conference room?
**Putem merge în sala de conferinţe?**

Who's the guest speaker?
**Cine este invitatul?**

Here's a copy of the paper.
**Iată un exemplar din lucrare.**

There will be discussion after the lecture.
**Conferinţa va fi urmată de discuţii.**

What is the subject of today's talk?
**Care este subiectul prelegerii de astăzi?**

## Health and Medical Aid

### GENERAL EXPRESSIONS

What's the trouble?
**Ce vă supără?**

I am sick.
**Sînt bolnav/ă.**

How long have you been feeling sick?
**De cînd nu vă simţiţi bine?**

Where does it hurt?
**Unde vă doare?**

It hurts here.
**Mă doare aici.**

I've been vomiting.
**Am vomat.**

I feel dizzy.
**Am vertij.**

I can't eat.
**Nu am poftă de mîncare.**

I can't sleep.
**Nu pot dormi.**

I feel worse.
**Mă simt mai rău.**

I feel better.
**Mă simt mai bine.**

May I see a doctor?
**Mă poate consulta un doctor?**

# Health and Medical Aid

I'm pregnant.
**Sînt însărcinată.**

Is it serious?
**Este ceva serios (grav)?**

I've missed a period.
**Menstruaţia întîrzie.**

Could the doctor come and see me here?
**Ar putea veni doctorul să mă consulte aici?**

## PARTS OF THE BODY

| | |
|---|---|
| appendix | **apendice** |
| arm | **braţ** |
| artery | **arteră** |
| back | **spate** |
| bladder | **vezica urinară** |
| bone | **os** |
| bowels | **intestine** |
| breast | **sîn** |
| chest | **piept** |
| ear | **ureche** |
| eye | **ochi** |
| face | **faţă** |
| finger | **deget** |
| foot | **picior** |
| genitals | **organe genitale** |
| gland | **glandă** |
| head | **cap** |
| heart | **inimă** |
| intestines | **intestine** |
| jaw | **maxilar** |
| joint | **articulaţie** |
| kidney | **rinichi** |
| knee | **genunchi** |
| leg | **picior** |
| lip | **buză** |

| liver | ficat |
| lung | plămîn |
| mouth | gură |
| muscle | muşchi |
| neck | gît |
| nerve | nerv |
| nose | nas |
| penis | penis |
| rib | coastă |
| shoulder | umăr |
| skin | piele |
| spine | coloana vertebrală |
| stomach | stomac |
| tendon | tendon |
| throat | esofag |
| toe | călcîi |
| tongue | limbă |
| tonsils | amigdale |
| vagina | vagin |
| vein | venă |
| wrist | încheietura mîinii |

## ACCIDENTS AND INJURIES

Help!
**Ajutor!**

There's someone drowning.
**Cineva se îneacă.**

I'm having a heart attack.
**Am un atac de cord.**

Call an ambulance, please.
**Chemaţi salvarea, vă rog.**

He/she is bleeding heavily.
**El/ea are hemoragie puternică.**

He/she is unconscious.
**El/ea şi-a pierdut cunoştinţa.**

My child has hurt his head.
**Copilul meu s-a lovit la cap.**

He's seriously injured.
**El s-a rănit grav.**

She can't move her arm.
**Ea nu-şi poate mişca braţul.**

I'm afraid I have food poisoning.
**Mă tem că am o intoxicaţie alimentară.**

I've been stung by a bee.
**M-a înţepat o albină.**

I've been bitten by a dog/snake.
**M-a muşcat un cîine/şarpe.**

My child ingested poison.
**Copilul meu a înghiţit otravă.**

I am experiencing shortness of breath, sweating and
weakness.
**Am dificultăţi de respiraţie, transpir şi am o stare de
slăbiciune.**

This person choked and cannot speak.
**Această persoană s-a sufocat şi nu poate vorbi.**

He has suffered broken bones.
**El are oasele fracturate.**

I scalded my hands with boiling water.
**Mi-am opărit mîinile cu apă fiartă.**

I've got a...
**Am...**

      ...boil.
      **...un furuncul.**

      ...bruise.
      **...o contuzie.**

      ...burn.
      **...o arsură.**

      ...cut.
      **...o tăietură**

      ...rash.
      **...o iritaţie.**

      ...strained muscle.
      **...o întindere de muşchi.**

      ...swelling.
      **...o umflătură.**

      ...wound.
      **...o rană.**

## SYMPTOMS AND CONDITIONS

I feel faint/feverish/shivery.
**Am o stare de slăbiciune/febră/frisoane.**

I've got diarrhea.
**Am diaree.**

I have...
**Am...**

      ...an allergy.
      **...o alergie.**

...cramps.
**...crampe.**

...fever.
**...febră.**

...an infection.
**...o infecţie.**

...an itch.
**...o iritaţie.**

...a temperature.
**...temperatură.**

I have a cold.
**Am o răceală.**

I have a cough.
**Tuşesc.**

I have a headache.
**Am o migrenă.**

I have a toothache.
**Am o nevralgie.**

I have a sore throat.
**Mă doare în gît.**

I have a stomach ache.
**Mă doare stomacul.**

I have a backache.
**Mă doare spatele.**

I have constipation.
**Sînt constipat/ă.**

I have a heart condition.
**Am o afecţiune cardiacă.**

I've got…
**Am…**

…high blood pressure.
**…tensiune ridicată.**

…low blood pressure.
**…tensiune scăzută.**

…indigestion.
**…indigestie.**

…palpitations.
**…palpitații.**

…rheumatism.
**…reumatism.**

…sunstroke.
**…insolație.**

I'm allergic to…
**Sînt alergic la…**

…cats.
**…pisici.**

…dust.
**…praf.**

…insect bites.
**…înțepături de insecte.**

…penicillin.
**…penicilină.**

…pollen.
**…polen.**

### DISEASES

| | |
|---|---|
| AIDS | **sida** |
| anxiety | **nevroză anxioasă** |
| appendicitis | **apendicită** |
| arteriosclerosis | **ateroscleroză** |
| arthritis | **artrită** |
| asthma | **astmă** |
| cancer | **cancer** |
| cholera | **holeră** |
| cold | **răceală** |
| cystitis | **cistită** |
| depression | **depresiune nervoasă** |
| diabetes | **diabet zaharat** |
| flu | **gripă** |
| hepatitis | **hepatită** |
| jaundice | **icter** |
| kidney stone | **calculi renali** |
| phobia | **fobie** |
| pneumonia | **pneumonie** |
| prostatitis | **prostată** |
| rheumatism | **reumatism** |
| ulcer | **ulcer** |
| venereal disease | **boală venerică** |

### DOCTOR

I need a doctor, quickly.
**Am nevoie urgent de un doctor.**

Can you get me a doctor?
**Puteți chema un doctor?**

Can you recommend a(n)...
**Îmi puteți recomanda un...**

    ...acupuncturist?
    **...specialist în acupunctură?**

...anesthesiologist?
**...anestezist?**

...cardiologist?
**...cardiolog?**

...gynecologist?
**...ginecolog?**

...internist?
**...internist?**

...neurologist?
**...neurolog?**

...ophthalmologist?
**...oftalmolog?**

...pediatrician?
**...pediatru?**

...psychiatrist?
**...psihiatru?**

...surgeon?
**...chirurg?**

...urologist?
**...urolog?**

Can I have an appointment...
**Pot fixa o oră de consultaţie...**

...for today?
**...pentru astăzi?**

...for tomorrow?
**...pentru mîine?**

...as soon as possible?
**...cît se poate de repede?**

# Health and Medical Aid

I am not feeling well.
**Nu mă simt bine.**

I feel very tired.
**Mă simt foarte obosit/ă.**

I have difficulty urinating.
**Urinez cu dificultate.**

I have a nosebleed.
**Am hemoragie nazală.**

I feel a squeezing pain in my chest.
**Mă apasă o durere în piept.**

It's a dull/stabbing/constant pain.
**E o durere surdă/ascuţită/permanentă.**

Is it infected?
**E infectat?**

I need a painkiller.
**Am nevoie de un calmant.**

This is the first time I've had this.
**Este prima dată cînd am aşa ceva.**

I have been feeling like this for a week.
**Mă simt astfel de o săptămînă.**

## GYNECOLOGIST

I'm on the pill.
**Iau pilule anticoncepţionale.**

I haven't had my period for two months.
**Nu am mai avut menstruaţie de două luni.**

I am four months pregnant.
**Sînt însărcinată în luna a patra.**

I have menstrual cramps.
**Am dureri de menstruație.**

I have a vaginal infection.
**Am o infecție vaginală.**

## Dentist

This tooth hurts.
**Dintele acesta mă doare.**

I don't want it extracted, if possible.
**Dacă e posibil nu aș vrea să mi-l scoateți.**

The gum is very sore.
**Gingia mă doare foarte tare.**

The gum bleeds here in front.
**Gingia sîngerează aici în față.**

Could you give me an anesthetic?
**Mi-ați putea da un anestezic?**

I've lost a filling.
**Mi-a căzut o plombă.**

Can you fix it temporarily?
**Puteți s-o tratați provizoriu?**

Don't eat anything for... hours.
**Nu mîncați nimic... ore.**

## Ophthalmologist

I'd like to have my eyesight checked.
**Aș vrea să fac un control ocular.**

I'm nearsighted/farsighted.
**Sînt miop/presbit.**

I have low vision.
**Nu văd prea bine. (Am vederea slabă).**

My eyesight isn't good.
**Nu am vederea bună.**

I've got something in my eye.
**Mi-a intrat ceva în ochi.**

How much do I owe you?
**Cît vă datorez?**

## PRESCRIPTION AND TREATMENT

Can you give me a prescription for this?
**Îmi puteţi da o reţetă pentru aceasta?**

I am taking this medicine.
**Iau medicamentul acesta.**

How do I take this medicine?
**Cum trebuie să iau acest medicament?**

So I'll take one pill with a glass of water...
**Deci voi lua o pilulă cu un pahar de apă...**

...three times a day.
**...de trei ori pe zi.**

...before/after each meal.
**...înainte/după fiecare masă.**

I don't tolerate drugs.
**Nu suport medicamentele.**

I'm allergic to antibiotics.
**Sînt alergic la antibiotice.**

Can you prescribe a sleeping pill or a tranquilizer?
**Îmi puteţi prescrie un somnifer sau un tranchilizant?**

I need medication for...
**Îmi trebuie medicamente pentru...**

How many times a day must I take it?
**De cîte ori pe zi trebuie să-l iau?**

When should I stop?
**Cînd trebuie să întrerup?**

I have been vaccinated.
**Sînt vaccinat/ă.**

Is it possible for me to travel?
**Pot să călătoresc?**

## HOSPITAL

What are the visiting hours?
**Care sînt orele de vizitare?**

When will the doctor come to see me?
**Cînd va veni doctorul să mă vadă?**

I'm in pain.
**Am dureri.**

He's had a blood transfusion.
**I s-a făcut o transfuzie.**

He's had leg surgery.
**A fost operat la picior.**

Where is the nurse?
**Unde este infirmiera?**

She gave me an injection.
**Mi-a făcut o injecție.**

# Health and Medical Aid

### Payment and Insurance

How much do I owe you?
**Cît vă datorez?**

I have insurance.
**Am asigurare.**

Can I have a receipt for my health insurance?
**Îmi puteți da o chitanță pentru asigurare?**

Would you fill in this health insurance form, please?
**Vreți să completați formularul acesta de asigurare, vă rog?**

Can I have a medical certificate?
**Îmi puteți elibera un certificat medical?**

# Appendix

## MONTHS AND DAYS

| | |
|---|---|
| January | **ianuarie** |
| February | **februarie** |
| March | **martie** |
| April | **aprilie** |
| May | **mai** |
| June | **iunie** |
| July | **iulie** |
| August | **august** |
| September | **septembrie** |
| October | **octombrie** |
| November | **noiembrie** |
| December | **decembrie** |

| | |
|---|---|
| Monday | **luni** |
| Tuesday | **marţi** |
| Wednesday | **miercuri** |
| Thursday | **joi** |
| Friday | **vineri** |
| Saturday | **sîmbătă** |
| Sunday | **duminică** |

## WEIGHTS AND MEASURES

| | |
|---|---|
| gram | **gram** |
| kilogram | **kilogram** |
| pound | **livră** |
| ton | **tonă** |
| millimiter | **milimetru** |
| centimeter | **centimetru** |
| decimeter | **decimetru** |
| meter | **metru** |
| kilometer | **kilometru** |
| square kilometer | **kilometru pătrat** |
| hectare | **hectar** |

# Appendix

| | |
|---|---|
| acre | **acru** |
| square meter | **metru pătrat** |
| cubic meter | **metru cub** |
| hectoliter | **hectolitru** |
| liter | **litru** |

## CARDINAL NUMBERS

| | |
|---|---|
| 0 | **zero** |
| 1 | **unu, una** |
| 2 | **doi, două** |
| 3 | **trei** |
| 4 | **patru** |
| 5 | **cinci** |
| 6 | **şase** |
| 7 | **şapte** |
| 8 | **opt** |
| 9 | **nouă** |
| 10 | **zece** |
| 11 | **unsprezece** |
| 12 | **doisprezece, douăsprezece** |
| 13 | **treisprezece** |
| 14 | **paisprezece** |
| 15 | **cincisprezece** |
| 16 | **şaisprezece** |
| 17 | **şaptesprezece** |
| 18 | **optsprezece** |
| 19 | **nouăsprezece** |
| 20 | **douăzeci** |
| 21 | **douăzeci şi unu** |
| 22 | **douăzeci şi doi** |
| 30 | **treizeci** |
| 40 | **patruzeci** |
| 50 | **cincizeci** |
| 60 | **şaizeci** |
| 70 | **şaptezeci** |
| 80 | **optzeci** |
| 90 | **nouăzeci** |
| 100 | **o sută** |
| 101 | **o sută unu** |

| | |
|---|---|
| 132 | o sută treizeci şi doi |
| 200 | două sute |
| 300 | trei sute |
| 405 | patru sute cinci |
| 1,000 | o mie |
| 2,000 | două mii |
| 5,000 | cinci mii |
| 6,400 | şase mii patru sute |
| 10,000 | zece mii |
| 1,000,000 | un milion |
| 1,000,000,000 | un miliard |
| 2,000,000,000 | două miliarde |

## ORDINAL NUMBERS

| | |
|---|---|
| first | primul, prima |
| second | al doilea, a doua |
| third | al treilea, a treia |
| fourth | al patrulea, a patra |
| fifth | al cincilea, a cincea |
| sixth | al şaselea, a şasea |
| seventh | al şaptelea, a şaptea |
| eighth | al optulea, a opta |
| ninth | al nouălea, a noua |
| tenth | al zecelea, a zecea |
| eleventh | al unsprezecelea, a unsprezecea |
| twelfth | al doisprezecelea, a douăsprezecea |
| thirteenth | al treisprezecelea, a treisprezecea |
| fourteenth | al paisprezecelea, a paisprezecea |
| fifteenth | al cincisprezecelea, a cincisprezecea |
| sixteenth | al şaisprezecelea, a şaisprezecea |
| seventeenth | al şaptesprezecelea, a şaptesprezecea |

| | |
|---|---|
| eighteenth | **al optsprezecelea, a optsprezecea** |
| nineteenth | **al nouăsprezecelea, a nouăsprezecea** |
| twentieth | **al douăzecilea, a douăzecea** |
| twenty first | **al douăzecişiunulea, a douăzecişiuna** |
| twenty second | **al douăzecişidoilea, a douăzecişidoua** |
| thirtieth | **al treizecilea, a treizecea** |
| fortieth | **al patruzecilea, a patruzecea** |
| fiftieth | **al cincizecilea, a cincizecea** |
| sixtieth | **al şaizecilea, a şaizecea** |
| seventieth | **al şaptezecilea, a şaptezecea** |
| eightieth | **al optzecilea, a optzecea** |
| ninetieth | **al nouăzecilea, a nouăzecea** |
| one hundredth | **al o sutălea, a o suta** |
| one thousandth | **al o mielea, a o mia** |

## FRACTIONAL NUMBERS

| | |
|---|---|
| one half | **o jumătate** |
| one third | **o treime** |
| one fourth | **o pătrime** |
| one fifth | **o cincime** |
| one tenth | **o zecime** |
| two thirds | **două treimi** |
| three fourths | **trei pătrimi** |
| two fifths | **două cincimi** |
| three tenths | **trei zecimi** |
| one and a half | **o dată şi jumătate** |
| five and three eights | **cinci şi trei optimi** |
| one point one (1.1) | **unu virgulă unu (1,1)** |

## RESPONSES FOR ALL OCCASIONS

I like that.
**Îmi place asta.**

I like you.
**Dumneata îmi placi.**

That's cool.
**Asta-i grozav (formidabil).**

Great!
**Nemaipomenit! Fantastic!**

Perfect.
**Perfect.**

Funny.
**Amuzant.**

Interesting.
**Interesant.**

I don't smoke.
**Eu nu fumez.**

Really?
**Serios?**

Congratulations!
**Felicitări!**

Well done!
**Bravo! (Foarte bine!)**

You're welcome.
**Pentru puțin (N-aveți pentru ce).**

It's nothing.
**Pentru nimic.**

Bless you! (*after sneeze*)
**Sănătate!**

Excuse me.
**Scuzaţi-mă, vă rog.**

What a pity.
**Ce păcat.**

That's life.
**Asta-i viaţa.**

No problem.
**Nici o problemă.**

O.K.
**De acord (În ordine).**

This is the good life!
**Ce frumoasă este viaţa!**

Have a good day.
**Vă doresc o zi bună.**

Good luck!
**Noroc!**

Let's go!
**Să mergem!**

# BIBLIOGRAPHY

Călinescu, George. *History of Romanian Literature.*
(Translated by Leon Levițchi.) Rome, 1994.

*Dicționar Englez-Român (English-Romanian Dictionary).* Bucharest: Editura Academiei, 1974.

Georgescu, Vlad. *The Romanians, A History.* Columbus:
Ohio State University Press, 1991.

Hitchins, Keith. *Romania, 1866–1947.* Oxford: Clarendon
Press, 1994.

——. *The Romanians, 1774–1866.* Oxford: Clarendon
Press, 1996.

McNulty, Karsten D. *Romanian Folk Art: A Guide to
Living Traditions.* Farmington, Connecticut: 1999.

Pop, Ioan Aurel. *Romanians and Romania, A Brief History.* New York: Columbia University Press, 2000.

Treptow, Kurt W., ed. *A History of Romania*, Iași, New
York: Columbia University Press, 1996.